CHEAT CODE

EXPLOSION

FOR CONSOLES

**FLIP THIS BOOK OVER
FOR HANDHELD SYSTEMS**

Mobile Games

Nintendo DS™ & 3DS™

PlayStation® Portable

PlayStation® Vita

**LOOK FOR
CODEY**

When you see
Codey's face next to a game
title, you've found the newest
and coolest codes!

PLAYSTATION® 3

3D DOT GAME HEROES................................3

BAKUGAN: DEFENDERS OF THE CORE............3

BAND HERO...4

BATMAN: ARKHAM CITY...............................4

THE BEATLES: ROCK BAND...........................4

BEJEWELED 3...5

BEN 10 GALACTIC RACING...........................5

CARS 2: THE VIDEO GAME............................5

DISGAEA 4: A PROMISE UNFORGOTTEN...........5

DJ HERO 2..6

DOUBLE DRAGON: NEON..............................6

DRIVER: SAN FRANCISCO..............................6

EARTH DEFENSE FORCE: INSECT ARMAGEDDON......7

FAT PRINCESS...7

FINAL FANTASY XIII-2...................................7

FROGGER: HYPER ARCADE EDITION.................7

GRAN TURISMO 5..8

GREG HASTINGS PAINTBALL 2.......................8

GUITAR HERO 5..9

GUITAR HERO: VAN HALEN...........................10

GUITAR HERO:
WARRIORS OF ROCK....................................11

HARRY POTTER AND THE
DEATHLY HALLOWS: PART 1..........................11

HEROES OVER EUROPE.................................12

JIMMIE JOHNSON'S
ANYTHING WITH AN ENGINE........................12

JUST DANCE 3...12

THE KING OF FIGHTERS XIII..........................12

LARA CROFT AND THE GUARDIAN OF LIGHT......13

LEGO BATMAN 2: DC SUPER HEROES..............13

LEGO HARRY POTTER: YEARS 1-4...................14

LEGO HARRY POTTER: YEARS 5-7...................15

LEGO INDIANA JONES 2:
THE ADVENTURE CONTINUES.........................16

LEGO PIRATES OF THE CARIBBEAN:
THE VIDEO GAME..17

LEGO STAR WARS III: THE CLONE WARS...........17

LITTLEBIGPLANET..19

MADAGASCAR 3: THE VIDEO GAME.................19

MADDEN NFL 12...20

MARVEL VS. CAPCOM ORIGINS.......................20

MONSTER WORLD IV.....................................21

NARUTO SHIPPUDEN:
ULTIMATE NINJA STORM GENERATIONS............22

NASCAR THE GAME 2011...............................23

NBA 2K11...23

NBA 2K12...24

NBA 2K13...24

NBA JAM...25

NEED FOR SPEED: THE RUN............................25

NFL BLITZ..25

NHL 12...28

NIGHTS INTO DREAMS...................................28

ONE PIECE: PIRATE WARRIORS.......................29

PHINEAS AND FERB:
ACROSS THE 2ND DIMENSION.........................29

PLANTS VS. ZOMBIES...................................29

RATCHET & CLANK.......................................30

THE RATCHET & CLANK COLLECTION................30

RATCHET & CLANK FUTURE: A CRACK IN TIME....31

THE REVENGE OF SHINOBI.............................32

ROCK BAND 3...32

ROCKSMITH..32

THE SIMPSONS ARCADE GAME.......................32

THE SIMS 3..32

THE SIMS 3: PETS..32

SKYLANDERS GIANTS....................................33

THE SLY COLLECTION....................................36

SONIC GENERATIONS....................................37

SOULCALIBUR V..38

SPACE CHANNEL 5 PART 2.............................39

SPIDER-MAN: EDGE OF TIME.........................39

SPIDER-MAN: SHATTERED DIMENSIONS.............40

STAR TREK: D-A-C..40

SUPER HANG-ON...40

SUPER STREET FIGHTER IV.............................41

THOR: GOD OF THUNDER...............................41

TIGER WOODS PGA TOUR 12: THE MASTERS......41

THE TOMB RAIDER TRILOGY...........................41

TONY HAWK'S PRO SKATER HD.......................42

TOY STORY 2: BUZZ LIGHTYEAR TO THE RESCUE!......43

TRANSFORMERS: DARK OF THE MOON...............43

VIRTUA TENNIS 4..43

WWE '12...43

WWE ALL STARS..44

WWE SMACKDOWN VS. RAW 2011...................44

X-MEN DESTINY...44

3D DOT GAME HEROES

HIDE SHIELD

Pause the game and press Up, Up, Down, Down, Left, Right, Left, Right, ⬤, ▲. Re-enter the code to show the shield again.

TOGGLE SWAY IN WALKING

Pause the game and press L1, R1, L1, R1, L1, L1, R1, R1, ⬤. Re-enter to turn this back on.

SPELUNKER MODE

Enter your name as SPELUNKER. In this mode, you will die with one hit — along with some dialogue changes.

BAKUGAN: DEFENDERS OF THE CORE

HIDDEN ITEMS

Select Unlock Codes from Collection and enter HXV6Y7BF. Now you can enter up to eight of your unique Bakugan Dimensions codes.

The codes unlock the following:

10,000 Core Energy	Light Arrow
Ten Vexos Passes	Tornado Vortex
Earthen Armor	Water Pillar
Fire Spirit	Zorch Thunder

Here are eight codes:

2FKRRMNCDQ	QY8CLD5NJE
82D77YK6P8	TD4UMFSRW3
HUUH8ST7AR	YJ7RGG7WGZ
JJUZDEACXX	YQLHBBSMDC

BAND HERO

MOST CHARACTERS UNLOCKED

Select Input Cheats from the options and enter Blue, Yellow, Green, Yellow, Red, Green, Red, Yellow.

ELECTRIKA STEEL UNLOCKED

Select Input Cheats from the options and enter Blue, Blue, Red, Yellow, Red, Yellow, Blue, Blue.

ALL HOPO MODE

Select Input Cheats from the options and enter Red, Green, Blue, Green, Blue, Green, Red, Green.

ALWAYS SLIDE

Select Input Cheats from the options and enter Yellow, Green, Yellow, Yellow, Yellow, Red, Blue, Red.

AUTO KICK

Select Input Cheats from the options and enter Yellow, Green, Yellow, Blue, Blue, Red, Blue, Red.

FOCUS MODE

Select Input Cheats from the options and enter Yellow, Yellow, Green, Green, Red, Red, Blue, Blue.

HUD FREE MODE

Select Input Cheats from the options and enter Green, Red, Green, Red, Yellow, Blue, Green, Red.

PERFORMANCE MODE

Select Input Cheats from the options and enter Yellow, Yellow, Blue, Green, Blue, Red, Red, Red.

AIR INSTRUMENTS

Select Input Cheats from the options and enter Blue, Yellow, Blue, Red, Red, Yellow, Green, Yellow.

INVISIBLE ROCKER

Select Input Cheats from the options and enter Green, Red, Yellow, Green, Yellow, Blue, Yellow, Green.

BATMAN: ARKHAM CITY

ALL BATMAN SKINS

This code allows you to start the campaign with all of the skins that you have downloaded, purchased, or unlocked. After selecting your save slot, press Left, Left, Down, Down, Left, Left, Right, Up, Up, Down at the main menu. You are then given the opportunity to select a skin.

BIG HEAD MODE

In the game, select the Cryptographic Sequencer. Hold L2 and then hold R2 to get Batman to use the device. Next, rotate the right analog stick clockwise while rotating the left analog stick counter-clockwise. Eventually, you notice Batman's head enlarge. Enemies and other characters' heads are also big. This works in Normal, Hard, and New Game +.

THE BEATLES: ROCK BAND

BONUS PHOTOS

At the title screen, press Blue, Yellow, Orange, Orange, Orange, Blue, Blue, Blue, Yellow, Orange.

BEJEWELED 3

BUTTERFLIES MODE

Reach Level 5 in Zen Mode.

DIAMOND MINE MODE

In Quest Mode, unlock the second relic by completing four challenges of the first.

ICE STORM MODE

Score over 100,000 points in Lightning Mode.

POKER MODE

Reach Level 5 in Classic Mode.

BEN 10 GALACTIC RACING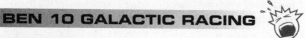

KINECELARATOR

Select Promotional Codes from Extras and enter Ben, Spidermonkey, Kevin Levin, Ultimate Echo Echo.

CARS 2: THE VIDEO GAME

ALL MODES AND TRACKS

Select Enter Codes from the Options and enter 959595.

LASER GUIDED

Select Enter Codes from the Options and enter 123456. Select Cheats to toggle the cheat on and off.

UNLIMITED ENERGY

Select Enter Codes from the Options and enter 721953. Select Cheats to toggle the cheat on and off.

DISGAEA 4: A PROMISE UNFORGOTTEN

EXTRA CHARACTERS

After completing the story, extra battles become available from the Senate. Clear these to unlock the following characters.

CHARACTER	CLEAR EXTRA BATTLE	CHARACTER	CLEAR EXTRA BATTLE
Axel	1	Laharl	5
Flonne	2	Asagi	6
Raspberyl	3	Kurtis	7
Etna	4	Zetta	9

DJ HERO 2

ALL BONUS CONTENT

Select Cheats from the Options. Choose Retail Cheats and enter VIP Pass.

DAVID GUETTA

Select Cheats from the Options. Choose Retail Cheats and enter Guetta Blaster.

DEADMAU5

Select Cheats from the Options. Choose Retail Cheats and enter Open The Trap.

INVISIBLE DJ

Select Cheats from the Options. Choose Retail Cheats and enter Now You See Me.

AUTO CROSSFADE

Select Cheats from the Options. Choose Retail Cheats and enter I Hate Crossfading. This disables Leaderboards.

AUTO SCRATCH

Select Cheats from the Options. Choose Retail Cheats and enter Soothing. This disables Leaderboards.

AUTO TAP

Select Cheats from the Options. Choose Retail Cheats and enter Look No Hands! This disables Leaderboards.

DOUBLE DRAGON: NEON

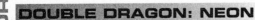

PLAY AS A RO-BRO

At the stage select, hold L1 + L2 + L3 + R1 + R2 + R3 + Select + Start. Enter again to return to normal.

CONCEPT ART GALLERY

Complete the game to unlock this gallery at the main menu.

DRAGON DIFFICULTY

Defeat the game on Normal difficulty.

DOUBLE DRAGON DIFFICULTY

Defeat the game on Dragon difficulty.

DRIVER: SAN FRANCISCO

MOVIE SCENE CHALLENGES

As you collect the 130 Movie Tokens in the game, Movie Scene Challenges are unlocked as shown below.

MOVIE SCENE CHALLENGE	VEHICLE GIVEN	# MOVIE TOKENS
Gone In 60 Seconds	1973 Ford Mustang Mach I	10
Starsky & Hutch	1974 Dodge Monaco Cop	20
Bullitt	1968 Ford Mustang GT Fastback	30
The French Connection	1971 Pontiac LeMans	40
Blues Brothers	1974 Dodge Monaco	50

6

MOVIE SCENE CHALLENGE	VEHICLE GIVEN	# MOVIE TOKENS
Cannonball Run	1978 Lamborghini Countach LP400S	60
Dukes of Hazard	1969 Dodge Charger R/T	70
Vanishing Point	1970 Dodge Challenger R/T	80
The Driver	1965 Chevrolet S-10	90
Redline	2011 McLaren MP4-12C	100
Smokey & The Bandit	1977 Pontiac TransAm Firebird	110
Test Drive	1987 RUF CT-R Yellow Bird	120
The Italian Job	1972 Lamborghini Miura	130

EARTH DEFENSE FORCE: INSECT ARMAGEDDON

HIDDEN IMAGES IN GALLERY

Select Gallery from the Extras menu. At the gallery press ●, ●, ▲, ●, L1, R1.

FAT PRINCESS

GRIM REAPER!

Select Play With Yourself and then Mess About. Start a game, pause, and press Up, Up, Down, Down, Left, Right, Left, Right, Select, Start, ●.

FINAL FANTASY XIII-2

LIGHTNING THEME

This theme is unlocked if you have a save game for Final Fantasy XIII on your console.

ANOTHER LIGHTNING THEME

Earn the Master of Time Trophy.

MOG THEME

Earn the Fair Fighter Trophy.

NOEL THEME

Earn the Chronosavior Trophy.

SERAH THEME

Earn the Defragmented Trophy.

FROGGER: HYPER ARCADE EDITION

CONTRA STYLE

At the style select, highlight Contra and enter Up, Up, Down, Down, Left, Right, Left, Right, ●, ✕.

GRAN TURISMO 5

B LICENSE TESTS

Buy a car.

A LICENSE TESTS

Reach Level 3 and complete the B License Tests.

INTERNATIONAL C LICENSE TESTS

Reach Level 6 and complete the A License Tests.

INTERNATIONAL B LICENSE TESTS

Reach Level 9 and complete the International C License Tests.

INTERNATIONAL A LICENSE TESTS

Reach Level 12 and complete the International B License Tests.

S LICENSE TESTS

Reach Level 15 and complete the International A License Tests.

TOP GEAR TEST TRACK

Complete Top Gear Challenge Beginner with gold.

NÜRBURGRING NORDSCHLEIFE

Complete all AMG Challenge Intermediate with at least bronze.

NÜRBURGRING NORDSCHLEIFE 4-HOUR CIRCUIT WITHOUT TIME AND WEATHER CHANGE

Complete all AMG Challenge Intermediate with at least silver.

NÜRBURGRING NORDSCHLEIFE 24-HOUR CIRCUIT WITH TIME AND WEATHER CHANGE

Complete all AMG Challenge Intermediate with gold.

GREG HASTINGS PAINTBALL 2

GUN AND PRO PLAYER

At any time, hold R2 and press Up, Up, Down, Right, Left, Left, Right, Up.

ALL HOPOS

Select Input Cheats from the Options menu and enter Green, Green, Blue, Green, Green, Green, Yellow, Green.

ALWAYS SLIDE

Select Input Cheats from the Options menu and enter Green, Green, Red, Red, Yellow, Blue, Yellow, Blue.

AUTO KICK

Select Input Cheats from the Options menu and enter Yellow, Green, Red, Blue, Blue, Blue, Blue, Red.

FOCUS MODE

Select Input Cheats from the Options menu and enter Yellow, Green, Red, Green, Yellow, Blue, Green, Green.

HUD FREE MODE

Select Input Cheats from the Options menu and enter Green, Red, Green, Green, Yellow, Green, Green, Green.

PERFORMANCE MODE

Select Input Cheats from the Options menu and enter Yellow, Yellow, Blue, Red, Blue, Green, Red, Red.

AIR INSTRUMENTS

Select Input Cheats from the Options menu and enter Red, Red, Blue, Yellow, Green, Green, Green, Yellow.

INVISIBLE ROCKER

Select Input Cheats from the Options menu and enter Green, Red, Yellow, Yellow, Yellow, Blue, Blue, Green.

ALL CHARACTERS

Select Input Cheats from the Options menu and enter Blue, Blue, Green, Green, Red, Green, Red, Yellow.

CONTEST WINNER 1

Select Input Cheats from the Options menu and enter Green, Green, Red, Red, Yellow, Red, Yellow, Blue.

GUITAR HERO: VAN HALEN

ALWAYS DRUM FILL

Select Input Cheats from the Options menu and enter Red, Red, Red, Blue, Blue, Green, Green, Yellow.

ALWAYS SLIDE

Select Input Cheats from the Options menu and enter Green, Green, Red, Red, Yellow, Red, Yellow, Blue.

AUTO KICK

Select Input Cheats from the Options menu and enter Yellow, Green, Red, Blue, Blue, Blue, Blue, Red.

HYPERSPEED

Select Input Cheats from the Options menu and enter Green, Blue, Red, Yellow, Yellow, Red, Green, Green. This allows you to enable Hyperguitar, Hyperbass, and Hyperdrums.

PERFORMANCE MODE

Select Input Cheats from the Options menu and enter Yellow, Yellow, Blue, Red, Blue, Green, Red, Red.

AIR INSTRUMENTS

Select Input Cheats from the Options menu and enter Red, Red, Blue, Yellow, Green, Green, Green, Yellow.

INVISIBLE ROCKER

Select Input Cheats from the Options menu and enter Green, Red, Yellow, Yellow, Yellow, Blue, Blue, Green.

BLACK HIGHWAY

Select Input Cheats from the Options menu and enter Yellow, Red, Green, Red, Green, Red, Red, Blue.

FLAME COLOR

Select Input Cheats from the Options menu and enter Green, Red, Green, Blue, Red, Red, Yellow, Blue.

GEM COLOR

Select Input Cheats from the Options menu and enter Blue, Red, Red, Green, Red, Green, Red, Yellow.

STAR COLOR

Select Input Cheats from the Options menu and enter Red, Red, Yellow, Red, Blue, Red, Red, Blue.

VOCAL FIREBALL

Select Input Cheats from the Options menu and enter Red, Green, Green, Yellow, Blue, Green, Yellow, Green.

EXTRA LINE 6 TONES

Select Input Cheats from the Options menu and enter Green, Red, Yellow, Blue, Red, Yellow, Blue, Green.

GUITAR HERO: WARRIORS OF ROCK

Select Extras from Options to toggle the following on and off. Some cheats will disable Achievements.

ALL CHARACTERS

Select Cheats from the Options menu and enter Blue, Green, Green, Red, Green, Red, Yellow, Blue.

ALL VENUES

Select Cheats from the Options menu and enter Red, Blue, Blue, Red, Red, Blue, Blue, Red.

ALWAYS SLIDE

Select Cheats from the Options menu and enter Blue, Green, Green, Red, Red, Yellow, Blue, Yellow.

ALL HOPOS

Select Cheats from the Options menu and enter Green (x3), Blue, Green (x3), Yellow. Most notes become hammer-ons or pull-offs.

INVISIBLE ROCKER

Select Cheats from the Options menu and enter Green, Green, Red, Yellow (x3), Blue, Blue.

AIR INSTRUMENTS

Select Cheats from the Options menu and enter Yellow, Red, Red, Blue, Yellow, Green (x3).

FOCUS MODE

Select Cheats from the Options menu and enter Green, Yellow, Green, Red, Green, Yellow, Blue, Green. This removes the busy background.

HUD FREE MODE

Select Cheats from the Options menu and enter Green, Green, Red, Green, Green, Yellow, Green, Green.

PERFORMANCE MODE

Select Cheats from the Options menu and enter Red, Yellow, Yellow, Blue, Red, Blue, Green, Red.

COLOR SHUFFLE

Select Cheats from the Options menu and enter Blue, Green, Blue, Red, Yellow, Green, Red, Yellow.

MIRROR GEMS

Select Cheats from the Options menu and enter Blue, Blue, Red, Blue, Green, Green, Red, Green.

RANDOM GEMS

Select Cheats from the Options menu and enter Green, Green, Red, Red, Yellow, Red, Yellow, Blue.

HARRY POTTER AND THE DEATHLY HALLOWS: PART 1

SUPER STRENGTH POTIONS

Select Unlock Menu from the Options and enter ✖, Left, Right, ✖, R2, R1.

ELITE CHALLENGES

Select Unlock Menu from the Options and enter ▲, Up, ✖, L2, R2, ✖.

AUGMENTED REALITY CHEAT FROM BOX (PROTEGO TOTALUM)

Select Unlock Menu from the Options and enter ▲, ⬤, Up, Left, R2, and Right.

HEROES OVER EUROPE

Cheats disable saving and Trophies.

CHEAT MODE

At the main menu, press ⬤, L2, Left on D-pad, R2, Right on D-pad, L1.

ALL MISSIONS

At the main menu, press Up on right analog stick, Down on right analog stick, L1, R1, Left on right analog stick, Right on right analog stick.

ALL PLANES

At the main menu, press L2, Left on right analog stick, R2, Right on right analog stick, L1, ⬤.

BF109 G10

At the main menu, press Left on left analog stick, Right on left analog stick, L2, R2, Left on right analog stick, Right on right analog stick.

SPITFIRE MK IX-C

At the main menu, press Up on left analog stick, Down on left analog stick, L2, R2, Up on right analog stick, Down on right analog stick.

JIMMIE JOHNSON'S ANYTHING WITH AN ENGINE

ALL RACERS

At the main menu, hold Right Trigger + Left Trigger + Right Bumper + Left Bumper and press Up, Right, Down, Left, Up, Left, Down, Right, click the Right Thumbstick, click the Left Thumbstick.

JUST DANCE 3

BARBRA STREISAND SPECIAL CHOREOGRAPHY

At the title screen (Press Start), press Up, Up, Down, Down, Left, Right, Left, Right.

THE KING OF FIGHTERS XIII

ALTERNATE COSTUMES AND COLOR PALETTES

Before selecting the color for the following fighters, press Select to get the alternate outfit.

FIGHTER	OUTFIT	FIGHTER	OUTFIT
Andy	Ninja Mask	Raiden	Big Bear
Elisabeth	KOF XI	Ralf	Camouflage
Joe	Tiger-Striped Boxers	Takuma	Mr. Karate
K'	Dual-Colored	Yuri	Braided Ponytail
Kyo	Orochi Saga		

EXTRA COLORS IN COLOR EDIT

Extra colors become available in color edit mode for every ten times you select a specific character.

BILLY KANE

Successfully pull off two target actions in each fight in Arcade Mode until Billy Kane challenges you. Defeat him to unlock him.

SAIKI

Successfully pull off five target actions in each fight in Arcade Mode until Saiki challenges you. Defeat him to unlock him.

LARA CROFT AND THE GUARDIAN OF LIGHT

LARA CROFT HEAVY JUNGLE OUTFIT

Complete the game.

LARA CROFT JUNGLE OUTFIT

Score 1,410,000 points.

LARA CROFT BIKER OUTFIT

Score 1,900,000 points.

LARA CROFT LEGEND OUTFIT

Defeat Xolotl.

DOPPELGANGER OUTFIT

Score 2,400,000 points.

LEGO BATMAN 2: DC SUPER HEROES

RED BRICK CODES

Pause the game, select Extras, and then choose Enter Code. Enter the following:

CHEAT	CODE	CHEAT	CODE
Attract Studs	MNZER6	Minikit Finder	LRJAG8
Beep Beep	ZHAXFH	Peril Finder	RYD3SJ
Character Studs	TPJ37T	Red Brick Finder	5KKQ6G
Disguises	BWQ2MS	Regenerate Hearts	ZXEX5D
Extra Hearts	4LGJ7T	Studs x 2	74EZUT
Extra Toggle	7TXH5K	Super Build	JN2J6V
Fall Rescue	TPGPG2	Vine Grapples	JXN7FJ
Gold Brick Finder	MBXW7V		

CHARACTERS AND VEHICLE

Pause the game, select Extras, and then choose Enter Code. Enter the following:

CHEAT	CODE	CHEAT	CODE
Clown Goon	9ZZZBP	Riddler Goon	Q285LK
LexBot	W49CSJ	Two-Face Goon	95KPYJ
Mime Goon	ZQA8MK	Harley Quinn's Motorbike	C79LVH
Policeman	V9SAGT		

LEGO HARRY POTTER: YEARS 1-4

RED BRICK EXTRAS

Once you have access to The Leaky Cauldron, enter Wiseacre's Wizarding Supplies from Diagon Alley. Go upstairs to enter the following. Pause the game and select Extras to toggle the cheats on or off.

CHEAT	CODE	CHEAT	CODE
Carrot Wands	AUC8EH	Invincibility	QQWC6B
Character Studs	H27KGC	Red Brick Detector	7AD7HE
Character Token Detector	HA79V8	Regenerate Hearts	89ML2W
Christmas	T7PVVN	Score x2	74YKR7
Disguise	4DMK2R	Score x4	J3WHNK
Fall Rescue	ZEX7MV	Score x6	XK9ANE
Extra Hearts	J9U6Z9	Score x8	HUFV2H
Fast Dig	Z9BFAD	Score x10	H8X69Y
Fast Magic	FA3GQA	Silhouettes	HZBVX7
Gold Brick Detector	84QNQN	Singing Mandrake	BMEU6X
Hogwarts Crest Detector	TTMC6D	Stud Magnet	67FKWZ
Ice Rink	F88VUW		

WISEACRE SPELLS

Once you have access to The Leaky Cauldron, enter Wiseacre's Wizarding Supplies from Diagon Alley. Go upstairs to enter the following. You need to learn Wingardium Leviosa before you can use these cheats.

SPELL	CODE	SPELL	CODE
Accio	VE9VV7	Incarcerous	YEB9Q9
Anteoculatia	QFB6NR	Locomotor Mortis	2M2XJ6
Calvorio	6DNR6L	Multicorfors	JK6QRM
Colovaria	9GJ442	Redactum Skullus	UW8LRH
Engorgio Skullus	CD4JLX	Rictusempra	2UCA3M
Entomorphis	MYN3NB	Slugulus Eructo	U6EE8X
Flipendo	ND2L7W	Stupefy	UWDJ4Y
Glacius	ERA9DR	Tarantallegra	KWWQ44
Herbifors	H8FTHL	Trip Jinx	YZNRF6

EEYLOPS GOLD BRICKS

Once you have access to The Leaky Cauldron, enter Wiseacre's Wizarding Supplies from Diagon Alley. Go upstairs to enter the following. To access the LEGO Builder, visit Gringott's Bank at the end of Diagon Alley.

GOLD BRICK	CODE	GOLD BRICK	CODE
1	QE4VC7	7	XY6VYZ
2	FY8H97	8	TUNC4W
3	3MQT4P	9	EJ42Q6
4	PQPM7Z	10	GFJCV9
5	ZY2CPA	11	DZCY6G
6	3GMTP6		

LEGO HARRY POTTER: YEARS 5-7

CHEATS

Pause the game and select Extras. Go to Enter Code and enter the following:

CHEAT	CODE	CHEAT	CODE
Carrot Wands	AUC8EH	Ghost Coins	2FLY6B
Character Studs	H27KGC	Gold Brick Detector	84QNQN
Character Token Detector	HA79V8	Hogwarts Crest Detector	TTMC6D
Christmas	T7PVVN	Invincibility	QQWC6B
Collect Ghost Studs	2FLY6B	Red Brick Detector	7AD7HE
Extra Hearts	J9U6Z9	Score x2	74YKR7
Fall Rescue	ZEX7MV	Score x6	XK9ANE
Fast Dig	Z9BFAD	Score x8	HUFV2H

LEGO INDIANA JONES 2: THE ADVENTURE CONTINUES

Pause the game, select Enter Secret Code from the Extras menu, and enter the following:

CHARACTERS

CHARACTER	CODE	CHARACTER	CODE
Belloq (Priest)	FTL48S	Indiana Jones (Officer)	3FQFKS
Dovchenko	WL4T6N	Interdimensional Being	PXT4UP
Enemy Boxer	7EQF47	Lao Che	7AWX3J
Henry Jones	4CSAKH	Mannequin (Boy)	2UJQWC
Indiana Jones	PGWSEA	Mannequin (Girl)	3PGSEL
Indiana Jones: 2	FGLKYS	Mannequin (Man)	QPWDMM
Indiana Jones (Collect)	DZFY9S	Mannequin (Woman)	U7SMVK
Indiana Jones (Desert)	M4C34K	Mola Ram	82RMC2
Indiana Jones (Desert Disguise)	2W8QR3	Mutt	2GKS62
Indiana Jones (Dinner Suit)	QUNZUT	Salah	E88YRP
Indiana Jones (Kali)	J2XS97	Willie	94RUAJ

EXTRAS

EFFECT	CODE	EFFECT	CODE
Beep Beep	UU3VSC	Score x3	PEHHPZ
Disguise	Y9TE98	Score x4	UXGTB3
Fast Build	SNXC2F	Score X6	XWLJEY
Fast Dig	XYAN83	Score x8	S5UZCP
Fast Fix	3Z7PJX	Score x10	V7JYBU
Fearless	TUXNZF	Silhouettes	FQGPYH
Ice Rink	TY9P4U	Snake Whip	2U7YCV
Invincibility	6JBB65	Stud Magnet	EGSM5B
Poo Money	SZFAAE		

LEGO PIRATES OF THE CARIBBEAN: THE VIDEO GAME

CODES

Pause the game and select Extras. Choose Enter Code and enter the following codes:

EFFECT	PASSWORD	EFFECT	PASSWORD
Ammand the Corsair	EW8T6T	Jack Sparrow (Musical)	VDJSPW
Angelica (Disguised)	DLRR45	Jacoby	BWO656
Angry Cannibal	VGF32C	Jimmy Legs	13GLW5
Blackbeard	D3DW0D	King George	RKED43
Clanker	ZM37GT	Koehler	RT093G
Clubba	644THF	Mistress Ching	GDETDE
Davy Jones	4DJLKR	Phillip	WEV040
Govorner Weatherby Swann	LD9454	Quartermaster	RX58HU
Gunner	Y611WB	The Spaniard	P861J0
Hungry Cannibal	64BNHG	Twigg	KDLFKD

LEGO STAR WARS III: THE CLONE WARS

Pause the game and select the Extras menu to enter the following codes:

CHARACTERS

CHARACTER	CODE	CHARACTER	CODE
Aayla Secura	2VG95B	Captain Antilles (Classic)	D8SNGJ
Adi Gallia	G2BFEN	Captain Rex	MW3QYH
Admiral Ackbar (Classic)	272Y9Q	Captain Typho	GD6FX3
Admiral Yularen	NG6PYX	Chancellor Palpatine	5C62YQ
Ahsoka	2VJ9TH	Chewbacca (Classic)	66UU3T
Anakin Skywalker	F9VUYJ	Clone Pilot	HQ7BVD
Anakin Skywalker (Geonosian Arena)	9AA4DW	Clone Shadow Trooper (Classic)	7GFNCQ
Asajj Ventress	YG9DD7	Clone Trooper	NP5GTT
Aurra Sing	M2V1JV	Commander Bly	7CB6NS
Bail Organa	GEHX6C	Commander Cody	SMN259
Barriss Offee	BTVTZ5	Commander Fil	U25HFC
Battle Droid	5Y7MA4	Commander Ponds	JRPR2A
Battle Droid Commander	LSU4LJ	Commander Stone	5XZQSV
Bib Fortuna	9U4TF3	Commando Droid	QEGU64
Boba Fett (Classic)	TY2BYJ	Count Dooku	EWR7WM
Boil	Q5Q39P	Darth Maul (Classic)	QH68AK
Bossk	2KLW5R	Darth Sidious (Classic)	QXY5XN
C-3PO	574226	Darth Vader (Classic)	FM4JB7
Cad Bane	NHME85	Darth Vader Battle Damaged (Classic)	NMJFBL

CHARACTER	CODE	CHARACTER	CODE
Destroyer Droid	9MUTS2	Obi-Wan Kenobi (Geonosian Arena)	5U9FJK
Dr. Nuvo Vindi	MB9EMW	OG-9 Homing Spider Droid	7NEC36
Echo	JB9E5S	Onaconda Farr	DB7ZQN
Eeth Koth	WUFDYA	Padmé Amidala (Geonosian Arena)	SZ824Q
Gammorean Guard	WSFZZQ	Padmé Amidala	8X87U6
General Grievous	7FNU4T	Pirate Ruffian	BH2EHU
Geonosian Guard	GAFZUD	Plo Koon	BUD4VU
Gold Super Battle Droid	2C8NHP	Poggle The Lesser	4592WM
Gonk Droid	C686PK	Princess Leia (Classic)	2D3D3L
Grand Moff Tarkin	NH2405	Probe Droid	U2T4SP
Greedo (Classic)	FUW4C2	Queen Neeyutnee	ZQRN85
Hailfire Droid	T7XF9Z	Qui-Gon Jinn (Classic)	LKHD3B
Han Solo (Classic)	KFDBXF	R2-D2	RZ5HUV
Heavy Super Battle Droid	G65KJJ	R3-S6	Z87PAU
Heavy Weapons Clone Trooper	WXUTWY	R4-P17	5MXSYA
HELIOS 3D	4AXTY4	R6-H5	7PMC3C
Hevy	EUB8UG	Rebel Commando (Classic)	PZMQNK
Hondo Ohnaka	5A7XYX	Robonino	2KLW5R
IG-86	EABPCP	Rys	4PTP53
Imperial Guard (Classic)	5W6FGD	Savage Oppress	MELL07
Jango Fett	5KZQ4D	Senate Commando	EPBPLK
Jar Jar Binks	MESPTS	Senate Commando (Captain)	S4Y7VW
Jek	AYREC9	Senator Kharrus	EA4E9S
Ki-Adi-Mundi	HGBCTQ	Senator Philo	9Q7YCT
Kit Fitso	PYWJ6N	Shahan Alama	G4N7C2
Lando Calrissian (Classic)	ERAEWE	Sionver Boll	5C62YQ
LEP Servent Droid	SM3Y9B	Stormtrooper (Classic)	HPE7PZ
Lieutenant Thire	3NEUXC	Super Battle Droid	MJKDV5
Lok Durd	TKCYUZ	Tee Watt Kaa	FYVSHD
Luke Skywalker (Classic)	PG73HF	Turk Falso	HEBHW5
Luminara Unduli	MKUYQ8	Tusken Raider (Classic)	GC2XSA
Lurmen Villager	R35Y7N	TX-20	PE7FGD
Luxury Droid	V4WMJN	Undead Geonosian	QGENFD
Mace Windu	8NVRWJ	Vader's Apprentice (Classic)	EGQQ4V
MagnaGuard	2KEF2D	Wag Too	VRUVSZ
MSE-6	S6GRNZ	Wat Tambor	ZP8XVH
Nahdar Vebb	ZKXG43	Waxer	BNJE79
Neimoidian	BJB94J	Wedge Antilles (Classic)	DRGLWS
Nute Gunray	QFYXMC	Whorm Loathsom	4VVYQV
Obi-Wan Kenobi	J9HNF9	Workout Clone Trooper	MP9DRE
Obi-Wan Kenobi (Classic)	FFBU5M	Yoda	CSQTMB

VEHICLES

VEHICLE	CODE
Dwarf Spider Droid	NACMGG
Geonosian Solar Sailor	PJ2U3R
Geonosian Starfighter	EDENEC

VEHICLE	CODE
Slave I	KDDQVD
The Twilight	T4K5L4
Vulture Droid	7W7K7S

RED BRICKS

CHEAT	CODE
Character Studs	QD2C31
Dark Side	X1V4N2
Dual Wield	C4ES4R
Fast Build	GCHP7S
Glow in the Dark	4GT3VQ
Invincibility	J46P7A
Minikit Detector	CSD5NA
Perfect Deflect	3F5L56
Red Brick Detector	N3R01A

CHEAT	CODE
Regenerate Hearts	2D7JNS
Score x2	YZPHUV
Score x4	43T5E5
Score x6	SEBHGR
Score x8	BYFSAQ
Score x10	N1CKR1
Stud Magnet	6MZ5CH
Super Saber Cut	BS828K
Super Speeders	B1D3W3

LITTLEBIGPLANET

CHEAT PAST ALL THE CREATE MODE TUTORIALS

As the credits roll press Down, Up, L1, L2, R2, R1, ⬤, ✕.

MADAGASCAR 3: THE VIDEO GAME

ALL DISGUISES

Select Promotion from Extras and enter Pineapple, Strawberry, Grapes, Apple.

BANANA DASH MINI-GAME IN LONDON

Select Promotion from Extras and enter Strawberry, Orange, Apple, Grapes.

BANANA DASH MINI-GAME IN PARIS

Select Promotion from Extras and enter Pineapple, Grapes, Pineapple, Banana.

BANANA DASH MINI-GAME IN PISA

Select Promotion from Extras and enter Orange, Banana, Orange, Apple.

BANANA DASH MINI-GAME IN ROME

Select Promotion from Extras and enter Grape, Apple, Grape, Strawberry.

MADDEN NFL 12

MADDEN NFL 12 DEVELOPERS TEAM IN EXHIBITION

Select Exhibition from Play Now. At the team select, press the Random Team button, L2, until the Developers team shows up. Once you have entered a game as the team, they will always be on the list.

MARVEL VS. CAPCOM ORIGINS

MARVEL SUPER HEROES

PLAY AS ANITA

At the characters select, press MP, LP, Left, LK, MK.

PLAY AS DR DOOM

At the characters select, press MK, LP, Down, LK, MP.

PLAY AS THANOS

At the characters select, press HK, MP, MP, Up.

EXTRA POWER

After selecting your character, press player 1 and player 2 start.

USE GEMS

At the versus screen, hold both Starts.

MARVEL VS. CAPCOM: CLASH OF SUPER HEROES

PLAY AS GOLD WAR MACHINE

Highlight Zangief and press Left, Left, Down, Down, Right, Right, Down, Down, Left, Left, Up, Up, Up, Up, Right, Right, Left, Left, Down, Down, Down, Down, Right, Right, Up, Up, Left, Left, Down, Down, Right, Right, Up, Up, Up, Up, Up.

PLAY AS HYPER VENOM

Highlight Chun-Li and press Right, Down, Down, Down, Down, Left, Up, Up, Up, Up, Right, Right, Down, Down, Left, Left, Down, Down, Right, Right, Up, Up, Up, Up, Left, Left, Up.

PLAY AS LILITH

Highlight Zangief and press Left, Left, Down, Down, Right, Right, Up, Up, Down (x4), Left, Left, Up (x4), Right, Left, Down (x4), Right, Right, Up (x4), Left, Left, Down (x4), Right, Down.

PLAY AS ORANGE HULK

Highlight Chun-Li and press Right, Right, Down, Down, Left, Left, Right, Right, Down, Down, Left, Left, Up (x4), Down, Down, Right, Right, Up, Up, Down (x4), Up (x4), Left, Up.

PLAY AS ROLL

Highlight Zangief and press Left, Left, Down, Down, Right, Right, Down, Down, Left, Left, Up, Right, Up, Up, Right, Right.

PLAY AS SHADOW LADY

Highlight Morrigan and press Up, Right, Right, Down (x4), Left, Left, Up (x4), Right, Right, Left, Left, Down, Down, Right, Right, Down, Down, Left, Left, Up, Up, Right, Right, Up, Up, Left, Left, Down (x5).

SELECT PARTNER

Select your two characters then hold Start and the following buttons:

CHARACTER	CODE
Anita	Weak Punch, Medium Punch, High Punch
Arthur	Weak Punch, Medium Punch
Colossus	Weak Punch, Medium Punch, Medium Kick
Cyclops	Weak punch, Weak Kick, Medium Punch
Devilot	Medium Punch
Iceman	Medium Punch, Medium Kick
Jubilee	Weak Kick, Medium Punch, High Punch
Juggernaut	Weak Punch, Medium Kick
Lou	Medium Punch
Magneo	Weak Kick, High Punch
Michelle Hart	Weak Punch, Weak Kick
Psylocke	Medium Kick
Pure and Fur	Weak Kick
Rogue	Weak Punch, Weak Kick, Medium Punch, High Punch
Saki	High Punch
Sentinel	Medium Punch, Medium Kick, High Punch
Shadow	Weak Punch, Medium Kick, High Punch
Storm	Weak Punch, Weak Kick, High Punch
Thor	Weak Kick, Medium Punch
Ton-Pooh	Weak Punch, High Punch
Unknown Soldier	Weak Punch
US Agent	High Punch, Medium Kick

MONSTER WORLD IV

SOUND TEST

Highlight New Game and press Up, Down, Up, Down, Left, Left, Right, Right.

NARUTO SHIPPUDEN: ULTIMATE NINJA STORM GENERATIONS

NINJA CARD PASSWORDS

Select Enter Password from the Collection Screen and enter the following. Each password unlocks one Ninja Info Card.

OOHNWGTFV8	BL770WJT70	MKKJMC7CWF
OB7JLNHXA4	BQ7207JT80	MMD4M2BK7K
OCKC96JGVL	BVKHANGBKR	MSJ1BFU4JB
OLP3WPBQ7B	CODGMFHCCD	MUW7LMT1WG
17769QUOKT	CE8Q9UKG8N	NDD9LGOEVO
1TFLMLP4BE	CJE20EPKWV	PLESLFPVKK
1V8WD29DBJ	CVJVLP6PVS	PQVGOKUCLO
1WQ4WR17VV	D53XB9P4LP	PSA21VB6M2
28G1D0FSBS	DCF515Q8X9	Q8M8P2J295
2DRA0BDFAR	DS1BXA13LD	QCS5D53XBA
2LM5CHLVX1	DX0L0382NT	QEB22X9LNP
2MFFXGNKWL	E23G24EB0B	QTBT1W97M2
39PXPFXEDW	EL52EVS00X	R4C43XB8PD
3ET93PHNNM	ENE5N43M9L	R8JE3QS6QT
3J6R2NS6B4	ERCKGKSN1P	RE6KE7GPCC
3USV86L2HM	F515Q009CE	S5JVSL6DDC
4HB5ELA91R	F6DTQBCXCF	S85PRDRU1T
4LTP2Q6U26	F7T1103JNS	SAUFE2T72U
4RTCRU4BWD	FMBB22KR0J	SKJERP5K15
53HXEB6EQ1	G12P36C5QW	TEP2FTPH4A
5DFQ45CJF0	GB7FS2G8EV	TH9NGBKRFF
5FUU285P1D	GR56DKG1CP	TVQ7HC2PQ5
6PF63C1C35	GWQ8EKCNEG	U3GQH7R65P
6QDPEH0HQL	H3D14HNF2X	U59BHXUEF3
6RQD5KD6GN	HH88SX6Q4P	UCM26NV9TW
6UB06B8FS2	HWR9FKDPFH	UFG3GKQJ5B
794L5RFD5J	HX3CS22CEG	UL4KS3Q2SU
7DEDGW26R1	J22C572J3P	UMK7SHU2QQ
7KXC71MSTS	JFXC608F44	UTG4GWQ65P
8CTCJFSQ6L	JMV3HRHBR7	V9TW64S2JJ
8EJ57XFMJ3	JSB8UFKXHL	VG63VA3W6D
8JPPVC8TUG	JXF97FR2F7	VLGL6FEQSU
8Q1VK79N7B	K1C6VJKXHL	VML7SHV3RR
96XD609G54	KEB84GXKREE	W1X6BJWX5C
9FP7L7N1H1	KF4RT7RU4B	W57HWX4B7S
9P8BLJ6FXX	KTS46B3JUP	WHOBJBA5HF
ADUMLGTR7M	L3PAK7BPUM	WV72WQ4B7R
ALNQK2L6VS	L6N0B1XT65	XH5G7ASAHD
AQUOKTTFCB	LMTA6QSEJV	XVN2VPX5TT
B7JHWCTWU3	MB3GA4DK88	XXPF0EMWKV

NASCAR THE GAME 2011

MARK MARTIN PAINT SCHEMES

At the garage main menu, press Down, Down, Up, Up, Right, Left, Right, Left. Enter
godaddy.com.

KYLE BUSH NOS ENERGY DRINK CAR

At the garage main menu, press Down, Down, Up, Up, Right, Left, Right, Left. Enter drinknos.

NBA 2K11

MJ: CREATING A LEGEND

In Features, select Codes from the Extras menu. Choose Enter Code and enter icanbe23.

2K CHINA TEAM

In Features, select Codes from the Extras menu. Choose Enter Code and enter 2kchina.

2K SPORTS TEAM

In Features, select Codes from the Extras menu. Choose Enter Code and enter 2Ksports.

NBA 2K TEAM

In Features, select Codes from the Extras menu. Choose Enter Code and enter nba2k.

VC TEAM

In Features, select Codes from the Extras menu. Choose Enter Code and enter vcteam.

ABA BALL

In Features, select Codes from the Extras menu. Choose Enter Code and enter payrespect.

2011 ALL-STAR UNIFORMS

In Features, select Codes from the Extras menu. Choose Enter Code and enter wydololoh.

SECONDARY ROAD UNIFORM

In Features, select Codes from the Extras menu. Choose Enter Code and enter ronoilnm. This unlocks the secondary road uniform for the Hornets, Magic, and Timberwolves.

ORANGE SPLIT DUNK

In Features, select Codes from the Extras menu. Choose Enter Code and enter SPRITEDUNK1. Go to Sprite Slam Dunk Showdown and use the help menu to find out more.

SPIN TOMMY DUNK

In Features, select Codes from the Extras menu. Choose Enter Code and enter SPRITEDUNK2. Go to Sprite Slam Dunk Showdown and use the help menu to find out more.

THE VILLAIN DUNK

In Features, select Codes from the Extras menu. Choose Enter Code and enter SPRITEDUNK3. Go to Sprite Slam Dunk Showdown and use the help menu to find out more.

NBA 2K12

ABA BALL

Select Extras from the Features menu. Choose Codes and enter payrespect. This can be toggled on and off from this Codes menu.

2K CHINA TEAM

Select Extras from the Features menu. Choose Codes and enter 2kchina.

2K SPORTS TEAM

Select Extras from the Features menu. Choose Codes and enter 2ksports.

UNLOCK NBA 2K TEAM

Select Extras from the Features menu. Choose Codes and enter nba2k.

VC TEAM

Select Extras from the Features menu. Choose Codes and enter vcteam.

JORDAN RETRO COLLECTION

Select Extras from the Features menu. Choose Codes and enter 23.

SECONDARY ROAD UNIFORMS

Select Extras from the Features menu. Choose Codes and enter hcsilapadatu. This unlocks uniforms for 76ers, Jazz, Kings, and Mavericks.

CHRISTMAS UNIFORMS

Select Extras from the Features menu. Choose Codes and enter ibyasmliancbhlald. This unlocks uniforms for Bulls, Celtics, Heat, Knicks, Lakers, and Mavericks.

HEAT BACK IN BLACK UNIFORM

Select Extras from the Features menu. Choose Codes and enter albkbinkcca.

RAPTORS MILITARY NIGHT UNIFORM

Select Extras from the Features menu. Choose Codes and enter liyrimta.

NBA 2K13

ABA BALL

Select Features from the main menu and then go to Codes. Enter payrespect.

UA TORCH SHOE

Select Features from the main menu and then go to Codes. Enter underarmour.

SPRITE EFFECT BONUS

Select Features from the main menu and then go to Codes. Enter spriteeffect. This adds +3 to Ball handling.

NBA JAM

BEASTIE BOYS

At the title screen, press Up, Up, Down, Down, Left, Right, Left, Right, ●, ✕. This team includes Ad Rock, MCA, and Mike D.

J. COLE AND 9TH WONDER

At the title screen, press Up, Left, Down, Right, Up, Left, Down, Right, ●, ✕.

DEMOCRATS TEAM

At the title screen, press Left (x13), ✕. This team includes Barack Obama, Joe Biden, Bill Clinton, and Hillary Clinton.

REPUBLICANS TEAM

At the title screen, press Right (x13), ✕. The team includes George W. Bush, Sarah Palin, Dick Cheney, and John McCain.

ESPN'S SPORTSNATION

Select Play Now. When entering the initials, enter ESP for P1 and NSN for P2. Advance to the Choose Teams screen to find the team. This team includes the hosts of the show; Colin Cowherd and Michelle Beadle.

NBA MASCOTS

Select Play Now. When entering the initials, enter MAS for P1 and COT for P2.

ORIGINAL GENERATION JAM

Select Play Now. When entering the initials, enter MJT for P1. Advance to the Choose Teams screen to find the team. This team includes Mark Turmell and Tim Kitzrow.

NEED FOR SPEED: THE RUN

AEM INTAKE CHALLENGE SERIES

Select Enter Cheat Code from Extras and enter aemintakes.

NFL BLITZ

Select Cheats from the Blitz Store to purchase the following cheats. They are entered with ■, ▲, ●. Press these buttons until the three given icons are shown. The number indicates how many times each button is pressed. ■ is the first number, ▲ the second, and ● is the third.

GAMEPLAY CHEATS

Buy these cheats to change the game to your advantage.

CHEAT	CODE
Tournament Mode	Goalpost, Goalpost, Goalpost (4 4 4)
Faster Passes	Helmet, NFL, NFL (5 1 1)
Speedster	Goalpost, NFL, EA Sports (4 1 0)
Fast Turbo Drain	Helmet, Headset, NFL (5 3 1)
More Fumbles	Helmet, Goalpost, NFL (5 4 1)
No First Downs	Goalpost, Headset, Goalpost (4 3 4)

CHEAT	CODE
No Fumbles	Helmet, EA Sports, Headset (5 0 3)
No Interceptions	Helmet, Helmet, EA Sports (5 5 0)
No Onside Kicks	Goalpost, Foam Finger, Foam Finger (4 2 2)
No Punting	Goalpost, Goalpost, EA Sports (4 4 0)
Power Defense	Goalpost, Whistle, Goalpost (4 8 4)
Power Offense	Helmet, Foam Finger, Helmet (5 2 5)
No Stepping out of Bounds	Helmet, EA Sports, EA Sports (5 0 0)
Unlimited Turbo	Helmet, NFL, Goalpost (5 1 4)

VISUAL CHEATS

Your team will get a Blitz makeover after you buy these cheats.

CHEAT	CODE
Big Head Player	Foam Finger, Helmet, EA Sports (2 5 0)
Big Head Team	Foam Finger, NFL, Foam Finger (2 1 2)
Tiny Head Team	Foam Finger, Goalpost, Headset (2 4 3)
Tiny Head Player	Headset, EA Sports, Foam Finger (3 0 2)
Huge Head Team	Headset, NFL, Foam Finger (3 1 2)
Huge Head Player	Foam Finger, EA Sports, NFL (2 0 1)
Super Ball Trail	EA Sports, NFL, Football (0 1 6)
Black & Red Ball	EA Sports, EA Sports, Foam Finger (0 0 2)
Camouflage Ball	EA Sports, EA Sports, Helmet (0 0 5)
Chrome Ball	EA Sports, Foam Finger, EA Sports (0 2 0)
Flames Ball	EA Sports, Goalpost, Foam Finger (0 4 2)
Ice Cream Ball	EA Sports, Foam Finger, Marker (0 2 7)
B-52 Ball	NFL, EA Sports, Goalpost (1 0 4)
Beachball	NFL, EA Sports, NFL (1 0 1)
Glow Ball	EA Sports, Marker, EA Sports (0 7 0)
Meat Ball	EA Sports, Football, EA Sports (0 6 0)
Pumpkin Ball	Whistle, Headset, NFL (8 3 1)
Soup Can Ball	Marker, NFL, EA Sports (7 1 0)
Blitz Team Ball	NFL, NFL, NFL (1 1 1)
USA Ball	Headset, NFL, Helmet (3 1 5)
Blitz Stadium	EA Sports, NFL, Goalpost (0 1 4)
Cardinals Stadium	EA Sports, Foam Finger, Foam Finger (0 2 2)
Falcons Stadium	EA Sports, Headset, EA Sports (0 3 0)
Ravens Stadium	EA Sports, Headset, Helmet (0 3 5)
Bills Stadium	EA Sports, Headset, Marker (0 3 7)
Panthers Stadium	EA Sports, Goalpost, Goalpost (0 4 4)
Bears Stadium	EA Sports, Goalpost, Football (0 4 6)
Bengals Stadium	EA Sports, Goalpost, Whistle (0 4 8)
Browns Stadium	EA Sports, Helmet, Headset (0 5 3)
Cowboys Stadium	EA Sports, Helmet, Helmet (0 5 5)

CHEAT	CODE
Broncos Stadium	EA Sports, EA Sports, Marker (0 0 7)
Lions Stadium	EA Sports, Helmet, Marker (0 5 7)
Packers Stadium	EA Sports, Football, Foam Finger (0 6 2)
Texans Stadium	EA Sports, Football, Goalpost (0 6 4)
Colts Stadium	EA Sports, Football, Football (0 6 6)
Jaguars Stadium	EA Sports, Marker, Foam Finger (0 7 2)
Chiefs Stadium	EA Sports, Whistle, EA Sports (0 8 0)
Dolphins Stadium	EA Sports, Marker, Marker (0 7 7)
Vikings Stadium	NFL, EA Sports, Football (1 0 6)
Patriots Stadium	NFL, NFL, Goalpost (1 1 4)
Saints Stadium	NFL, Foam Finger, Headset (1 2 3)
Giants Stadium	NFL, Headset, EA Sports (1 3 0)
Jets Stadium	NFL, EA Sports, Whistle (1 0 8)
Raiders Stadium	NFL, Foam Finger, Helmet (1 2 5)
Eagles Stadium	NFL, Headset, Headset (1 3 3)
Steelers Stadium	NFL, Headset, Helmet (1 3 5)
Chargers Stadium	NFL, Helmet, EA Sports (1 5 0)
Seahawks Stadium	Foam Finger, Foam Finger, EA Sports (2 2 0)
49ers Stadium	Foam Finger, NFL, EA Sports (2 1 0)
Rams Stadium	Foam Finger, Headset, EA Sports (2 3 0)
Bucs Stadium	Foam Finger, Goalpost, EA Sports (2 4 0)
Titans Stadium	Headset, EA Sports, Headset (3 0 3)
Redskins Stadium	Goalpost, EA Sports, NFL (4 0 1)
Day	EA Sports, Whistle, Foam Finger (0 8 2)
Twilight	NFL, NFL, Marker (1 1 7)
Night	NFL, Whistle, Marker (1 8 7)

SETTINGS CHEATS

Change certain game settings when you buy these cheats.

CHEAT	CODE
Hide Player Name	EA Sports, Foam Finger, Goalpost (0 2 4)
Extra Code Time	Helmet, Helmet, Helmet (5 5 5)
No Ball Target	EA Sports, Helmet, NFL (0 5 1)
Wide Camera	NFL, NFL, Foam Finger (1 1 2)
Show Field Goal Percentage	EA Sports, NFL, Foam Finger (0 1 2)
All-Time QB Coop	Headset, Headset, EA Sports (3 3 0)
All-Time WR Coop	EA Sports, Headset, Headset (0 3 3)
Icon Passing	Headset, Helmet, Headset (3 5 3)
No Player Icon	EA Sports, Goalpost, EA Sports (0 4 0)

FANTASY CHARACTERS

Buy these cheats to play as your favorite characters. Characters must be unlocked by defeating them in Blitz Gauntlet first.

UNLOCKABLE CHARACTERS

CHEAT	CODE
Bigfoot	Headset, Headset, Headset (3 3 3)
Bigfoot Team	Marker, EA Logo, EA Logo (7 0 0)
Cowboy	Headset, Foam Finger, Headset (3 2 3)
Cowboy Team	Goalpost, Marker, Goalpost (4 7 4)
Gladiator	Foam Finger, Whistle, Foam Finger (2 8 2)
Gladiator Team	Helmet, NFL, Marker (5 1 7)
Horse	NFL, Marker, NFL (1 7 1)
Horse Team	Foam Finger, Football, Foam Finger (2 6 2)
Hot Dog	NFL, Football, NFL (1 6 1)
Hot Dog Team	Foam Finger, Headset, Foam Finger (2 3 2)
Lion	Foam Finger, EA Sports, Foam Finger (2 0 2)
Lion Team	Headset, Goalpost, Headset (3 4 3)
Ninja	Foam Finger, Marker, Foam Finger (2 7 2)
Ninja Team	Football, NFL, Football (6 1 6)
Pirate	NFL, Foam Finger, NFL (1 2 1)
Pirate Team	Helmet, Headset, Helmet (5 3 5)

NHL 12

3RD JERSEYS

Select NHL 12 Code Entry from My NHL 12 and enter 2wg3gap9mvrth6kq. This unlocks uniforms for Florida, New York Islanders, Ottawa, and Toronto.

NIGHTS INTO DREAMS

UNLOCK EVERYTHING

At the title screen, press Left, Right, ■, ◎, ✖, ▲, R1, R2, Down, Up, L1, L2. Trophies, saving, and posting high scores are disabled until the game is restarted.

ONE PIECE: PIRATE WARRIORS

SEVEN LUFFY COSTUMES

Complete the Main Log.

SANJI'S NEW WORLD COSTUME

Complete Sanji's Another Log.

ZORO'S NEW WORLD COSTUME

Complete Zoro's Another Log.

PHINEAS AND FERB: ACROSS THE 2ND DIMENSION

SKIN FOR AGENT P: PERRY THE PLATTYBORG

Pause the game, select Enter Code from Extras, and enter
◎, ✕, ◎, △, ▣, △.

PLANTS VS. ZOMBIES

If a code does not work, your Tree of Wisdom may not be tall enough.
Try again later.

ALTERNATE LAWN MOWER

During a game, press R1 + R2 + L1
+ L2 and enter trickedout.

ZOMBIE SHADES

During a game, press R1 + R2 + L1
+ L2 and enter future.

ZOMBIES HAVE A MUSTACHE

During a game, press R1 + R2 + L1
+ L2 and enter mustache.

ZOMBIES DANCE

During a game, press R1 + R2 + L1
+ L2 and enter dance.

DEAD ZOMBIES LEAVE DAISIES BEHIND

During a game, press R1 + R2 + L1
+ L2 and enter daisies.

CANDY SHOWER WHEN ZOMBIE DIES

During a game, press R1 + R2 + L1
+ L2 and enter piñata.

CHANGES ZOMBIES SOUND

During a game, press R1 + R2 + L1
+ L2 and enter sukhbir.

RATCHET & CLANK

The following cheats can be activated only after defeating Drek. After getting the Cheat Enabled message, go to Cheats in the Goodies Menu and toggle it on or off.

CLANK BIG HEAD

During a game, perform the following: Flip Back, Hyper-Strike, Comet-Strike, Double Jump, Hyper-Strike, Flip Left, Flip Right, Full Second Crouch.

RATCHET BIG HEAD

During a game, perform the following: Flip Back (X3), Full Second Crouch, Stretch Jump, Full Second Glide.

ENEMY BIG HEAD

During a game, perform the following: Stretch Jump, Flip Back (x3), Stretch Jump, Flip Back (x3), Stretch Jump, Flip Back (x3), Full Second Crouch.

NPC BIG HEAD

During a game, perform the following: Flip Left, Flip Right, Flip Back (x3), Comet-Strike, Double Jump, Comet-Strike, Hyper-Strike.

INVINCIBILITY

During a game, perform the following: Comet-Strike (x4), Flip Back, Full Second Crouch, Flip Back, Full Second Crouch, Comet-Strike (x4).

MIRRORED LEVELS

During a game, perform the following: Flip Left (x4), Multi-Strike, Hyper-Strike, Flip Right, Flip Right, Double Jump, Flip Right, Flip Right, Double Jump, Full Second Crouch.

TRIPPY CONTRAILS

During a game, perform the following: Wall Jump (x10), Double Jump, Hyper-Strike. This adds effect behind Ratchet during rail slide.

THE RATCHET & CLANK COLLECTION

RATCHET & CLANK

The following cheats can be activated only after defeating Drek. After getting the Cheat Enabled message, go to Cheats in the Goodies Menu and toggle it on or off.

CLANK BIG HEAD

During a game, perform the following: Flip Back, Hyper-Strike, Comet-Strike, Double Jump, Hyper-Strike, Flip Left, Flip Right, Full Second Crouch.

RATCHET BIG HEAD

During a game, perform the following: Flip Back (X3), Full Second Crouch, Stretch Jump, Full Second Glide.

ENEMY BIG HEAD

During a game, perform the following: Stretch Jump, Flip Back (x3), Stretch Jump, Flip Back (x3), Stretch Jump, Flip Back (x3), Full Second Crouch.

NPC BIG HEAD

During a game, perform the following: Flip Left, Flip Right, Flip Back (x3), Comet-Strike, Double Jump, Comet-Strike, Hyper-Strike.

INVINCIBILITY

During a game, perform the following: Comet-Strike (x4), Flip Back, Full Second Crouch, Flip Back, Full Second Crouch, Comet-Strike (x4).

MIRRORED LEVELS

During a game, perform the following: Flip Left (x4), Multi-Strike, Hyper-Strike, Flip Right, Flip Right, Double Jump, Flip Right, Flip Right, Double Jump, Full Second Crouch.

TRIPPY CONTRAILS

During a game, perform the following: Wall Jump (x10), Double Jump, Hyper-Strike. This adds effect behind Ratchet during rail slide.

RATCHET & CLANK: UP YOUR ARSENAL

DUAL BLADE LASER SWORD

Pause the game and press ◉, ◉, ◉, ◉, Up, Down, Left, Left.

QWARK'S ALTERNATE COSTUME

Start a game of Qwark Vid-Comic and press Up, Up, Down, Down, Left, Right, ◉, ◉, ◉.

SQUAT STATS

At the online menu, highlight Stats and press Up, Down, Left, Right, ◉.

PIRATE VS NINJA MINI-GAME

At the Qwark Comics Issue select, press ◉ to bring up a password screen. Enter _MEGHAN_ as a password.

RATCHET & CLANK FUTURE: A CRACK IN TIME

DISCOUNT AT WEAPON VENDORS

Have a save game for Ratchet and Clank Future: Tools of Destruction.

PIRATE HAT SKIN

Have a save game for Ratchet and Clank Future: Quest for Booty.

BANCHO RATCHET SKIN

Pause the game and enter Up, Right, Down, Left, Triangle, Square, X, Circle, R3.

THE REVENGE OF SHINOBI

STAGE PRACTICE

At the title screen, hold A + B + C and press Start. This unlocks the mode at the main menu.

ROCK BAND 3

GUILD X-79 GUITAR

At the main menu, press Blue, Orange, Orange, Blue, Orange, Orange, Blue, Blue.

OVATION D-2010 GUITAR

At the main menu, press Orange, Blue, Orange, Orange, Blue, Blue, Orange, Blue.

STOP! GUITAR

At the main menu, press Orange, Orange, Blue, Blue, Orange, Blue, Blue, Orange.

ROCKSMITH

UNLOCKABLE SONGS

As you achieve Double Encores, the following songs are unlocked randomly.

Boss by Chris Lee

Jules by Seth Chapla

Ricochet by Brian Adam McCune

Six AM Salvation by Versus Them

Space Ostrich by Disonaur

The Star Spangled Banner by Seth Chapla

THE SIMPSONS ARCADE GAME

ALL EXTRAS

At the title screen, press Up, Up, Down, Down, Left, Right, Left, Right, ◉, ✖.

THE SIMS 3

CHEATS

Load your family, press Start, and hold L1 + L2 + R1 + R2. The game prompts you to save another file before activating the cheats. Spoot the Llama is now available in Misc Décor. Place it in your lot and click it to access the cheats. This disables Trophies and challenges.

THE SIMS 3: PETS

CREATION MODE

32   Pause the game and press L2 + L1 + R2 + R1. This disables trophies.

SKYLANDERS SPECIFIC QUESTS

Skylanders Giants includes quests specific to each Skylander as a way to improve them. Here we list each Skylander with their quest and tips on how to complete it.

SKYLANDER	QUEST	HOW TO COMPLETE
Bash	On a Roll: Defeat 10 enemies with one roll attack.	If you have trouble completing this quest, opt for the Pulver Dragon upgrade path.
Boomer	On a Troll: Defeat five enemies with one kicked Troll Bomb.	Once you have Troll Bomb Boot, look for a group of tight-knit Chompies. Chapter 1: Time of the Giants has several groupings of five Chompies.
Bouncer	Stay on Target!: Target enemies 100 times with laser-guided Shoulder Rockets.	You must purchase the Targeting Computer upgrade for Bouncer's Shoulder Rockets.
Camo	Garden Gorger: Eat 10 watermelons.	If you aren't in a rush to complete a level, switch to Camo when a watermelon appears.
Chill	Ice Sore: Defeat six enemies with one Ice Narwhal attack.	Try to find six enemies that are grouped together at a medium distance, such as in an arena.
Chop Chop	Stalwart Defender: Absorb 1,000 damage with your shield.	To complete this quest safely, block attacks from a small group of weaker enemies near a food item (just in case they sneak in some unexpected damage).
Crusher	High Roller: Defeat 100 enemies with boulders.	Use Rockslide defeat enemies until you have completed this quest.
Cynder	On the Haunt: Defeat 50 enemies with your Ghost Ally.	Ghost Ally does not inflict much damage so focus on saving low-health enemies, like Chompies, for the Ghost to attack. The Ghost attacks while Cynder is flying, so consider circling an area with Chompies.
Dino-Rang	Fooderang: Pick up 20 food items with boomerangs.	After acquiring Sticky Boomerangs, use it to grab any food found in the area. In the Arena Challenges on Flynn's Ship, the audience throws food items into the arena between rounds.
Double Trouble	Big Bomb Trouble: Defeat 10 enemies with one Magic Bomb attack.	Find a group of 10 or more Chompies and set off a bomb. A good place to earn this is any of of Brock's Arena Challenges with regular Chompies.
Drill Sergeant	Drill Skill: Defeat Drill-X without changing Skylanders.	Drill Sergeant must defeat Drill-X (the final boss in Chapter 11: Drill-X's Big Rig) solo. Use Adventure items (like Healing Potion) to survive the battle. You can complete it on Easy difficulty with a fully-upgraded Drill Sergeant.
Drobot	Feed the Burn: Defeat 50 enemies with Afterburners.	It's easiest to hit enemies with Afterburners when Drobot first takes off.
Eruptor	Pizza Burp: Eat 10 Pizzas.	If you want to have a greater chance of encountering a pizza, equip Lucky Wheel of Health in the Luck-O-Tron.
Eye Brawl	Gold Search: Collect 5,000 gold with the eyeball detached.	Remember to detach Eye-Brawl's eye before collecting any treasure from chests or enemies.
Flameslinger	Circular Combustion: Defeat 10 enemies with one column of Fire Flame Dash.	There are two upgrades you can get to help you on this quest. The first is Column of Fire. The second is Supernova in the Pyromancer Path.
Flashwing	Let It Shine: Defeat 20 enemies with one Crystal Lighthouse.	Since Crystal Lighthouse is stationary, this is a tricky quest. The best candidate for this is one of the arena maps, particularly Kaos' Royal Flush (the second challenge, Birthday Bash). Set up the Lighthouse in the middle of the birthday cake.
Fright Rider	Delving Throw: Toss 50 enemies into the air.	The power to use for this quest is Burrow Bomber. Hit any medium or small enemy with the attack to pop them up in the air and register a toss.
Ghost Roaster	Grave Circumstances: Defeat 100 enemies with Skull Charge.	Repeatedly use Skull Charge to attack enemies and you should complete this quest in no time.

SKYLANDER	QUEST	HOW TO COMPLETE
Gill Grunt	Anchors Away!: Defeat six enemies with one Anchor Attack.	Line up a group of Chompies with your Anchor Cannon and let loose to complete the quest. If you have Series 2 Gill Grunt, Anchor's Away! makes completing the quest easier.
Hex	Noggin Knocker: Knock away 100 enemies with your Skull Rain.	Once Hex has Skull Shield, allow enemies to get within melee range while Hex is charging that attack. If they get too close, they get knocked back, tallying a point for this quest.
Hot Dog	Animal Aggravator: Scare away 20 birds.	Look for the small birds pecking at the ground in each level. These birds are the ones you need to scare with Hot Dog for this achievement. Chapter 13: The Oracle and Chapter 1: Time of Giants both have plenty of birds.
Hot Head	Buggy Breakthrough: Destroy 20 walls in Hot Rod mode.	The walls this quest is referring to are the walls that can only be crushed by a Giant or a bomb. Whenever you encounter one of these walls, switch to Hot Head. A good spot with plenty of these types of walls is Chapter 2: Junkyard Isles.
Ignitor	Tinder Trekker: Travel 26,000 feet in Flame Form.	Use Flame Form often and this number will accumulate quickly.
Jet-Vac	Bird Cleaner: Suck up 50 birds in your Suction Gun.	Look for tiny birds on the ground throughout most levels with green grass. Chapter 13: The Oracle and Chapter 1: Time of Giants both have plenty of birds.
Lightning Rod	Current Event: Defeat 10 enemies with one Grand Lightning strike.	You need to find a group of 10 Chompies in one area and use the Grand Lightning to blast them all. Choosing the Lord of Lightning Path makes this easier since the Grand Lightning attack lasts longer.
Ninjini	Bottle Beatdown: Defeat 5 enemies within five seconds of exiting your bottle.	Transform Ninjini into the bottle and move into a large group of small enemies. Follow up the bottle attack with her swords.
Pop Fizz	Rampage: Do 200 HP of damage in a single run in Beast Form.	Transform into Beast Form in a large group of enemies and destroy everything in sight to complete the quest.
Prism Break	Bifurcation Sensation: Defeat 100 enemies with double refraction.	A beam must pass through two Shards before hitting an enemy to count. Unlock the Chained Refractions upgrade and place plenty of Crystal Shards. Fire an Energy Beam through them to indirectly take out nearby enemies.
Shroomboom	Lunching Launch: Eat a watermelon while performing a Self-Slingshot!	When you find a watermelon, blast Shroomboom through it with the Self-Slingshot power to complete the quest.
Slam Bam	Ice to Meet You: Trap 100 enemies in your Ice Blocks.	You do not need to damage or freeze enemies with Ice Block; it counts if you just hit them with the Ice Block.
Sonic Boom	Sonic Squeak: Babies defeat 50 enemies.	Upgrade Sonic Boom's egg attack powers and keep babies summoned at all times.
Sprocket	Mined Your Step: Defeat 50 enemies using the Landmine Golf attack.	Once you unlock the Landmine Golf ability, use it often. A quick way to complete this quest is to load up one of the easier Arena levels.
Spyro	Full Charge: Collect 3 gold, eat 1 food item, and defeat 2 enemies in 1 Sprint Charge.	Look for two low-health enemies (Chompies are a good choice) as well as some food and gold on the screen. Purchase the Sprint Charge upgrade to increase the distance of Spyro's sprint.
Stealth Elf	Stealth Health: Gain 1,000 HP while stealthed.	You need to first purchase Sylvan Regeneration. Once you do, you get credit towards the 1,000 HP every time you heal while Stealth Elf is in the Stealthier Decoy mode.
Stump Smash	Meganut Bowling: Defeat five enemies with one Meganut.	Meganuts are powerful, and bowling over five Chompies with one is no problem. The upgrade Acorn Croquet makes this much easier to achieve since you can wack the acorn directly at enemies.
Sunburn	Immolation Itinerant: Travel 1 mile using Immolation Teleport.	Use Immolation Teleport regularly to tally up the distance towards one full mile. The quickest way to complete this quest is to unlock the Flight of the Phoenix and the Guided Teleportation upgrades.

SKYLANDER	QUEST	HOW TO COMPLETE
Swarm	Swarm Feelings: Defeat 100 enemies in Swarm Form.	While you can complete this quest without pursuing the Wasp Stormer Path, it's extremely difficult, and you must focus on weaker enemies.
Terrafin	Land Lubber: Eat 20 food items while burrowing.	Once you have Surface Feeder, stay underground and collect Food Items as they drop.
Thumpback	Beached Whale: Defeat 8 enemies with one Belly Flop.	Upgrade Thumpback's Belly Flop attack with Slippery Belly. If you are having trouble getting this quest, invest in the Up Close and Personal path to further increase the strength of the Belly Flop attack.
Tree Rex	Timberrrrr!: Defeat 50 enemies by landing on them. Chompies don't count!	Unfortunately, Elbow Drop doesn't work for this quest. Tree Rex must crush enemies by landing on them. The best way to do this is to find a bounce pad in an area with plenty of Chompies.
Trigger Happy	Holding Gold: Save up 50,000 Gold.	This is one of the hardest quests any character has in the game. Not because it's difficult, but because it will take some time to collect 50,000 Gold.
Voodood	Trickwire: Defeat six enemies at once with your tripwire.	Find a group of six or more low-health enemies, like Bone Chompies, and set up the Tripwire near them. Chapter 1: Time of the Giants has several good spots to try for this quest.
Warnado	Chompy Catcher: Catch 100 Chompies in tornadoes.	The best place to do this is in the Arena Challenges. Head to any of the early challenges and there are plenty of Chompies. High Winds also helps gather up more Chompies at once.
Wham-Shell	Irate Invertebrate: Defeat 6 enemies with one Poseidon Strike.	To get the most out of Poseidon Strike, invest in the Captain Crustacean path. Once you have unlocked Mace of the Deep, go for this quest by finding a group of Chompies and blasting them.
Whirlwind	What does it mean?: Create 50 double rainbows.	Unlock the Dual Rainbows ability, then fire out a Tempest cloud and following up with a Rainbow of Doom. Rainbows made via the Double Dose of Doom power don't count unless they hit a Tempest Cloud. Triple rainbows created via Triple Tempest count as one double rainbow.
Wrecking Ball	Competitive Eater: Swallow 100 Enemies.	Purchase Enemy Slurp and swallow as many enemies as you can. Any medium-sized and smaller enemy can be eaten.
Zap	In the Slimelight: Defeat 50 enemies by electrifying them in Sea Slime.	Use Sea Slime to electrify enemies regularly and you'll complete this quest in no time.
Zook	Spore It On: Absorb 1,000 points of damage with a Foliage Barrier.	Use Foliage Barrier often and you will complete this quest quickly.

THE SLY COLLECTION

SLY 2: BAND OF THIEVES

RESTART CURRENT EPISODE

Pause the game and press Left, R1, Up, Down, Up, Left.

TUTORIAL

Pause the game and press Right, Left, Up, Up, Up, R1.

SKIP TO EPISODE 1

Pause the game and press Down, R1, Left, Right, R1, Down.

SKIP TO EPISODE 2

Pause the game and press R1, Left, Right, R1, Left, Down.

SKIP TO EPISODE 3

Pause the game and press Up, Left, Right, Left, Down, Up.

SKIP TO EPISODE 4

Pause the game and press Up, Right, Right, Up, Left, Left.

SKIP TO EPISODE 5

Pause the game and press Left, R1, Down, Down, Up, Right.

SKIP TO EPISODE 6

Pause the game and press Down, Up, R1, R1, Left, Down.

SKIP TO EPISODE 7

Pause the game and press Left, Left, Left, Down, Down, R1.

SKIP TO EPSIODE 8

Pause the game and press Down Up, Left, Left, R1, Right.

UNLOCK TOM GADGET

Pause the game and press Left, Left, Down, Right, Left, Right.

TIME RUSH ABILITY

Pause the game and press Down, Down, Up, Down, Right, Left.

SLY 3: HONOR AMONG THIEVES

FLY THE TOONAMI PLANE

While in the regular plane, pause the game and press R1, R1, Right, Down, Down, Right.

RESTART MISSIONS

Pause the game and enter the following codes to restart the corresponding missions:

RESTART THIS MISSION	ENTER THIS CODE
Episode 1, Day 1	Left, R2, Right, L1, R2, L1
Episode 1, Day 2	Down, L2, Up, Left, R2, L2
Episode 2, Day 1	Right, L2, Left, Up, Right, Down
Episode 2, Day 2	Down, Up, R1, Up, R2, L2
Episode 3, Day 1	R2, R1, L1, Left, L1, Down
Episode 3, Day 2	L2, R1, R2, L2, L1, Up
Episode 4, Day 1	Left, Right, L1, R2, Right, R2
Episode 4, Day 2	L1, Left, L2, Left, Up, L1
Episode 5, Day 1	Left, R2, Right, Up, L1, R2
Episode 5, Day 2	R2, R1, L1, R1, R2, R1
Operation Laptop Retrieval	L2, Left, R1, L2, L1, Down
Operation Moon Crash	L2, Up, Left, L1, L2, L1
Operation Reverse Double Cross	Right, Left, Up, Left, R2, Left
Operation Tar Be-Gone	Down, L2, R1, L2, R1, Right
Operation Turbo Dominant Eagle	Down, Right, Left, L2, R1, Right
Operation Wedding Crasher	L2, R2, Right, Down, L1, R2

SONIC GENERATIONS

SECRET STATUE ROOM

In the Collection Room, hold Select for a few seconds. Sonic jumps into the statue room below. Once there, press Select and enter the following.

STATUE	CODE	STATUE	CODE
Aero-Cannon	329 494	Chopper	639 402
Amy Rose	863 358	Classic Eggman	103 729
Big the Cat	353 012	Classic Sonic	171 045
Blaze the Cat	544 873	Classic Tails	359 236
Booster	495 497	Cop Speeder	640 456
Buzz Bomber	852 363	Crabmeat	363 911
Capsule	777 921	Cream the Rabbit	332 955
Chao	629 893	Cucky/Picky/Flicky/Pecky	249 651
Chaos Emerald	008 140	Dark Chao	869 292
Charmy Bee	226 454	Dr. Eggman	613 482
Chip	309 511	E-123 Omega	601 409

STATUE	CODE
Egg Chaser	200 078
Egg Fighter	851 426
Egg Launcher	973 433
Egg Pawn	125 817
Eggrobo	360 031
Espio the Chameleon	894 526
Goal Plate	933 391
Goal Ring	283 015
Grabber	275 843
Gun Beetle	975 073
Gun Hunter	668 250
Hero Chao	507 376
Iblis Biter	872 910
Iblis Taker	513 929
Iblis Worm	711 268
Item Box	209 005
Jet the Hawk	383 870

STATUE	CODE
Knuckles the Echidna	679 417
Metal Sonic	277 087
Miles "Tails" Prower	632 951
Moto Bug	483 990
Omochao	870 580
Ring	390 884
Rouge the Bat	888 200
Sandworm	548 986
Shadow the Hedgehog	262 416
Silver the Hedgehog	688 187
Sonic the Hedgehog	204 390
Spinner	530 741
Spiny	466 913
Spring – Star	537 070
Spring	070 178
Vector the Crocodile	868 377

SOULCALIBUR V

ALGOL FEAR AND TOWER OF GLORY: MOST HOLY DICHOTOMY STAGE

Defeat Algol Fear in Legendary Souls or Quick Battle.

ALPHA PATROKLOS AND ASTRAL CHAOS: PATHWAY STAGE

Defeat Patrolklos in Quick Battle.

EDGE MASTER AND TOWER OF GLORY: SPIRAL OF GOOD AND EVIL

Complete chapter 17 of story mode to unlock Edge Master and his stage. You can also be obtained by defeating him in Arcade, Legendary Souls, or Quick Battle.

ELYSIUM AND UTOPIA OF THE BLESSED

Complete the final chapter of s tory mode.

KILIK AND THE PENITENTIARY OF DESTINY STAGE

Defeat Kilik in Arcade or Legendary Souls.

PYRRHA OMEGA AND DENEVER CASTLE: EYE OF CHAOS

Complete chapter 19 of story mode.

DEVIL JIN STYLE

Defeat Harada in Quick Battle or Legendary Souls. Go to Customization and then to Original Characters. At the style select at the bottom of the list is Devil Jin (Tekken).

SPACE CHANNEL 5 PART 2

LET CPU TAKE OVER

Pause the game, hold L1 + R1 and press ◉, ▲, ■. The CPU takes over, but trophies are disabled.

SPIDER-MAN: EDGE OF TIME

SHATTERED DIMENSIONS BONUS SUITS

If you have a saved game data for Spider-Man: Shattered Dimensions on your system, eight new Alternate Suits become available in the Bonus Gallery.

AMAZING SPIDER-MAN #500 SUIT (AMAZING)

Select Enter Code from VIP Unlock Code and enter laststand. Go to the Bonus Gallery to access the alternate suits.

POISON SUIT (2099)

Select Enter Code from VIP Unlock Code and enter innerspider. Go to the Bonus Gallery to access the alternate suits.

SPIDEY VS WOLVERINE SUIT (AMAZING) – WHAT IF? SPIDERMAN

Select Enter Code from VIP Unlock Code and enter coldhearted. Go to the Bonus Gallery to access the alternate suits.

2099 ARENA CHALLENGE AND AMAZING ARENA CHALLENGE

Select Enter Code from VIP Unlock Code and enter twospidersenter. Select Arenas from the Main Menu.

BIG TIME SUIT (2099)

At the main menu, press Right, Down, Down, Up, Left, Down, Down, Right.

FUTURE FOUNDATION SUIT (AMAZING)

At the main menu, press Up, Down, Left, Up, Down, Left, Right, Left.

SPIDER-MAN: SHATTERED DIMENSIONS

The following can be entered after completing the tutorial. The suits can be found in the Bonus Gallery under Alternate Suits.

IRON SPIDER SUIT

At the main menu, press Up, Right, Right, Right, Left, Left, Left, Down, Up.

NEGATIVE ZONE SUIT

At the main menu, press Left, Right, Right, Down, Right, Down, Up, Left.

SCARLET SPIDER SUIT

At the main menu, press Right, Up, Left, Right, Up, Left, Right, Up, Left, Right.

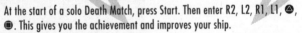

STAR TREK: D-A-C

KOBAYASHI MARU SECRET ACHIEVEMENT

At the start of a solo Death Match, press Start. Then enter R2, L2, R1, L1, ▲, ●. This gives you the achievement and improves your ship.

SUPER HANG-ON

START ARCADE MODE WITH $10,000

Highlight Arcade Mode and press Up, Left, A, B, Start.

SUPER STREET FIGHTER IV

BARREL BUSTER AND CAR CRUSHER BONUS STAGES

Beat Arcade Mode in any difficulty.

COLORS AND TAUNTS

Colors 1 and 2 plus the first taunt for each fighter are available from the start. For colors 11 & 12, start a game with a Street Fighter IV save game on your system. To earn the rest of the colors and taunts, you need to fight a certain number of matches with that character.

COLOR	# OF MATCHES		TAUNT	# OF MATCHES
3	2		2	1
4	4		3	3
5	6		4	5
6	8		5	7
7	10		6	9
8	12		7	11
9	14		8	13
10	16		9	15
			10	16

THOR: GOD OF THUNDER

NEW GAME PLUS

After defeating the game, select New Game Plus to use your stats and powers from the beaten game.

TIGER WOODS PGA TOUR 12: THE MASTERS

50,000 XP

If you have a save game from Tiger Woods PGA Tour 2011, you receive 50,000 XP.

THE TOMB RAIDER TRILOGY

TOMB RAIDER: LEGEND

The following codes must be unlocked in the game before using them.

BULLETPROOF

During a game, hold L1 and press
❌, R1, ▲, R1, ⬛, L2.

DRAIN ENEMY HEALTH

During a game, hold L1 and press
⬛, ⬤, ❌, L2, R1, ▲.

INFINITE ASSAULT RIFLE AMMO

During a game, hold L2 and press
❌, ⬤, ❌, L1, ⬛, ▲.

INFINITE GRENADE LAUNCHER AMMO

During a game, hold L2 and press L1, △, R1, ◉, L1, ◉.

INFINITE SHOTGUN AMMO

During a game, hold L2 and press R1, ◉, ◉, L1, ◉, ✖.

INFINITE SMG AMMO

During a game, hold L2 and press ◉, △, L1, R1, ✖, ◉.

EXCALIBUR

During a game, hold L2 and press △, ✖, ◉, R1, △, L1.

SOUL REAVER

During a game, hold L2. Then press: ✖, R1, ◉, R1, L1, ◉.

ONE SHOT KILL

During a game, hold L1 and press △, ✖, △, ◉, L2, ◉.

TEXTURELESS MODE

During a game, hold L1 and press L2, ✖, ◉, ✖, △, R1.

TOMB RAIDER: UNDERWORLD

INVINCIBLE

During a game, hold L2 and press ✖, R2, △, R2, ◉, L1.

ONE SHOT KILLS

During a game, hold L2 and press hold R2 and press △, ✖, △, ◉, L1, ◉.

SHOW ENEMY HEALTH

During a game, hold L2 and press ◉, ◉, ✖, L1, R2, △.

TONY HAWK'S PRO SKATER HD

ALL CHEATS

At the skater select, hold L2 and press ✖, ◉, △.

ALL GAME MODES

At the skater select, hold L2 and press ✖, △, ◉.

ALL LEVELS

At the skater select, hold L2 and press △, ◉, ◉.

ALL SKATERS

At the skater select, hold L2 and press △, ◉, ◉.

ALL TRICKS

At the skater select, hold L2 and press ✖, ◉, △.

MAX ALL STATS

At the skater select, hold L2 and press △, ◉, ✖.

MAX MONEY

At the skater select, hold L2 and press △, ◉, ✖. This gives you $999,999,999.

TOY STORY 2: BUZZ LIGHTYEAR TO THE RESCUE!

LEVEL SELECT

At the Options menu, press Right, Left, ◉, ▲, ▲.

ALL LEVELS

At the title screen, press Up (x4), Down, Down, Up, Up, Down (x3).

DEBUG MODE

At the title screen, press ✕, ◉, ■.

TRANSFORMERS: DARK OF THE MOON

RATCHET IN MULTIPLAYER

Select Unlockables from the Extras and enter Up, Right, Down, Left, Up, Start.

VIRTUA TENNIS 4

THERON TENNIEL

At the player select, select Load to access Custom Players. Next, press L1.

VICKY BARNEY

At the player select, select Load to access Custom Players. Next, press R1.

WWE '12

WWE ATTITUDE ERA HEAVYWEIGHT CHAMPIONSHIP

Select Options from My WWE. Next, choose Cheat Codes and enter OhHellYeah!.

WWE ALL STARS

UNLOCK ARENAS, WRESTLERS, AND ATTIRE

At the main menu, press Left, ▲, Down, Left, ▲, ●, Left, ●, ▲, Down, Right, ●, Left, Up, ●, Right.

AUSTIN AND PUNK ATTIRES

At the main menu, press Left, Left, Right, Right, Up, Down, Up, Down.

ROBERTS AND ORTON ATTIRES

At the main menu, press Up, Down, Left, Right, Up, Up, Down, Down.

SAVAGE AND MORRISON ATTIRES

At the main menu, press Down, Left, Up, Right, Right, Up, Left, Down.

WWE SMACKDOWN VS. RAW 2011

JOHN CENA (ENTRANCE/CIVILIAN)

In My WWE, select Cheat Codes from the Options and enter SLURPEE.

ALL OF RANDY ORTON'S COSTUMES

In My WWE, select Cheat Codes from the Options and enter apexpredator.

TRIBUTE TO THE TROOPS ARENA

In My WWE, select Cheat Codes from the Options and enter 8thannualtribute.

CRUISERWEIGHT TITLE, HARDCORE TITLE, AND MILLION DOLLAR TITLE

In My WWE, select Cheat Codes from the Options and enter Historicalbelts.

X-MEN DESTINY

JUGGERNAUT SUIT

At the title screen, hold L1 + R1 and press Down, Right, Up, Left, ▲, ●.

EMMA FROST SUIT

At the title screen, hold L1 + R1 and press Up, Down, Right, Left, ●, ▲.

NINTENDO Wii™

THE AMAZING SPIDER-MAN

CLASSIC SPIDER-MAN SUIT

Complete all petty crimes.

BAKUGAN: DEFENDERS OF THE CORE

HIDDEN ITEMS

Select Unlock Codes from Collection and enter HXV6Y7BF. Now you can enter up to eight of your unique Bakugan Dimensions codes.

The codes unlock the following:

Here are eight codes:

The codes unlock the following:	Here are eight codes:
10,000 Core Energy	2FKRRMNCDQ
Ten Vexos Passes	82D77YK6P8
Earthen Armor	HUUH8ST7AR
Fire Spirit	JJUZDEACXX
Light Arrow	QY8CLD5NJE
Tornado Vortex	TD4UMFSRW3
Water Pillar	YJ7RGG7WGZ
Zorch Thunder	YQLHBBSMDC

BATMAN: THE BRAVE AND THE BOLD—THE VIDEOGAME

BATMAN COSTUMES

Access the terminal on the left side of the Batcave and enter the

COSTUME	CODE
Dark Batsuit	3756448
Medieval Batsuit	5644863
Rainbow Suit	7629863

CHALLENGE MAPS

CHALLENGE MAP	CODE
Gotham 1 & 2	4846348
Proto Sparring	6677686
Science Island 1 & 2	7262348

WEAPONS

WEAPON	CODE
Barrier	2525655
Belt Sword	2587973
Flashbangs	3527463
Smoke Pellets	7665336

BATTLE OF GIANTS: DINOSAURS STRIKE

ARMORED

DINOSAUR	PASSWORD
Cassosaurus	09182
Gastonia	69281
Hillierosaurus	27139
NeoAnkylosaurus	13579
NeoDacentrurus	81726

DINOSAUR	PASSWORD
NeoEdmontonia	90817
NeoMiragaia	23071
NeoScolosaurus	86420
NeoStegosaurus	84570
Wuerhosaurus	18963

PREDATORS

DINOSAUR	PASSWORD
Neo Baryonyx	75139
NeoCarcharodon	37452
NeoCarnotaurus	4629
NeoCeratosaur	20135

DINOSAUR	PASSWORD
NeoDilophosaurus	43782
NeoTrex	73096
Suchominus	03275

HORNED

DINOSAUR	PASSWORD
Chasmosaurus	46135
Naxocertops	16948
NeoEiniosaurus	31946

DINOSAUR	PASSWORD
NeoStyracosaurus	25378
NeoTriceratops	18275

RAPTORS

DINOSAUR	PASSWORD
Allosaurus	35274
Gorgoraptor	23587
NeoJuravenator	74312

DINOSAUR	PASSWORD
NeoOviraptor	93245
NeoVelociraptor	10927
Trodon	51274

BEN 10 ALIEN FORCE: VILGAX ATTACKS

LEVEL SKIP

Pause the game and enter Portal in the Cheats menu.

UNLOCK ALL SPECIAL ATTACKS FOR ALL FORMS

Pause the game and enter Everythingproof in the Cheats menu.

UNLOCK ALL ALIEN FORMS

Pause the game and enter Primus in the Cheats menu.

TOGGLE INVULNERABILITY ON AND OFF

Pause the game and enter Xlmrsmoothy in the Cheats menu.

GIVES PLAYER FULL HEALTH

Pause the game and enter Herotime in the Cheats menu.

QUICK ENERGY REGENERATION

Pause the game and enter Generator in the Cheats menu.

BEN 10 ULTIMATE ALIEN: COSMIC DESTRUCTION

To remove the cheats, you will need to start a new game.

1,000,000 DNA

Pause the game, select Cheats, and enter Cash.

REGENERATE HEALTH

Pause the game, select Cheats, and enter Health.

REGENERATE ENERGY

Pause the game, select Cheats, and enter Energy.

UPGRADE EVERYTHING

Pause the game, select Cheats, and enter Upgrade.

ALL LEVELS

Pause the game, select Cheats, and enter Levels.

ENEMIES DO DOUBLE DAMAGE/ PLAYER DOES 1/2 DAMAGE

Pause the game, select Cheats, and enter Hard.

CARS 2: THE VIDEO GAME

ALL MODES AND TRACKS

Select Enter Codes from the Options and enter 959595.

UNLIMITED ENERGY

Select Enter Codes from the Options and enter 721953. Select Cheats to toggle the cheat on and off.

LASER GUIDED

Select Enter Codes from the Options and enter 123456. Select Cheats to toggle the cheat on and off.

CENTIPEDE: INFESTATION

MISSILE COMMAND PACK

Select Enter Code from Extras and enter 111771.

DOKAPON KINGDOM

DOUBLE THE TAXES FROM A TOWN

After saving a town, hold the controller sideways and press A, A + 2.

FAST—RACING LEAGUE

NEUTRON SIBERIA LEAGUE

Complete Neutron Shima League.

NEUTRON SUNAHARA LEAGUE

Complete Neutron Siberia League.

PROTON SHIMA LEAGUE

Complete Neutron Sunahara League.

PROTON SIBERIA LEAGUE

Complete Proton Shima League.

PROTON SUNAHARA LEAGUE

Complete Proton Siberia League.

FAIA VM SHIP

Place in the Neutron Shima league.

DT BOSUTON SHIP

Place in the Neutron Siberia league.

DENKOU QX SHIP

Place in the Proton Siberia league.

KAN Y SHIP

Place in the Proton Sunahara league.

BOOST AT START OF RACE

Right when the announcers says Go, press the accelerator.

FROGGER: HYPER ARCADE EDITION

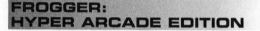

CONTRA STYLE

At the style select, highlight Contra and enter Up, Up, Down, Down, Left, Right, Left, Right, 1, 2.

JERRY RICE & NITUS' DOG FOOTBALL

THREE OF ALL TREATS AND GAME BALLS

At the player select, press Down, A, +, A.

B BUTTON FOR BOOST

At the player select, press Up, Left, +, Right, A.

CPU VS. CPU

At the player select, hold 2 as you select Play.

FIRST PERSON VIEW

At the player select, press Down, A, Right, +.

GENERIC FIELD

While selecting a field, hold 2.

CREDITS

At the title screen, press A, -, -, A.

JUST DANCE 3

BARBRA STREISAND SPECIAL CHOREOGRAPHY

At the title screen (Press Start), press Up, Up, Down, Down, Left, Right, Left, Right.

KARAOKE REVOLUTION GLEE: VOLUME 2

ICE ICE BABY

Select Unlockables from the Options and enter A64112.

PINK HOUSES

Select Unlockables from the Options and enter DD6C62.

KARAOKE REVOLUTION GLEE: VOLUME 3

BORN THIS WAY

Select Unlockables from the Options and enter 60328B.

TOXIC

Select Unlockables from the Options and enter B81120.

FIREWORK

Select Unlockables from the Options and enter 41025F.

KIRBY'S DREAM COLLECTION: SPECIAL EDITION

KIRBY 64: THE CRYSTAL SHARDS CHEATS

SOUND CHECK

Defeat Miracle Matter.

DARK STAR LEVEL

Collect 100 shards and defeat Miracle Matter.

BOSS BATTLES

Defeat 02.

MINI-GAME DIFFICULTIES

COMPLETE MINI-GAME ON...	UNLOCK DIFFICULTY
Easy	Normal
Normal	Hard
Hard	Intense

KIRBY'S ADVENTURE

EXTRA GAME

Defeat the game with 100%.

SOUND TEST

Defeat Extra Game with 100%.

KIRBY'S DREAM LAND

CONFIGURATION MODE

At the title screen, hold Down + Select + B.

BONUS GAME

At the title screen, hold Up + Select + A.

KIRBY'S DREAM LAND 2

OPTION MODE

Complete the game with 100% and then load up your file. Select Option to get a Sound Test, Boss Battle, and Bonus Game.

KIRBY'S DREAM LAND 3

J OPTION

Complete the M Option to get this Jumping mini-game.

? OPTION

Beat all other options to view all videos.

B OPTION

Defeat the final boss to unlock this option. It allows you to face all of the bosses with one life and no healing.

KIRBY SUPER STAR

REVENGE OF META-KNIGHT

Defeat DynaBlade.

THE ARENA

Defeat all other levels.

MILKY WAY WISHES

Defeat Great Cave Offensive and Revenge of Meta-Knight.

SOUND TEST

Defeat The Arena.

THE LEGEND OF ZELDA: SKYWARD SWORD

HERO MODE

After completing the main quest, you can choose to play Hero Mode, which is a tougher version of the regular game. Defeat the game on this mode to unlock a Tri-force next to
the save.

GRATITUDE CRYSTAL REWARDS

There are 80 Gratitude Crystals that can be found and received throughout the game — 65 come from completing side quests and the rest must be found. The following lists the rewards you gain by returning these Gratitude Crystals to Batreaux.

REWARD	NUMBER OF GRATITUDE CRYSTALS
Medium Wallet (500 Rupees)	5
Heart Piece	10
Big Wallet (1000 Rupees) and Cursed Medal	30
Gold Rupee	40
Giant Wallet (5,000 Rupees)	50
2 Gold Rupees	70
Tycoon Wallet (9,000 Rupees)	80

LEGO BATMAN 2: DC SUPER HEROES

RED BRICK CODES

Pause the game, select Extras, and then choose Enter Code. Enter the following:

CHEAT	CODE	CHEAT	CODE
Attract Studs	MNZER6	Minikit Finder	LRJAG8
Beep Beep	ZHAXFH	Peril Finder	RYD3SJ
Character Studs	TPJ37T	Red Brick Finder	5KKQ6G
Disguises	BWQ2MS	Regenerate Hearts	ZXEX5D
Extra Hearts	4LGJ7T	Studs x 2	74EZUT
Extra Toggle	7TXH5K	Super Build	JN2J6V
Fall Rescue	TPGPG2	Vine Grapples	JXN7FJ
Gold Brick Finder	MBXW7V		

CHARACTERS AND VEHICLE

Pause the game, select Extras, and then choose Enter Code. Enter the following:

CHEAT	CODE	CHEAT	CODE
Clown Goon	9ZZZBP	Riddler Goon	Q285LK
LexBot	W49CSJ	Two-Face Goon	95KPYJ
Mime Goon	ZQA8MK	Harley Quinn's Motorbike	C79LVH
Policeman	V9SAGT		

LEGO HARRY POTTER: YEARS 1-4

RED BRICK EXTRAS

Once you have access to The Leaky Cauldron, enter Wiseacre's Wizarding Supplies from Diagon Alley. Go upstairs to enter the following. Pause the game and select Extras to toggle the cheats on or off.

CHEAT	CODE
Carrot Wands	AUC8EH
Character Studs	H27KGC
Character Token Detector	HA79V8
Christmas	T7PVVN

CHEAT	CODE
Disguise	4DMK2R
Fall Rescue	ZEX7MV
Extra Hearts	J9U6Z9
Fast Dig	Z9BFAD
Fast Magic	FA3GQA
Gold Brick Detector	84QNQN

CHEAT	CODE
Hogwarts Crest Detector	TTMC6D
Ice Rink	F88VUW
Invincibility	QQWC6B
Red Brick Detector	7AD7HE
Regenerate Hearts	89ML2W
Score x2	74YKR7
Score x4	J3WHNK
Score x6	XK9ANE
Score x8	HUFV2H
Score x10	H8X69Y
Silhouettes	HZBVX7
Singing Mandrake	BMEU6X
Stud Magnet	67FKWZ

WISEACRE SPELLS

Once you have access to The Leaky Cauldron, enter Wiseacre's Wizarding Supplies from Diagon Alley. Go upstairs to enter the following. You need to learn Wingardium Leviosa before you can use these cheats.

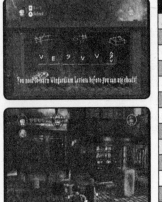

SPELL	CODE
Accio	VE9VV7
Anteoculatia	QFB6NR
Calvorio	6DNR6L
Colovaria	9GJ442
Engorgio Skullus	CD4JLX
Entomorphis	MYN3NB
Flipendo	ND2L7W
Glacius	ERA9DR
Herbifors	H8FTHL
Incarcerous	YEB9Q9
Locomotor Mortis	2M2XJ6
Multicorfors	JK6QRM
Redactum Skullus	UW8LRH
Rictusempra	2UCA3M
Slugulus Eructo	U6EE8X
Stupefy	UWDJ4Y
Tarantallegra	KWWQ44
Trip Jinx	YZNRF6

EEYLOPS GOLD BRICKS

Once you have access to The Leaky
Cauldron, enter Wiseacre's Wizarding
Supplies from Diagon Alley. Go
upstairs to enter the following.
To access the LEGO Builder, visit
Gringott's Bank at the end of
Diagon Alley.

GOLD BRICK	CODE
1	QE4VC7
2	FY8H97
3	3MQT4P
4	PQPM7Z
5	ZY2CPA
6	3GMTP6

GOLD BRICK	CODE
7	XY6VYZ
8	TUNC4W
9	EJ42Q6
10	GFJCV9
11	DZCY6G

LEGO HARRY POTTER: YEARS 5-7

CHEATS

Pause the game and select Extras. Go to Enter Code and enter the following:

CHEAT	CODE
Carrot Wands	AUC8EH
Character Studs	H27KGC
Character Token Detector	HA79V8
Christmas	T7PVVN
Collect Ghost Studs	2FLY6B
Extra Hearts	J9U6Z9
Fall Rescue	ZEX7MV
Fast Dig	Z9BFAD
Ghost Coins	2FLY6B

CHEAT	CODE
Gold Brick Detector	84QNQN
Hogwarts Crest Detector	TTMC6D
Invincibility	QQWC6B
Red Brick Detector	7AD7HE
Score x2	74YKR7
Score x6	XK9ANE
Score x8	HUFV2H
Score x10	H8X69Y
Super Strength	BMEU6X

LEGO INDIANA JONES 2: THE ADVENTURE CONTINUES

Pause the game, select Enter Secret Code from the Extras menu, and enter the following.

CHARACTERS

CHARACTER	CODE
Belloq (Priest)	FTL48S
Dovchenko	WL4T6N
Enemy Boxer	7EQF47
Henry Jones	4CSAKH
Indiana Jones	PGWSEA
Indiana Jones: 2	FGLKYS
Indiana Jones (Collect)	DZFY9S
Indiana Jones (Desert)	M4C34K
Indiana Jones (Desert Disguise)	2W8QR3
Indiana Jones (Dinner Suit)	QUNZUT
Indiana Jones (Kali)	J2XS97
Indiana Jones (Officer)	3FQFKS
Interdimensional Being	PXT4UP
Lao Che	7AWX3J
Mannequin (Boy)	2UJQWC

CHARACTER	CODE
Mannequin (Girl)	3PGSEL
Mannequin (Man)	QPWDMM
Mannequin (Woman)	U7SMVK
Mola Ram	82RMC2
Mutt	2GKS62
Salah	E88YRP
Willie	94RUAJ

EXTRAS

EFFECT	CODE
Beep Beep	UU3VSC
Disguise	Y9TE98
Fast Build	SNXC2F
Fast Dig	XYAN83
Fast Fix	3Z7PJX
Fearless	TUXNZF
Ice Rink	TY9P4U
Invincibility	6JBB65
Poo Money	SZFAAE
Score x3	PEHHPZ
Score x4	UXGTB3
Score X6	XWLJEY

EFFECT	CODE
Score x8	S5UZCP
Score x10	V7JYBU
Silhouettes	FQGPYH
Snake Whip	2U7YCV
Stud Magnet	EGSM5B

LEGO PIRATES OF THE CARIBBEAN: THE VIDEO GAME

CODES

Pause the game and select Extras. Choose Enter Code and enter the following codes:

EFFECT	PASSWORD
Ammand the Corsair	EW8T6T
Blackbeard	D3DW0D
Clubba	644THF
Davy Jones	4DJLKR
Governor Weatherby Swann	LD9454
Gunner	Y611WB
Hungry Cannibal	64BNHG
Jack Sparrow	VDJSPW

EFFECT	PASSWORD
Jacoby	BW0656
Jimmy Legs	13GLW5
Koehler	RT093G
Mistress Ching	GDETDE
Philip	WEV040
Quartermaster	RX58HU
The Spaniard	P861J0
Twigg	KDLFKD

LEGO STAR WARS III: THE CLONE WARS

Pause the game, select Enter Code from Extras and enter the following:

CHARACTERS

CHARACTER	CODE
Aayla Secura	2VG95B
Adi Gallia	G2BFEN
Admiral Ackbar (Classic)	272Y9Q
Admiral Yularen	NG6PYX
Ahsoka	2VJ9TH
Anakin Skywalker	F9VUYJ
Anakin Skywalker (Geonosian Arena)	9AA4DW
Asajj Ventress	YG9DD7
Aurra Sing	M2V1JV
Bail Organa	GEHX6C
Barriss Offee	BTVTZ5
Battle Droid	5Y7MA4
Battle Droid Commander	LSU4LJ
Bib Fortuna	9U4TF3
Boba Fett (Classic)	TY2BYJ

CHARACTER	CODE
Boil	Q5Q39P
Bossk	2KLW5R
C-3PO	574226
Cad Bane	NHME85
Captain Antilles (Classic)	D8SNGJ
Captain Rex	MW3QYH
Captain Typho	GD6FX3
Chancellor Palpatine	5C62YQ
Chewbacca (Classic)	66UU3T
Clone Pilot	HQ7BVD
Clone Shadow Trooper (Classic)	7GFNCQ
Clone Trooper	NP5GTT
Commander Bly	7CB6NS
Commander Cody	SMN259
Commander Fil	U25HFC
Commander Ponds	JRPR2A

CHARACTER	CODE	CHARACTER	CODE
Commander Stone	5XZQSV	Neimoidian	BJB94J
Commando Droid	QEGU64	Nute Gunray	QFYXMC
Count Dooku	EWR7WM	Obi-Wan Kenobi	J9HNF9
Darth Maul (Classic)	QH68AK	Obi-Wan Kenobi (Classic)	FFBU5M
Darth Sidious (Classic)	QXY5XN	Obi-Wan Kenobi (Geonosian Arena)	5U9FJK
Darth Vader (Classic)	FM4JB7	OG-9 Homing Spider Droid	7NEC36
Darth Vader Battle Damaged (Classic)	NMJFBL	Onaconda Farr	DB7ZQN
Destroyer Droid	9MUTS2	Padmé Amidala (Geonosian Arena)	SZ824Q
Dr. Nuvo Vindi	MB9EMW	Padmé Amidala	8X87U6
Echo	JB9E5S	Pirate Ruffian	BH2EHU
Eeth Koth	WUFDYA	Plo Koon	BUD4VU
Gammorean Guard	WSFZZQ	Poggle The Lesser	4592WM
General Grievous	7FNU4T	Princess Leia (Classic)	2D3D3L
Geonosian Guard	GAFZUD	Probe Droid	U2T4SP
Gold Super Battle Droid	2C8NHP	Queen Neeyutnee	ZQRN85
Gonk Droid	C686PK	Qui-Gon Jinn (Classic)	LKHD3B
Grand Moff Tarkin	NH2405	R2-D2	RZ5HUV
Greedo (Classic)	FUW4C2	R3-S6	Z87PAU
Hailfire Droid	T7XF9Z	R4-P17	5MXSYA
Han Solo (Classic)	KFDBXF	R6-H5	7PMC3C
Heavy Super Battle Droid	G65KJJ	Rebel Commando (Classic)	PZMQNK
Heavy Weapons Clone Trooper	WXUTWY	Robonino	2KLW5R
Helios 3D	4AXTY4	Rys	4PTP53
Hevy	EUB8UG	Savage Oppress	MELL07
Hondo Ohnaka	5A7XYX	Senate Commando	EPBPLK
IG-86	EABPCP	Senate Commando (Captain)	S4Y7VW
Imperial Guard (Classic)	5W6FGD	Senator Kharrus	EA4E9S
Jango Fett	5KZQ4D	Senator Philo	9Q7YCT
Jar Jar Binks	MESPTS	Shahan Alama	G4N7C2
Jek	AYREC9	Sionver Boll	5C62YQ
Ki-Adi-Mundi	HGBCTQ	Stormtrooper (Classic)	HPE7PZ
Kit Fitso	PYWJ6N	Super Battle Droid	MJKDV5
Lando Calrissian (Classic)	ERAEWE	Tee Watt Kaa	FYVSHD
LEP Servent Droid	SM3Y9B	Turk Falso	HEBHW5
Lieutenant Thire	3NEUXC	Tusken Raider (Classic)	GC2XSA
Lok Durd	TKCYUZ	TX-20	PE7FGD
Luke Skywalker (Classic)	PG73HF	Undead Geonosian	QGENFD
Luminara Unduli	MKUYQ8	Vader's Apprentice (Classic)	EGQQ4V
Lurmen Villager	R35Y7N	Wag Too	VRUVSZ
Luxury Droid	V4WMJN	Wat Tambor	ZP8XVH
Mace Windu	8NVRWJ	Waxer	BNJE79
MagnaGuard	2KEF2D	Wedge Antilles (Classic)	DRGLWS
MSE-6	S6GRNZ	Whorm Loathsom	4VVYQV
Nahdar Vebb	ZKXG43	Workout Clone Trooper	MP9DRE
		Yoda	CSQTMB

VEHICLES

VEHICLE	CODE		VEHICLE	CODE
Dwarf Spider Droid	NACMGG		Slave I	KDDQVD
Geonosian Solar Sailor	PJ2U3R		The Twilight	T4K5L4
Geonosian Starfighter	EDENEC		Vulture Droid	7W7K7S

RED BRICKS

CHEAT	CODE		CHEAT	CODE
Character Studs	QD2C31		Score x2	YZPHUV
Dark Side	X1V4N2		Score x4	43T5E5
Dual Wield	C4ES4R		Score x6	SEBHGR
Fast Build	GCHP7S		Score x8	BYFSAQ
Glow in the Dark	4GT3VQ		Score x10	N1CKR1
Invincibility	J46P7A		Stud Magnet	6MZ5CH
Minikit Detector	CSD5NA		Super Saber Cut	BS828K
Perfect Deflect	3F5L56		Super Speeders	B1D3W3
Regenerate Hearts	2D7JNS			

MADAGASCAR 3: THE VIDEO GAME

ALL DISGUISES

Select Promotion from Extras and enter Pineapple, Strawberry, Grapes, Apple.

BANANA DASH MINI-GAME IN LONDON

Select Promotion from Extras and enter Strawberry, Orange, Apple, Grapes.

BANANA DASH MINI-GAME IN PARIS

Select Promotion from Extras and enter Pineapple, Grapes, Pineapple, Banana.

BANANA DASH MINI-GAME IN PISA

Select Promotion from Extras and enter Orange, Banana, Orange, Apple.

BANANA DASH MINI-GAME IN ROME

Select Promotion from Extras and enter Grape, Apple, Grape, Strawberry.

MEGA MAN 5

ALL WEAPONS AND ITEMS PASSWORD

Enter Blue B4 D6 F1 and Red C1 D4 F6 as a password.

MONSTER WORLD IV

SOUND TEST

Highlight New Game and press Up, Down, Up, Down, Left, Left, Right, Right.

NASCAR THE GAME 2011

MARK MARTIN PAINT SCHEMES

At the garage main menu, press Down, Down, Up, Up, Right, Left, Right, Left. Enter godaddy.com.

NBA 2K12

ABA BALL

Select Extras from the Features menu. Choose Codes and enter payrespect. This can be toggled on and off from this Codes menu.

2K CHINA TEAM

Select Extras from the Features menu. Choose Codes and enter 2kchina.

2K SPORTS TEAM

Select Extras from the Features menu. Choose Codes and enter 2ksports.

UNLOCK NBA 2K TEAM

Select Extras from the Features menu. Choose Codes and enter nba2k.

VC TEAM

Select Extras from the Features menu. Choose Codes and enter vcteam.

JORDAN RETRO COLLECTION

Select Extras from the Features menu. Choose Codes and enter 23.

SECONDARY ROAD UNIFORMS

Select Extras from the Features menu. Choose Codes and enter hcsilapadatu. This unlocks uniforms for 76ers, Jazz, Kings, and Mavericks.

CHRISTMAS UNIFORMS

Select Extras from the Features menu. Choose Codes and enter ibyasmliancbhlald. This unlocks uniforms for Bulls, Celtics, Heat, Knicks, Lakers, and Mavericks.

HEAT BACK IN BLACK UNIFORM

Select Extras from the Features menu. Choose Codes and enter albkbinkcca.

RAPTORS MILITARY NIGHT UNIFORM

Select Extras from the Features menu. Choose Codes and enter liyrimta.

PHINEAS AND FERB: ACROSS THE 2ND DIMENSION

SKIN FOR AGENT P: PERRY THE PLATYBORG

During a game, press the Minus button to bring up the pause menu. Select Enter Code from Extras and enter BAB121.

POKÉMON RUMBLE

POKEMON PASSWORDS

Go to the recruitment building in the terminal and enter the following passwords to get the corresponding Pokemon.

POKEMON	PASSWORD	POKEMON	PASSWORD
Blastoise	9580-1423	Mew	9561-8808
Charizard	7968-4528	Piplup	9900-2455
Charmander	7927-6161	Shaymin (Sky Form)	5468-6284
Cherrim Positive Forme	7540-5667	Shiny Bidoof	5575-2435
Chimchar	8109-8384	Shiny Rattata	9849-3731
Eevee	0511-0403	Squirtle	6824-2045
Giratina (Origin Form)	8322-3706	Turtwig	8672-1076
		Venusaur	1589-3955

POKEPARK WII: PIKACHU'S ADVENTURE

CELEBI APPEARS

Enter 58068773 as a password.

DARKRAI APPEARS

Enter 65967413 as a password.

GROUDON APPEARS

Enter 49446209 as a password.

JIRACHI APPEARS

Enter 73938790 as a password.

PIKACHU'S BALLOONS

Enter 99930457 as a password.

PIKACHU'S SNOWBOARD

Enter 67446162 as a password.

PIKACHU'S SURFBOARD

Enter 02970626 as a password.

POKÉPARK 2: WONDERS BEYOND

KECLEON'S AWARDS

Befriend Kecleon by using Snivy to clear the southeastern buildings in Cove Town. Examine the red stripe to gain access to Kecleon. Here you can check your Records and the following Awards.

AWARD	EARNED BY
Ace Strikers	Score 100 goals.
Attraction Elite	Score first place in the four Attractions at Wish Park.
Battle Experts	Win all battles, including the Battle Tournament.
Battle Tournament Champs	Win the Battle Tournament after finishing the game.
Berry Rich	Collect 50,000 Berries.
Camera Czars	Take 100 Photos.
Chase Champions	Beat every Pokémon that plays Chase.
Collectors	Collect all Collection items.
Epic Explorers	Explore the Lighthouse, Stump, Cave, and Lab a lot.
Friendly Folk	Greet Pokémon 100 times.
Friends with Everyone	Befriend all 194 Pokémon.
Landscapers	Scatter plants 100 times.
Max Power	Get maximum Power Up for Pikachu and all his Pals.
Mighty Smashers	Hit Pokémon with Dash 500 times.
Portal Pros (Arbor)	Get 50,000 points when opening the Wish Park portal in Windmill Way.
Portal Pros (Cove)	Get 50,000 points when opening the Wish Park portal on Seaside Beach.
Portal Pros (Crag)	Get 50,000 points when opening the Wish Park portal in the Colosseum building.
Portal Pros (Tech)	Get 50,000 points when opening the Wish Park portal in the Scientorium.
Quillseekers	Collect all 40 Vast White Quills.
Sure Shots	Hit Pokémon 100 with objects.
Wrecking Crew	Destroy 100 objects in PokéPark.

POWER RANGERS SAMURAI

ALL RANGERS IN EVERY LEVEL

Complete Mission 15 and go through the credits.

RABBIDS GO HOME

ASSASSIN RABBID

Finish Nick of Time to unlock the
Rabbid customization option. Enter
this option and select a Rabbid.
Go to the menu and select Manage
Figurines from the Figurines screen.
Hold C + Z and press 2, 2, 1, 1, A,
A, 1, 1.

BEST BUY RABBID

Finish Nick of Time to unlock the
Rabbid customization option. Enter
this option and select a Rabbid.
Go to the menu and select Manage
Figurines from the Figurines screen.
Hold C + Z and press B, 1, 1, B, A,
2, 2, A.

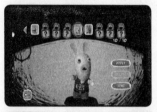

GEEK SQUAD RABBID

Finish Nick of Time to unlock the
Rabbid customization option. Enter
this option and select a Rabbid.
Go to the menu and select Manage
Figurines from the Figurines screen.
Hold C + Z and press A, A, 1, 1, 1,
1, 2, 2.

KANGAROO RABBID

Finish Nick of Time to unlock the
Rabbid customization option. Enter
this option and select a Rabbid.
Go to the menu and select Manage
Figurines from the Figurines screen.
Hold C + Z and press 1, 1, 1, 1, 1,
2, 1, 2.

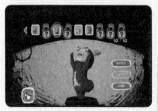

LEONARDO RABBID

Finish Nick of Time to unlock the Rabbid customization option. Enter this option and select a Rabbid. Go to the menu and select Manage Figurines from the Figurines screen. Hold C + Z and press 1, 1, 2, 2, A, A, 1, 1.

PRINCE RABBID

Finish Nick of Time to unlock the Rabbid customization option. Enter this option and select a Rabbid. Go to the menu and select Manage Figurines from the Figurines screen. Hold C + Z and press 1, 2, 1, 2, 1, 2, A, A.

SPLINTER CELL RABBID

Finish Nick of Time to unlock the Rabbid customization option. Enter this option and select a Rabbid. Go to the menu and select Manage Figurines from the Figurines screen. Hold C + Z and press B, B, B, B, A, A, A, A.

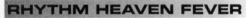

RHYTHM HEAVEN FEVER

THE CLAPPY TRIO GAME

Earn 35 Medals. Select the samurai head to play this game.

SNEAKY SPIRITS GAME

Earn 38 Medals. Select the samurai head to play this game.

POWER CALLIGRAPHY GAME

Earn 41 Medals. Select the samurai head to play this game.

TAP TRIAL GAME

Earn 44 Medals. Select the samurai head to play this game.

MR. UPBEAT ENDLESS GAME

Earn 3 Medals. Select the purple A button to play this game.

WAKE-UP CALLER ENDLESS GAME

Earn 11 Medals. Select the purple A button to play the game.

MUNCHY MONK ENDLESS GAME

Earn 23 Medals. Select the purple A button to play the game.

LADY CUPID ENDLESS GAME

Earn 32 Medals. Select the purple A button to play the game.

ENDLESS REMIX ENDLESS GAME

Earn a Perfect on all 50 games. Select the purple A button to play the game.

CLAP TRAP 2-PLAYER ENDLESS GAME

Earn 1 Duo Medal. Select the purple AA button to play the game.

MOCHI POUNDING 2-PLAYER ENDLESS GAME

Earn 2 Duo Medals. Select the purple AA button to play the game.

KUNG FU BALL 2-PLAYER ENDLESS GAME

Earn 4 Duo Medals. Select the purple AA button to play the game.

PIRATE CREW 2-PLAYER ENDLESS GAME

Earn 6 Duo Medals. Select the purple AA button to play the game.

BOSSA NOVA 2-PLAYER ENDLESS GAME

Earn 8 Duo Medals. Select the purple AA button to play the game.

TOY CAR RHYTHM TOY

Earn 1 Medal. Select the yellow smiley face to play around with it.

POLICE CALL RHYTHM TOY

Earn 7 Medals. Select the yellow smiley face to play around with it.

HI-HAT RHYTHM TOY

Earn 14 Medals. Select the yellow smiley face to play around with it.

RHYTHM FIGHTER RHYTHM TOY

Earn 21 Medals. Select the yellow smiley face to play around with it.

POLICE CALL RHYTHM TOY CODES

After unlocking the Police Call Rhythm Toy, the following can be entered for different effects:

BIRDS	MATCH
BOUTS	SEESAW
GOLFHERO	STAFF

SKYLANDERS GIANTS

SKYLANDERS SPECIFIC QUESTS

Skylanders Giants includes quests specific to each Skylander as a way to improve them.

Here we list each Skylander with their quest and tips on how to complete it.

SKYLANDER	QUEST	HOW TO COMPLETE
Bash	On a Roll: Defeat 10 enemies with one roll attack.	If you have trouble completing this quest, opt for the Pulver Dragon upgrade path.
Boomer	On a Troll: Defeat five enemies with one kicked Troll Bomb.	Once you have Troll Bomb Boot, look for a group of tight-knit Chompies. Chapter 1: Time of the Giants has several groupings of five Chompies.
Bouncer	Stay on Target!: Target enemies 100 times with laser-guided Shoulder Rockets.	You must purchase the Targeting Computer upgrade for Bouncer's Shoulder Rockets.
Camo	Garden Gorger: Eat 10 watermelons.	If you aren't in a rush to complete a level, switch to Camo when a watermelon appears.
Chill	Ice Sore: Defeat six enemies with one Ice Narwhal attack.	Try to find six enemies that are grouped together at a medium distance, such as in an arena.
Chop Chop	Stalwart Defender: Absorb 1,000 damage with your shield.	To complete this quest safely, block attacks from a small group of weaker enemies near a food item (just in case they sneak in some unexpected damage).

SKYLANDER	QUEST	HOW TO COMPLETE
Crusher	High Roller: Defeat 100 enemies with boulders.	Use Rockslide defeat enemies until you have completed this quest.
Cynder	On the Haunt: Defeat 50 enemies with your Ghost Ally.	Ghost Ally does not inflict much damage so focus on saving low-health enemies, like Chompies, for the Ghost to attack. The Ghost attacks while Cynder is flying, so consider circling an area with Chompies.
Dino-Rang	Fooderang: Pick up 20 food items with boomerangs.	After acquiring Sticky Boomerangs, use it to grab any food found in the area. In the Arena Challenges on Flynn's Ship, the audience throws food items into the arena between rounds.
Double Trouble	Big Bomb Trouble: Defeat 10 enemies with one Magic Bomb attack.	Find a group of 10 or more Chompies and set off a bomb. A good place to earn this is any of of Brock's Arena Challenges with regular Chompies.
Drill Sergeant	Drill Skill: Defeat Drill-X without changing Skylanders.	Drill Sergeant must defeat Drill-X (the final boss in Chapter 11: Drill-X's Big Rig) solo. Use Adventure items (like Healing Potion) to survive the battle. You can complete it on Easy difficulty with a fully-upgraded Drill Sergeant.
Drobot	Feed the Burn: Defeat 50 enemies with Afterburners.	It's easiest to hit enemies with Afterburners when Drobot first takes off.
Eruptor	Pizza Burp: Eat 10 Pizzas.	If you want to have a greater chance of encountering a pizza, equip Lucky Wheel of Health in the Luck-O-Tron.
Eye Brawl	Gold Search: Collect 5,000 gold with the eyeball detached.	Remember to detach Eye-Brawl's eye before collecting any treasure from chests or enemies.
Flameslinger	Circular Combustion: Defeat 10 enemies with one column of Fire Flame Dash.	There are two upgrades you can get to help you on this quest. The first is Column of Fire. The second is Supernova in the Pyromancer Path.
Flashwing	Let It Shine: Defeat 20 enemies with one Crystal Lighthouse.	Since Crystal Lighthouse is stationary, this is a tricky quest. The best candidate for this is one of the arena maps, particularly Kaos' Royal Flush (the second challenge, Birthday Bash). Set up the Lighthouse in the middle of the birthday cake.
Fright Rider	Delving Throw: Toss 50 enemies into the air.	The power to use for this quest is Burrow Bomber. Hit any medium or small enemy with the attack to pop them up in the air and register a toss.
Ghost Roaster	Grave Circumstances: Defeat 100 enemies with Skull Charge.	Repeatedly use Skull Charge to attack enemies and you should complete this quest in no time.
Gill Grunt	Anchors Away!: Defeat six enemies with one Anchor Attack.	Line up a group of Chompies with your Anchor Cannon and let loose to complete the quest. If you have Series 2 Gill Grunt, Anchor's Away! makes completing the quest easier.
Hex	Noggin Knocker: Knock away 100 enemies with your Skull Rain.	Once Hex has Skull Shield, allow enemies to get within melee range while Hex is charging that attack. If they get too close, they get knocked back, tallying a point for this quest.
Hot Dog	Animal Aggravator: Scare away 20 birds.	Look for the small birds pecking at the ground in each level. These birds are the ones you need to scare with Hot Dog for this achievement. Chapter 13: The Oracle and Chapter 1: Time of Giants both have plenty of birds.
Hot Head	Buggy Breakthrough: Destroy 20 walls in Hot Rod mode.	The walls this quest is referring to are the walls that can only be crushed by a Giant or a bomb. Whenever you encounter one of these walls, switch to Hot Head. A good spot with plenty of these types of walls is Chapter 2: Junkyard Isles.

SKYLANDER	QUEST	HOW TO COMPLETE
Ignitor	Tinder Trekker: Travel 26,000 feet in Flame Form.	Use Flame Form often and this number will accumulate quickly.
Jet-Vac	Bird Cleaner: Suck up 50 birds in your Suction Gun.	Look for tiny birds on the ground throughout most levels with green grass. Chapter 13: The Oracle and Chapter 1: Time of Giants both have plenty of birds.
Lightning Rod	Current Event: Defeat 10 enemies with one Grand Lightning strike.	You need to find a group of 10 Chompies in one area and use the Grand Lightning to blast them all. Choosing the Lord of Lightning Path makes this easier since the Grand Lightning attack lasts longer.
Ninjini	Bottle Beatdown: Defeat 5 enemies within five seconds of exiting your bottle.	Transform Ninjini into the bottle and move into a large group of small enemies. Follow up the bottle attack with her swords.
Pop Fizz	Rampage: Do 200 HP of damage in a single run in Beast Form.	Transform into Beast Form in a large group of enemies and destroy everything in sight to complete the quest.
Prism Break	Bifurcation Sensation: Defeat 100 enemies with double refraction.	A beam must pass through two Shards before hitting an enemy to count. Unlock the Chained Refractions upgrade and place plenty of Crystal Shards. Fire an Energy Beam through them to indirectly take out nearby enemies.
Shroomboom	Lunching Launch: Eat a watermelon while performing a Self-Slingshot!	When you find a watermelon, blast Shroomboom through it with the Self-Slingshot power to complete the quest.
Slam Bam	Ice to Meet You: Trap 100 enemies in your Ice Blocks.	You do not need to damage or freeze enemies with Ice Block; it counts if you just hit them with the Ice Block.
Sonic Boom	Sonic Squeak: Babies defeat 50 enemies.	Upgrade Sonic Boom's egg attack powers and keep babies summoned at all times.
Sprocket	Mined Your Step: Defeat 50 enemies using the Landmine Golf attack.	Once you unlock the Landmine Golf ability, use it often. A quick way to complete this quest is to load up one of the easier Arena levels.
Spyro	Full Charge: Collect 3 gold, eat 1 food item, and defeat 2 enemies in 1 Sprint Charge.	Look for two low-health enemies (Chompies are a good choice) as well as some food and gold on the screen. Purchase the Sprint Charge upgrade to increase the distance of Spyro's sprint.
Stealth Elf	Stealth Health: Gain 1,000 HP while stealthed.	You need to first purchase Sylvan Regeneration. Once you do, you get credit towards the 1,000 HP every time you heal while Stealth Elf is in the Stealthier Decoy mode.
Stump Smash	Meganut Bowling: Defeat five enemies with one Meganut.	Meganuts are powerful, and bowling over five Chompies with one is no problem. The upgrade Acorn Croquet makes this much easier to achieve since you can wack the acorn directly at enemies.
Sunburn	Immolation Itinerant: Travel 1 mile using Immolation Teleport.	Use Immolation Teleport regularly to tally up the distance towards one full mile. The quickest way to complete this quest is to unlock the Flight of the Phoenix and the Guided Teleportation upgrades.
Swarm	Swarm Feelings: Defeat 100 enemies in Swarm Form.	While you can complete this quest without pursuing the Wasp Stormer Path, it's extremely difficult, and you must focus on weaker enemies.
Terrafin	Land Lubber: Eat 20 food items while burrowing.	Once you have Surface Feeder, stay underground and collect Food Items as they drop.
Thumpback	Beached Whale: Defeat 8 enemies with one Belly Flop.	Upgrade Thumpback's Belly Flop attack with Slippery Belly. If you are having trouble getting this quest, invest in the Up Close and Personal path to further increase the strength of the Belly Flop attack.

SKYLANDER	QUEST	HOW TO COMPLETE
Tree Rex	Timberrrrr!: Defeat 50 enemies by landing on them. Chompies don't count!	Unfortunately, Elbow Drop doesn't work for this quest. Tree Rex must crush enemies by landing on them. The best way to do this is to find a bounce pad in an area with plenty of Chompies.
Trigger Happy	Holding Gold: Save up 50,000 Gold.	This is one of the hardest quests any character has in the game. Not because it's difficult, but because it will take some time to collect 50,000 Gold.
Voodood	Trickwire: Defeat six enemies at once with your tripwire.	Find a group of six or more low-health enemies, like Bone Chompies, and set up the Tripwire near them. Chapter 1: Time of the Giants has several good spots to try for this quest.
Warnado	Chompy Catcher: Catch 100 Chompies in tornadoes.	The best place to do this is in the Arena Challenges. Head to any of the early challenges and there are plenty of Chompies. High Winds also helps gather up more Chompies at once.
Wham-Shell	Irate Invertebrate: Defeat 6 enemies with one Poseidon Strike.	To get the most out of Poseidon Strike, invest in the Captain Crustacean path. Once you have unlocked Mace of the Deep, go for this quest by finding a group of Chompies and blasting them.
Whirlwind	What does it mean?: Create 50 double rainbows.	Unlock the Dual Rainbows ability, then fire out a Tempest cloud and following up with a Rainbow of Doom. Rainbows made via the Double Dose of Doom power don't count unless they hit a Tempest Cloud. Triple rainbows created via Triple Tempest count as one double rainbow.
Wrecking Ball	Competitive Eater: Swallow 100 Enemies.	Purchase Enemy Slurp and swallow as many enemies as you can. Any medium-sized and smaller enemy can be eaten.
Zap	In the Slimelight: Defeat 50 enemies by electrifying them with Sea Slime.	Use Sea Slime to electrify enemies regularly and you'll complete this quest in no time.
Zook	Spore It On: Absorb 1,000 points of damage with a Foliage Barrier.	Use Foliage Barrier often and you will complete this quest quickly.

SONIC COLORS

EXTRA LIVES

After completing a level, the results screen shows how well you did. Jump through the numbers until they break apart revealing gold rings and extra lives.

SPIDER-MAN: EDGE OF TIME

SHATTERED DIMENSIONS BONUS SUITS

If you have a saved game data for Spider-Man: Shattered Dimensions on your system, new Alternate Suits become available in the Bonus Gallery.

BIG TIME SUIT (2099)

At the main menu, press Right, Down, Down, Up, Left, Down, Down, Right.

FUTURE FOUNDATION SUIT (AMAZING)

At the main menu, press Up, Down, Left, Up, Down, Left, Right, Left.

SPIDER-MAN: SHATTERED DIMENSIONS

The following can be entered after completing the tutorial.

IRON SPIDER SUIT

At the main menu, press Up, Right, Right, Right, Left, Left, Left, Down, Up.

NEGATIVE ZONE SUIT

At the main menu, press Left, Right, Right, Down, Right, Down, Up, Left.

SCARLET SPIDER SUIT

At the main menu, press Right, Up, Left, Right, Up, Left, Right, Up, Left, Right.

STAR WARS THE CLONE WARS: LIGHTSABER DUELS

COUNT DOOKU

Select Cheats from Extras and press 2, 2, +, 2, 2, +, 2, 2, -, A, -, C, -, Z, +, Z.

GENERAL GRIEVOUS

Select Cheats from Extras and press 2, 2, +, 2, 2, +, 2, 2, -, Z, -, A, -, C, +, C.

ALL STORY MODE STAGES

Select Cheats from Extras and press A, +, 2, 2, +, C, +, 2, 2, +, Z, +, 2, 2.

MUSTAFAR STAGE

Select Cheats from Extras and press Z (x5), +, Z (x5), +, 1.

RAXUS PRIME STAGE

Select Cheats from Extras and press A (x5), +, A (x5), +, , 2.

SEPARATIST DROID FACTORY STAGE

Select Cheats from Extras and press C (x5), +, C (x5), +, 1.

CREDITS

Select Cheats from Extras and press 1, 2, +, 1.

GALLERY ONE

Select Cheats from Extras and press -, A, +, 1.

GALLERY TWO

Select Cheats from Extras and press -, A, +, 2.

GALLERY THREE

Select Cheats from Extras and press +, A, +, 1, +, 2.

GALLERY FOUR

Select Cheats from Extras and press +, A, +, 2, +, 2.

TIGER WOODS
PGA TOUR 12: THE MASTERS

ALL BALLS AVAILABLE AT SHOP

Select Passwords from the Options and enter tour proving.

ALL CLUBS AVAILABLE AT SHOP

Select Passwords from the Options and enter clubsoda.

ADIDAS EQUIPMENT

Select Passwords from the Options and enter ClimaCool.

FOOTJOY EQUIPMENT

Select Passwords from the Options and enter Dry Joys.

ALL PING CLUBS

Select Passwords from the Options and enter rapture.

TIGER WOODS APPAREL

Select Passwords from the Options and enter gearoftheTiger.

JEWELRY

Select Passwords from the Options and enter Platinum.

VIRTUA TENNIS 4

THERON TENNIEL

At the player select, select Load to access Custom Players. Next, press -.

VICKY BARNEY

At the player select, select Load to access Custom Players. Next, press +.

WWE '12

WWE ATTITUDE ERA HEAVYWEIGHT CHAMPIONSHIP

Select Options from My WWE. Next, choose Cheat Codes and enter OhHellYeah!.

WWE ALL STARS

UNLOCK EVERYTHING

At the main menu, press Left, Right, Left, Down, Up, Left, Right, Up on the D-pad. This code does not save, so it must be entered again after resetting the game.

WWE SMACKDOWN VS. RAW 2011

JOHN CENA (ENTRANCE/CIVILIAN)

In My WWE, select Cheat Codes from the Options and enter SLURPEE.

ALL OF RANDY ORTON'S COSTUMES

In My WWE, select Cheat Codes from the Options and enter apexpredator.

TRIBUTE TO THE TROOPS ARENA

In My WWE, select Cheat Codes from the Options and enter 8thannualtribute.

CRUISERWEIGHT TITLE, HARDCORE TITLE, AND MILLION DOLLAR TITLE

In My WWE, select Cheat Codes from the Options and enter Historicalbelts.

AAH IMPOSSIBLE RESCUE

NARRATOR

At the main menu, enter the following codes to change the narrator.

NARRATOR	CODE	NARRATOR	CODE
Anime-L22	Y, Y, Y, Y, X	Michelle Rakar	X, X, X, X, Y
Carole Clark	X, Y, Y, Y, X	Ofebriso	Y, Y, X, X, X
Geoff-Li	X, Y, X, X, X	Pia Lehtinen	X, X, Y, X, X
Hoegoeshinseki	Y, X, X, X, Y	Sanjikunsgirl	X, Y, X, Y, X
Lilfirebender	X, X, Y, Y, X	Skimlines	Y, Y, X, X, Y
Lucas Wilheim	Y, X, Y, X, Y	Teisei	Y, X, X, X, X
Meika	X, X, X, X, X		

ALAN WAKE'S AMERICAN NIGHTMARE

AVATAR AWARDS

AVATAR	EARNED BY
American Nightmare Hoodie	Purchase the Game and Meet Emma in the Game.
Night Springs T-Shirt	Unlock the first Nightmare Difficulty Arcade Level.
Old Gods of Asgard Tour T-Shirt	Complete Story Mode.

ANOMALY: WARZONE EARTH

AVATAR AWARDS

AVATAR	EARNED BY
Anomaly Battle Pants	Complete any tactical trial mission to unlock these pants.
Anomaly Battle Shirt	Complete 1st mission to unlock the battle shirt.
Anomaly Commander's Helmet	Finish the campaign to unlock the commander's helmet.

APPLES TO APPLES

BUMBLEBEE APPLE AVATAR

Select Enter Code from Unlockables and enter buzzworthy.

NINJA APPLE AVATAR

Select Enter Code from Unlockables and enter silentslice.

BAKUGAN BATTLE BRAWLERS

1,000 BP

Enter 33204429 as your name.

100,000 BP

Enter 18499753 as your name.

5,000 BP

Enter 42348294 as your name.

500,000 BP

Enter 26037947 as your name.

10,000 BP

Enter 46836478 as your name.

BAKUGAN: DEFENDERS OF THE CORE

HIDDEN ITEMS

Select Unlock Codes from Collection and enter HXV6Y7BF. Now you can enter up to eight of your unique Bakugan Dimensions codes.

The codes unlock the following:

10,000 Core Energy	Light Arrow
Ten Vexos Passes	Tornado Vortex
Earthen Armor	Water Pillar
Fire Spirit	Zorch Thunder

Here are eight codes:

2FKRRMNCDQ	QY8CLD5NJE
82D77YK6P8	TD4UMFSRW3
HUUH8ST7AR	YJ7RGG7WGZ
JJUZDEACXX	YQLHBBSMDC

BAND HERO

MOST CHARACTERS UNLOCKED

Select Input Cheats from the options and enter Blue, Yellow, Green, Yellow, Red, Green, Red, Yellow.

ELECTRIKA STEEL UNLOCKED

Select Input Cheats from the options and enter Blue, Blue, Red, Yellow, Red, Yellow, Blue, Blue.

ALL HOPO MODE

Select Input Cheats from the options and enter Red, Green, Blue, Green, Blue, Green, Red, Green.

ALWAYS SLIDE

Select Input Cheats from the options and enter Yellow, Green, Yellow, Yellow, Yellow, Red, Blue, Red.

AUTO KICK

Select Input Cheats from the options and enter Yellow, Green, Yellow, Blue, Blue, Red, Blue, Red.

FOCUS MODE

Select Input Cheats from the options and enter Yellow, Yellow, Green, Green, Red, Red, Blue, Blue.

HUD FREE MODE

Select Input Cheats from the options and enter Green, Red, Green, Red, Yellow, Blue, Green, Red.

INVISIBLE ROCKER

Select Input Cheats from the options and enter Green, Red, Yellow, Green, Yellow, Blue, Yellow, Green.

PERFORMANCE MODE

Select Input Cheats from the options and enter Yellow, Yellow, Blue, Green, Blue, Red, Red, Red.

AIR INSTRUMENTS

Select Input Cheats from the options and enter Blue, Yellow, Blue, Red, Red, Yellow, Green, Yellow.

BATMAN: ARKHAM CITY

ALL BATMAN SKINS

This code allows you to start the campaign with all of the skins that you have downloaded, purchased, or unlocked. After selecting your save slot, press Left, Left, Down, Down, Left, Left, Right, Up, Up, Down at the main menu. You are then given the opportunity to select a skin.

BIG HEAD MODE

In the game, select the Cryptographic Sequencer. Hold Left Trigger and then hold Right Trigger to get Batman to use the device. Next, rotate the right Thumbstick clockwise while rotating the left Thumbstick counter-clockwise. Eventually, you notice Batman's head enlarge. Enemies and other characters' heads are also big. This works in Normal, Hard, and New Game +.

THE BEATLES: ROCK BAND

BONUS PHOTOS

At the title screen, press Blue, Yellow, Orange, Orange, Orange, Blue, Blue, Blue, Yellow, Orange.

BEN 10: ALIEN FORCE VILGAX ATTACKS

LEVEL SKIP

Pause the game and enter Portal in the Cheats menu.

UNLOCK ALL SPECIAL ATTACKS FOR ALL FORMS

Pause the game and enter Everythingproof in the Cheats menu.

UNLOCK ALL ALIEN FORMS

Pause the game and enter Primus in the Cheats menu.

TOGGLE INVULNERABILITY ON AND OFF

Pause the game and enter XImrsmoothy in the Cheats menu.

GIVES PLAYER FULL HEALTH

Pause the game and enter Herotime in the Cheats menu.

QUICK ENERGY REGENERATION

Pause the game and enter Generator in the Cheats menu.

BEN 10 GALACTIC RACING

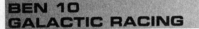

KINECELARATOR

Select Promotional Codes from Extras and enter Ben, Spidermonkey, Kevin Levin, Ultimate Echo Echo.

BEN 10 ULTIMATE ALIEN: COSMIC DESTRUCTION

These cheats disable Achievements. To remove the cheats, you will need to start a new game.

1,000,000 DNA

Pause the game, select Cheats, and enter Cash.

REGENERATE HEALTH

Pause the game, select Cheats, and enter Health.

REGENERATE ENERGY

Pause the game, select Cheats, and enter Energy.

UPGRADE EVERYTHING

Pause the game, select Cheats, and enter Upgrade.

ALL LEVELS

Pause the game, select Cheats, and enter Levels.

ENEMIES DO DOUBLE DAMAGE/ PLAYER DOES 1/2 DAMAGE

Pause the game, select Cheats, and enter Hard.

UNLOCKS RATH

Pause the game, select Cheats, and enter Primus.

BIOLOGY BATTLE

INCREASED CONFLICT LEVEL IN GLOBAL CHALLENGE MODE

At the Global Challenge Mode lobby, press A to access the game controls/start screen. At this screen, hold Y and press A.

BLUR

BMW CONCEPT 1 SERIES TII CHROME

In the Multiplayer Showroom, highlight the BMW Concept 1 Series tii and press Left Trigger, Right Trigger, Left Trigger, Right Trigger.

FULLY UPGRADE FORD BRONCO

In the Multiplayer Showroom, highlight the Ford Bronco and press Left Trigger, Right Trigger, Left Trigger, Right Trigger.

AVATAR AWARDS

AWARD	EARNED BY
Wreck Tee	Earn the Been there, got the T-shirt Achievement
Friend Rechallenge Tee	Defeat a friends rechallenge.
Legend Tee	Unlock first Legend Rank in multiplayer.
Showdown Tee	Complete Showdown
Sticker Tee	Complete the Sticker Book.

CARNIVAL GAMES: MONKEY SEE, MONKEY DO!

AVATAR AWARDS

AWARD	EARNED BY
Barker Bowler	Purchase Barker Bowler Prize.
Barker's Best	Purchase Barker's Best Prize.
Monkey Barker	Purchase Monkey Barker Prize.

CARS 2: THE VIDEO GAME

ALL MODES AND TRACKS

Select Enter Codes from the Options and enter 959595.

LASER GUIDED

Select Enter Codes from the Options and enter 123456. Select Cheats to toggle the cheat on and off.

UNLIMITED ENERGY

Select Enter Codes from the Options and enter 721953. Select Cheats to toggle the cheat on and off.

AVATAR AWARDS

AWARD	EARNED BY
Team Brazil Jumpsuit	Unlock this item by earning the In Your Face Achievement.
Team France Jumpsuit	Unlock this item by earning the Island Hopper Achievement.
Team Spain Jumpsuit	Unlock this item by earning the Smashing Achievement.

COSTUME QUEST

AVATAR AWARDS

AWARD	EARNED BY
Pumpkin Pail	Start a new game.
Pumpkin Mask	Complete the game.

CRIMSON ALLIANCE

AVATAR AWARDS

AWARD	EARNED BY
Pocket Shaman	Defeat a Primitive Shaman.
Death Knight Helm	20 Treasures.

CRIMSON DRAGON

AVATAR AWARDS

AVATAR	EARNED BY
Bloodskin Helmet	Complete the First Mission.
Bloodskin Suit (Top)	Raise the level of Bloodskin.
Bloodskin Suit (Bottom)	Get an S rank five times with Bloodskin.

DANCE CENTRAL 2

ANGEL'S DC CLASSIC OUTFIT

Select Gameplay Settings from the Options, choose Enter Cheats and enter Y, Right, Left, Up, X, X, Down, Y.

MISS AUBREY'S DC CLASSIC OUTFIT

Select Gameplay Settings from the Options, choose Enter Cheats and enter Left, Down, X, X, Down, Right.

EMILIA'S DC CLASSIC OUTFIT

Select Gameplay Settings from the Options, choose Enter Cheats and enter Left, Left, Up, Right, Right, X, Down, Y.

TAYE'S DC CLASSIC OUTFIT

Select Gameplay Settings from the Options, choose Enter Cheats and enter Up, Left, Y, X, Left, Up, X, Y.

AVATAR AWARDS

AWARD	EARNED BY
Bring It Tee	Play every song in the game in Perform It mode.
Neon Tee	Get a solo score of at least 2,000,000 points on a song.
Ribbon Tee	Earn Gold Stars on a song.

DEAD BLOCK

AVATAR AWARDS

AWARD	EARNED BY
Construction Worker Helmet	Collect the helmet in the tutorial.
Dead Block Shirt	Beat all singleplayer levels.

DEATH BY CUBE

LOSS - BLACK ROBOT

At the Upgrade screen, hold Left Trigger and press Right Trigger, Right Trigger, X, Y, X.

SELIS - PINK ROBOT

At the Upgrade screen, hold Right Trigger and press Left Trigger, Y, X, Left Trigger, Start.

DIRT 3

AVATAR AWARDS

AVATAR	EARNED BY
Racing Shoes	Reach Fan Level 12.
Racing Gloves	Reach Fan Level 24.
Racing Suit	Complete Season 1.
Rally Helmet	Complete Season 2.

DJ HERO 2

ALL BONUS CONTENT

Select Cheats from the Options. Choose Retail Cheats and enter VIP Pass.

DAVID GUETTA

Select Cheats from the Options. Choose Retail Cheats and enter Guetta Blaster.

DEADMAU5

Select Cheats from the Options. Choose Retail Cheats and enter Open The Trap.

INVISIBLE DJ

Select Cheats from the Options. Choose Retail Cheats and enter Now You See Me.

AUTO CROSSFADE

Select Cheats from the Options. Choose Retail Cheats and enter I Hate Crossfading. This disables Leaderboards.

AUTO SCRATCH

Select Cheats from the Options. Choose Retail Cheats and enter Soothing. This disables Leaderboards.

AUTO TAP

Select Cheats from the Options. Choose Retail Cheats and enter Look No Hands! This disables Leaderboards.

DOUBLE DRAGON: NEON

DOUBLE DRAGON 2 BILLY LEE GAMERPIC

As soon as you press Start at the title screen, this gamerpic becomes available.

PLAY AS A RO-BRO

At the stage select, hold Left Trigger + Left Bumper + click left analog stick + Right Trigger + Right Bumper + click right analog stick + Back + Start. Enter again to return to normal.

CONCEPT ART GALLERY

Complete the game to unlock this gallery at the main menu.

DRAGON DIFFICULTY

Defeat the game on Normal difficulty.

DOUBLE DRAGON DIFFICULTY

Defeat the game on Dragon difficulty.

DRAGON'S LAIR

AVATAR AWARDS

AWARD	EARNED BY
Dragon's Lair Logo T-Shirt	Free with your purchase of Dragon's Lair!
Dragon's Lair Castle T-Shirt	Unlock the Secret Achievement.
Dirk the Daring's Helmet	Beat the Game.

MOVIE SCENE CHALLENGES

As you collect the 130 Movie Tokens in the game, Movie Scene Challenges are unlocked as shown below.

MOVIE SCENE CHALLENGE	VEHICLE GIVEN	# MOVIE TOKENS
Gone In 60 Seconds	1973 Ford Mustang Mach I	10
Starsky & Hutch	1974 Dodge Monaco Cop	20
Bullitt	1968 Ford Mustang GT Fastback	30
The French Connection	1971 Pontiac LeMans	40
Blues Brothers	1974 Dodge Monaco	50
Cannonball Run	1978 Lamborghini Countach LP400S	60
Dukes of Hazard	1969 Dodge Charger R/T	70
Vanishing Point	1970 Dodge Challenger R/T	80
The Driver	1965 Chevrolet S-10	90
Redline	2011 McLaren MP4-12C	100
Smokey & The Bandit	1977 Pontiac TransAm Firebird	110
Test Drive	1987 RUF CT-R Yellow Bird	120
The Italian Job	1972 Lamborghini Miura	130

DUNGEON FIGHTER LIVE: FALL OF HENDON MYRE

AVATAR AWARDS

AVATAR	EARNED BY
Goblin Mask	Complete your First Quest.
Slayer Bracelet	Reach Level 20.
Slayer T-Shirt	Clear the final dungeon in under 45 minutes with two or more players in your online party.

DUST: AN ELYSIAN TAIL

AVATAR AWARDS

AVATAR	EARNED BY
Dust Shirt	Wake up in The Glade.
Fidget Shirt	Make Fidget even more powerful.
Ahrah Shirt	Discover the Truth.

EARTH DEFENSE FORCE: INSECT ARMAGEDDON

HIDDEN IMAGES IN GALLERY

Select Gallery from the Extras menu. At the gallery press X, X, Y, X, Left Bumper, Right Bumper.

FABLE HEROES

AVATAR AWARDS

AVATAR	EARNED BY
Heroes T-Shirt	Unlock the Heroes T-Shirt by completing the Millfields level.
Jack of Blades Mask	Unlock the Jack of Blades Mask by purchasing all the abilities for the Jack of Blades puppet.

FABLE: THE JOURNEY

AVATAR AWARDS

AVATAR	EARNED BY
Fable: The Journey T-Shirt	Fable: The Journey T-Shirt can be unlocked by progressing through your Journey.
Mask of the Devourer	Mask of the Devourer can be unlocked by progressing through your Journey.
Theresa's Blindfold	Theresa's Blindfold can be unlocked by progressing through your Journey.

FANTASTIC PETS

AVATAR AWARDS

AWARD	EARNED BY
Fantastic T-Shirt	Reach Fantastic Pet trainer rank 2.
Cute Hat (Female)	Reach Fantastic Pet trainer rank 3.
Fierce Hat (Male)	Reach Fantastic Pet trainer rank 3.
Fantastic Gloves	Reach Fantastic Pet trainer rank 4.
Fantastic Shoes	Reach Fantastic Pet trainer rank 5.
Fantastic Pet	Reach Fantastic Pet trainer rank 6.

FEZ

FLY

In New Game + at any time, press Up, Up, Up, Up + A.

FINAL FANTASY XIII-2

LIGHTNING GAMER PICTURE

This gamer picture is unlocked if you have a save game for Final Fantasy XIII on your console.

ANOTHER LIGHTNING GAMER PICTURE

Earn all of the Achievements.

MOG GAMER PICTURE

Earn the Fair Fighter Achievement.

NOEL GAMER PICTURE

Earn the Chronosavior Achievement.

SERAH GAMER PICTURE

Earn the Defragmented Achievement.

FIRE PRO WRESTLING

AVATAR AWARDS

AVATAR	EARNED BY
Wrestler Mask	Win every match in the Tutorial Series.
Leather Boots	Win every match in the Campion Series.
Bottoms	Obtain every Costume piece.

FORZA MOTORSPORT 4

AVATAR AWARDS

AVATAR	EARNED BY
Autovista T-Shirt	Fully explore any car in Autovista.
Stopwatch Cap	Post a time in every Rivals Mode Event.

FROGGER: HYPER ARCADE EDITION

CONTRA STYLE

At the style select, highlight Contra and enter Up, Up, Down, Down, Left, Right, Left, Right, B, A.

FROM DUST

AVATAR AWARDS

AVATAR	EARNED BY
The Tribal Mask	Retrieve this mask by unlocking the complete version of "From Dust".

FRUIT NINJA KINECT

AVATAR AWARDS

AVATAR	EARNED BY
Fruit Ninja T-Shirt	Equip an Item in Sensei's Swag.
Kung Fu Pants	Complete 3 Multplayer Games.
Kung Fu Sensei Shirt	Complete 5 games of Classic, Zen or Arcade.

FULL HOUSE POKER

AVATAR AWARDS

AWARD	EARNED BY
Hoodie	Level up
Bulldog Helmet	Level up to 50

GAME ROOM

SWAP KONAMI AND ASTEROIDS CABINET STYLES

During a game or at a menu, press Up, Up, Down, Down, Left, Right, Left, Right, Ⓑ, Ⓐ.

GUARDIAN HEROES

AVATAR AWARDS

AVATAR	EARNED BY
Guardian Heroes Helmet	Scored 360 points in Arcade Mode.
Guardian Heroes T-Shirt	Unlocked at least 30 characters in Story Mode.

GUITAR HERO 5

ALL HOPOS

Select Input Cheats from the Options menu and enter Green, Green, Blue, Green, Green, Green, Yellow, Green.

ALWAYS SLIDE

Select Input Cheats from the Options menu and enter Green, Green, Red, Red, Yellow, Blue, Yellow, Blue.

AUTO KICK

Select Input Cheats from the Options menu and enter Yellow, Green, Red, Blue, Blue, Blue, Blue, Red.

FOCUS MODE

Select Input Cheats from the Options menu and enter Yellow, Green, Red, Green, Yellow, Blue, Green, Green.

HUD FREE MODE

Select Input Cheats from the Options menu and enter Green, Red, Green, Green, Yellow, Green, Green, Green.

PERFORMANCE MODE

Select Input Cheats from the Options menu and enter Yellow, Yellow, Blue, Red, Blue, Green, Red, Red.

AIR INSTRUMENTS

Select Input Cheats from the Options menu and enter Red, Red, Blue, Yellow, Green, Green, Green, Yellow.

INVISIBLE ROCKER

Select Input Cheats from the Options menu and enter Green, Red, Yellow, Yellow, Yellow, Blue, Blue, Green.

ALL CHARACTERS

Select Input Cheats from the Options menu and enter Blue, Blue, Green, Green, Red, Green, Red, Yellow.

CONTEST WINNER 1

Select Input Cheats from the Options menu and enter Green, Green, Red, Red, Yellow, Red, Yellow, Blue.

GUITAR HERO: VAN HALEN

ALWAYS DRUM FILL

Select Input Cheats from the Options menu and enter Red, Red, Red, Blue, Blue, Green, Green, Yellow.

ALWAYS SLIDE

Select Input Cheats from the Options menu and enter Green, Green, Red, Red, Yellow, Red, Yellow, Blue.

AUTO KICK

Select Input Cheats from the Options menu and enter Yellow, Green, Red, Blue, Blue, Blue, Blue, Red.

HYPERSPEED

Select Input Cheats from the Options menu and enter Green, Blue, Red, Yellow, Yellow, Red, Green, Green. This allows you to enable Hyperguitar, Hyperbass, and Hyperdrums.

PERFORMANCE MODE

Select Input Cheats from the Options menu and enter Yellow, Yellow, Blue, Red, Blue, Green, Red, Red.

AIR INSTRUMENTS

Select Input Cheats from the Options menu and enter Red, Red, Blue, Yellow, Green, Green, Green, Yellow.

INVISIBLE ROCKER

Select Input Cheats from the Options menu and enter Green, Red, Yellow, Yellow, Yellow, Blue, Blue, Green.

BLACK HIGHWAY

Select Input Cheats from the Options menu and enter Yellow, Red, Green, Red, Green, Red, Red, Blue.

FLAME COLOR

Select Input Cheats from the Options menu and enter Green, Red, Green, Blue, Red, Red, Yellow, Blue.

GEM COLOR

Select Input Cheats from the Options menu and enter Blue, Red, Red, Green, Red, Green, Red, Yellow.

STAR COLOR

Select Input Cheats from the Options menu and enter Red, Red, Yellow, Red, Blue, Red, Red, Blue.

VOCAL FIREBALL

Select Input Cheats from the Options menu and enter Red, Green, Green, Yellow, Blue, Green, Yellow, Green.

EXTRA LINE 6 TONES

Select Input Cheats from the Options menu and enter Green, Red, Yellow, Blue, Red, Yellow, Blue, Green.

XBOX 360®

CHEAT CODE EXPLOSION FOR CONSOLES

88

GUITAR HERO: WARRIORS OF ROCK

Select Extras from Options to toggle the following on and off. Some cheats will disable Achievements.

ALL CHARACTERS

Select Cheats from the Options menu and enter Blue, Green, Green, Red, Green, Red, Yellow, Blue.

ALL VENUES

Select Cheats from the Options menu and enter Red, Blue, Blue, Red, Red, Blue, Blue, Red.

ALWAYS SLIDE

Select Cheats from the Options menu and enter Blue, Green, Green, Red, Red, Yellow, Blue, Yellow.

ALL HOPOS

Select Cheats from the Options menu and enter Green (x3), Blue, Green (x3), Yellow. Most notes become hammer-ons or pull-offs.

INVISIBLE ROCKER

Select Cheats from the Options menu and enter Green, Green, Red, Yellow (x3), Blue, Blue.

AIR INSTRUMENTS

Select Cheats from the Options menu and enter Yellow, Red, Red, Blue, Yellow, Green (x3).

FOCUS MODE

Select Cheats from the Options menu and enter Green, Yellow, Green, Red, Green, Yellow, Blue, Green. This removes the busy background.

HUD FREE MODE

Select Cheats from the Options menu and enter Green, Green, Red, Green, Green, Yellow, Green, Green.

PERFORMANCE MODE

Select Cheats from the Options menu and enter Red, Yellow, Yellow, Blue, Red, Blue, Green, Red.

COLOR SHUFFLE

Select Cheats from the Options menu and enter Blue, Green, Blue, Red, Yellow, Green, Red, Yellow.

MIRROR GEMS

Select Cheats from the Options menu and enter Blue, Blue, Red, Blue, Green, Green, Red, Green.

RANDOM GEMS

Select Cheats from the Options menu and enter Green, Green, Red, Red, Yellow, Red, Yellow, Blue.

HALF-MINUTE HERO: SUPER MEGA NEO CLIMAX

AVATAR AWARDS

AVATAR	EARNED BY
Brave Vest	Cleared 1 quest after Quest 3 in 30 seconds.
Liar T-Shirt	Cleared 10 quests after Quest 3 in 30 seconds.

HARRY POTTER AND THE DEATHLY HALLOWS: PART 1

SUPER STRENGTH POTIONS

Select Unlock Menu from the Options and enter ❌, Left, Right, Ⓐ, 🎮, 🎮.

ELITE CHALLENGES

Select Unlock Menu from the Options and enter Ⓨ, Up, ❌, 🎮, 🎮, Ⓐ.

AUGMENTED REALITY CHEAT FROM BOX (PROTEGO TOTALUM)

Select Unlock Menu from the Options and enter Ⓨ, Ⓑ, Up, Left, 🎮, Right.

HARRY POTTER AND THE HALF-BLOOD PRINCE

BONUS TWO-PLAYER DUELING ARENA CASTLE GATES

At the Rewards menu, press Right, Right, Down, Down, Left, Right, Left, Right, Left, Right, Start.

UNLOCK EVERYTHING

At the Rewards menu, press Down, Left, Left, Left, Left, Left, Down, Down, Right, Down, Left.

HAUNT

AVATAR AWARDS

AVATAR	EARNED BY
Haunt Hoodie	Unlock the Full Game.
Haunt Jeans	Defeat one of each type of ghost.
Charger Ghost Mask	Successfully avoid five Charger ghost attacks.

HOLE IN THE WALL

AVATAR AWARDS

AVATAR	EARNED BY
Spandex Top	Win China Show.
Spandex Trousers	Win Russia Show.
Blue Helmet	Win USA Show.

HYBRID

AVATAR AWARDS

AVATAR	EARNED BY
Hybrid T-Shirt	T-Shirt with Hybrid Logo.
Variant T-Shirt	T-Shirt with Variant Logo.
Paladin T-Shirt	T-Shirt with Paladin Logo.

ILOMILO

ILOMILO SHUFFLE

At the main menu, press 🎮, 🎮, 🎮, 🎮.

AVATAR AWARDS

AWARD	EARNED BY
T-Shirt	Complete three levels.
Ilo And Milo	Collect enough memory fragments to unlock a full memory.

INSANELY TWISTED SHADOW PLANET

AVATAR AWARDS

AVATAR	EARNED BY
Shadow Planet Tee T-Shirt	Make it from your Homeworld to the Shadow Planet to unlock!
UFO Hero's Ship	Complete the Single-Player Campaign to unlock!

ISLANDS OF WAKFU

AVATAR AWARDS

AWARD	EARNED BY
Blue Platypus	Who's Who? Achievement
Merch T-Shirt	The Chosen One Achievement

JET SET RADIO

CUBE/COMBO

Complete Chapter 1

PLAY AS GARAM

To unlock Garam simply complete his challenges.

PLAY AS GOJI

To play as Goji, get a JET ranking on all the Grind City levels.

PLAY AS GUM

To unlock Gum simply finish her challenges at the beginning of the game.

PLAY AS LOVE SHOCKERS, NOISE TANKS, POISON JAM, AND GOJI

Beat the game with a JET ranking in all stages. This includes regular stages as well as Golden Rhino stages

PLAY AS MEW

Beat all the Benten-Cho (aka City of Night) levels with any ranking. After that, Mew will challenge you. Beat the three of her challenges, and she'll join you, allowing you to pick her as playable character.

PLAY AS POISON JAM

To play as Poison Jam, get a JET ranking on all of the Kogane-cho levels.

TAB

Unlock Gum and complete the challenges Tab gives you afterwards.

UNLOCK POTS, THE DOG!

To get to play as Pots, finish the game with the Jet ranking on every level. Every level, meaning both story mode and the basic areas.

SLATE

Play through the game until Slate challenges you to a race in Kogane-Cho. Beat him to unlock.

YO-YO

Progress through story mode until he challenges you. Beat his challenge to unlock.

AVATAR AWARDS

AVATAR	EARNED BY
Shirt	Unlock Gum and Tab.
Spray Can	Unlock Gum and Tab.

JIMMIE JOHNSON'S ANYTHING WITH AN ENGINE

ALL RACERS

At the main menu, hold R1 + L1 + R2 + L2 and press Up, Right, Down, Left, Up, Left, Down, Right, R3, L3.

JOE DANGER 2: THE MOVIE

AVATAR AWARDS

AVATAR	EARNED BY
Joe's Cosmic Helmet	Collect a set of D-A-N-G-E-R!
Joe's Jubilant Jetpack	Collect a second set of D-A-N-G-E-R!
Joe's Galactic Trousers	Collect a third set of D-A-N-G-E-R!

JOJO'S BIZARRE ADVENTURE HD VER.

FIGHT DEATH 13

Using one of the original six fighters, do not lose a match. After the fifth fight, Death 13 will challenge your fighter.

JOY RIDE TURBO

AVATAR AWARDS

AVATAR	EARNED BY
JR Turbo T	Win your first race to receive the official T shirt of the unofficial Joy Ride Turbo fan club.
Victory Pants	Purchase your first car in order to strut out of the dealership wearing a victorious pair of slacks.
Cacti Cap	Win a race on every track to unlock this trendy piece of headwear.

JUST DANCE 3

BARBRA STREISAND SPECIAL CHOREOGRAPHY

At the title screen (Press Start), press Up, Up, Down, Down, Left, Right, Left, Right.

KINECT DISNEYLAND ADVENTURES

AVATAR AWARDS

AVATAR	EARNED BY
Sorcerer Mickey Mouse Hat	Earn the Happiest Place on Earth Achievement.

KINECT PLAYFIT

AVATAR AWARDS

AVATAR	EARNED BY
Muscle Mass	Earn the 150K Ultra-Marathon Achievement.
Power Pants	Earn the Mount Everest Relay Achievement.

KINECT SPORTS

AVATAR	EARNED BY
Classic Kinect Sports Tee	Earn the Professional Sports Badge.
I Heart Kinect Sports Tee	Earn the Champion Sports Badge.
Kinect Sports Star Tee	Earn the Master Sports Badge.
Classic Kinect Sports Cap	Earn the Amateur Sports Badge.
Kinect Sports Champ Trophy	Earn the Legendary Sports Badge.

KINECT SPORTS SEASON TWO

AVATAR AWARDS

AVATAR	EARNED BY
Kinect Sports Darts Top Hat	Stay on target throughout your career with this awesome award for reaching level 5. Woohoo!
Kinect Sports Football Hat	Show your love for all things football with this award for reaching fan level 2. I'm so jealous!
Kinect Sports Golf Green Cap	Impress everyone at the clubhouse with this award for reaching the dizzy heights of fan level 10.

THE KING OF FIGHTERS XIII

ALTERNATE COSTUMES AND COLOR PALETTES

Before selecting the color for the following fighters, press Select to get the alternate outfit.

FIGHTER	OUTFIT	FIGHTER	OUTFIT
Andy	Ninja Mask	Raiden	Big Bear
Elisabeth	KOF XI	Ralf	Camouflage
Joe	Tiger-Striped Boxers	Takuma	Mr. Karate
K'	Dual-Colored	Yuri	Braided Ponytail
Kyo	Orochi Saga		

EXTRA COLORS IN COLOR EDIT

Extra colors become available in color edit mode for every 10 times you select a specific character.

BILLY KANE

Successfully pull off two target actions in each fight in Arcade Mode until Billy Kane challenges you. Defeat him to unlock him.

SAIKI

Successfully pull off five target actions in each fight in Arcade Mode until Saiki challenges you. Defeat him to unlock him.

LEGO BATMAN 2: DC SUPER HEROES

RED BRICK CODES

Pause the game, select Extras, then choose Enter Code. Enter the following:

CHEAT	CODE	CHEAT	CODE
Attract Studs	MNZER6	Minikit Finder	LRJAG8
Beep Beep	ZHAXFH	Peril Finder	RYD3SJ
Character Studs	TPJ37T	Red Brick Finder	5KKQ6G
Disguises	BWQ2MS	Regenerate Hearts	ZXEX5D
Extra Hearts	4LGJ7T	Studs x2	74EZUT
Extra Toggle	7TXH5K	Super Build	JN2J6V
Fall Rescue	TPGPG2	Vine Grapples	JXN7FJ
Gold Brick Finder	MBXW7V		

CHARACTERS AND VEHICLE

Pause the game, select Extras, then choose Enter Code. Enter the following:

CHEAT	CODE	CHEAT	CODE
Clown Goon	9ZZZBP	Riddler Goon	Q285LK
LexBot	W49CSJ	Two-Face Goon	95KPYJ
Mime Goon	ZQA8MK	Harley Quinn's Motorbike	C79LVH
Policeman	V9SAGT		

LEGO HARRY POTTER: YEARS 5-7

CHEATS

Pause the game and select Extras. Go to Enter Code and enter the following:

CHEAT	CODE	CHEAT	CODE
Carrot Wands	AUC8EH	Gold Brick Detector	84QNQN
Character Studs	H27KGC	Hogwarts Crest Detector	TTMC6D
Character Token Detector	HA79V8	Invincibility	QQWC6B
Christmas	T7PVVN	Red Brick Detector	7AD7HE
Collect Ghost Studs	2FLY6B	Score x2	74YKR7
Extra Hearts	J9U6Z9	Score x6	XK9ANE
Fall Rescue	ZEX7MV	Score x8	HUFV2H
Fast Dig	Z9BFAD	Score x10	H8X69Y
Ghost Coins	2FLY6B	Super Strength	BMEU6X

LEGO PIRATES OF THE CARIBBEAN: THE VIDEO GAME

CODES

Pause the game and select Extras. Choose Enter Code and enter the following codes:

EFFECT	PASSWORD	EFFECT	PASSWORD
Ammand the Corsair	EW8T6T	Clanker	ZM37GT
Angelica (Disguised)	DLRR45	Clubba	644THF
Angry Cannibal	VGF32C	Davy Jones	4DJLKR
Blackbeard	D3DW0D		

EFFECT	PASSWORD	EFFECT	PASSWORD
Govorner Weatherby Swann	LD9454	King George	RKED43
Gunner	Y611WB	Koehler	RT093G
Hungry Cannibal	64BNHG	Mistress Ching	GDETDE
Jack Sparrow (Musical)	VDJSPW	Phillip	WEV040
Jacoby	BWO656	Quartermaster	RX58HU
Jimmy Legs	13GLW5	The Spaniard	P861JO
		Twigg	KDLFKD

LEGO STAR WARS III: THE CLONE WARS

Pause the game, select Enter Code from Extras and enter the following:

CHARACTERS

CHARACTER	CODE	CHARACTER	CODE
Aayla Secura	2VG95B	Clone Shadow Trooper (Classic)	7GFNCQ
Adi Gallia	G2BFEN	Clone Trooper	NP5GTT
Admiral Ackbar (Classic)	272Y9Q	Commander Bly	7CB6NS
Admiral Yularen	NG6PYX	Commander Cody	SMN259
Ahsoka	2VJ9TH	Commander Fil	U25HFC
Anakin Skywalker	F9VUYJ	Commander Ponds	JRPR2A
Anakin Skywalker (Geonosian Arena)	9AA4DW	Commander Stone	5XZQSV
Asajj Ventress	YG9DD7	Commando Droid	QEGU64
Aurra Sing	M2V1JV	Count Dooku	EWR7WM
Bail Organa	GEHX6C	Darth Maul (Classic)	QH68AK
Barriss Offee	BTVTZ5	Darth Sidious (Classic)	QXY5XN
Battle Droid	5Y7MA4	Darth Vader (Classic)	FM4JB7
Battle Droid Commander	LSU4LJ	Darth Vader Battle Damaged (Classic)	NMJFBL
Bib Fortuna	9U4TF3	Destroyer Droid	9MUTS2
Boba Fett (Classic)	TY2BYJ	Dr. Nuvo Vindi	MB9EMW
Boil	Q5Q39P	Echo	JB9ESS
Bossk	2KLW5R	Eeth Koth	WUFDYA
C-3PO	574226	Gammorean Guard	WSFZZQ
Cad Bane	NHME85	General Grievous	7FNU4T
Captain Antilles (Classic)	D8SNGJ	Geonosian Guard	GAFZUD
Captain Rex	MW3QYH	Gold Super Battle Droid	2C8NHP
Captain Typho	GD6FX3	Gonk Droid	C686PK
Chancellor Palpatine	5C62YQ	Grand Moff Tarkin	NH2405
Chewbacca (Classic)	66UU3T	Greedo (Classic)	FUW4C2
Clone Pilot	HQ7BVD	Hailfire Droid	T7XF9Z

CHARACTER	CODE
Han Solo (Classic)	KFDBXF
Heavy Super Battle Droid	G65KJJ
Heavy Weapons Clone Trooper	WXUTWY
HELIOS 3D	4AXTY4
Hevy	EUB8UG
Hondo Ohnaka	5A7XYX
IG-86	EABPCP
Imperial Guard (Classic)	5W6FGD
Jango Fett	5KZQ4D
Jar Jar Binks	MESPTS
Jek	AYREC9
Ki-Adi-Mundi	HGBCTQ
Kit Fitso	PYWJ6N
Lando Calrissian (Classic)	ERAEWE
LEP Servent Droid	SM3Y9B
Lieutenant Thire	3NEUXC
Lok Durd	TKCYUZ
Luke Skywalker (Classic)	PG73HF
Luminara Unduli	MKUYQ8
Lurmen Villager	R35Y7N
Luxury Droid	V4WMJN
Mace Windu	8NVRWJ
MagnaGuard	2KEF2D
MSE-6	S6GRNZ
Nahdar Vebb	ZKXG43
Neimoidian	BJB94J
Nute Gunray	QFYXMC
Obi-Wan Kenobi	J9HNF9
Obi-Wan Kenobi (Classic)	FFBU5M
Obi-Wan Kenobi (Geonosian Arena)	5U9FJK
OG-9 Homing Spider Droid	7NEC36
Onaconda Farr	DB7ZQN
Padmé Amidala (Geonosian Arena)	SZ824Q
Padmé Amidala	8X87U6
Pirate Ruffian	BH2EHU

CHARACTER	CODE
Plo Koon	BUD4VU
Poggle The Lesser	4592WM
Princess Leia (Classic)	2D3D3L
Probe Droid	U2T4SP
Queen Neeyutnee	ZQRN85
Qui-Gon Jinn (Classic)	LKHD3B
R2-D2	RZ5HUV
R3-S6	Z87PAU
R4-P17	5MXSYA
R6-H5	7PMC3C
Rebel Commando (Classic)	PZMQNK
Robonino	2KLW5R
Rys	4PTP53
Savage Oppress	MELL07
Senate Commando	EPBPLK
Senate Commando (Captain)	S4Y7VW
Senator Kharrus	EA4E9S
Senator Philo	9Q7YCT
Shahan Alama	G4N7C2
Sionver Boll	5C62YQ
Stormtrooper (Classic)	HPE7PZ
Super Battle Droid	MJKDV5
Tee Watt Kaa	FYVSHD
Turk Falso	HEBHW5
Tusken Raider (Classic)	GC2XSA
TX-20	PE7FGD
Undead Geonosian	QGENFD
Vader's Apprentice (Classic)	EGQQ4V
Wag Too	VRUVSZ
Wat Tambor	ZP8XVH
Waxer	BNJE79
Wedge Antilles (Classic)	DRGLWS
Whorm Loathsom	4VVYQV
Workout Clone Trooper	MP9DRE
Yoda	CSQTMB

VEHICLES

VEHICLE	CODE
Dwarf Spider Droid	NACMGG
Geonosian Solar Sailor	PJ2U3R
Geonosian Starfighter	EDENEC

VEHICLE	CODE
Slave I	KDDQVD
The Twilight	T4K5L4
Vulture Droid	7W7K7S

RED BRICKS

CHEAT	CODE
Character Studs	QD2C31
Dark Side	X1V4N2
Dual Wield	C4ES4R
Fast Build	GCHP7S
Glow in the Dark	4GT3VQ
Invincibility	J46P7A
Minikit Detector	CSD5NA
Perfect Deflect	3F5L56
Regenerate Hearts	2D7JNS

CHEAT	CODE
Score x2	YZPHUV
Score x4	43T5E5
Score x6	SEBHGR
Score x8	BYFSAQ
Score x10	N1CKR1
Stud Magnet	6MZ5CH
Super Saber Cut	BS828K
Super Speeders	B1D3W3

MADAGASCAR 3: THE VIDEO GAME

ALL DISGUISES

Select Promotion from Extras and enter Pineapple, Strawberry, Grapes, Apple.

BANANA DASH MINI-GAME IN LONDON

Select Promotion from Extras and enter Strawberry, Orange, Apple, Grapes.

BANANA DASH MINI-GAME IN PARIS

Select Promotion from Extras and enter Pineapple, Grapes, Pineapple, Banana.

BANANA DASH MINI-GAME IN PISA

Select Promotion from Extras and enter Orange, Banana, Orange, Apple.

BANANA DASH MINI-GAME IN ROME

Select Promotion from Extras and enter Grape, Apple, Grape, Strawberry.

MADDEN NFL 12

MADDEN NFL 12 DEVELOPERS TEAM IN EXHIBITION

Select Exhibition from Play Now. At the team select, press the Random Team button, Left Trigger, until the Developers team shows up. Once you have entered a game as the team, they will always be on the list.

MAGIC: THE GATHERING— DUELS OF THE PLANESWALKERS 2013

BONUS FOIL CARDS

At the Player Status screen, select Magic the Gathering View Promotional Unlocks, and then click Enter Code. Enter the following to unlock a bonus foil promo card for each of the
original decks.

WMKFGC	GDZDJC
KWPMZW	HTRNPW
FNMDGP	NCTFJN
MWTMJP	PCNKGR
FXGJDW	GPCRSX

AVATAR AWARDS

AVATAR	EARNED BY
Avacynina Breastplate	Planeswalk to Innistard.
Garruk Wildspeaker Helmet	Defeat Garruk Wildspeaker in the Revenge Campaign.
Nicol Bolas Horns	Defeat Nicol Bolas in the Revenge Campaign.

MARS ROVER LANDING

AVATAR AWARDS

AVATAR	EARNED BY
Mars Rover Shirt	Touchdown safely 10 times.
Mars Surface Pants	Achieve five stars during the Entry phase five times.
Mars Rover Hat	Achieve a five star Landing rating five times.

MARVEL VS. CAPCOM ORIGINS

MARVEL SUPER HEROES

PLAY AS ANITA

At the characters select, press MP, LP, Left, LK, MK.

PLAY AS DR DOOM

At the characters select, press MK, LP, Down, LK, MP.

PLAY AS THANOS

At the characters select, press HK, MP, MP, Up.

EXTRA POWER

After selecting your character, press player 1 and player 2 start.

USE GEMS

At the versus screen, hold both Starts.

MARVEL VS. CAPCOM: CLASH OF SUPER HEROES

PLAY AS GOLD WAR MACHINE

Highlight Zangief and press Left, Left, Down, Down, Right, Right, Down, Down, Left, Left, Up, Up, Up, Up, Right, Right, Left, Left, Down, Down, Down, Down, Right, Right, Up, Up, Left, Left, Down, Down, Right, Right, Up, Up, Up, Up, Up.

PLAY AS HYPER VENOM

Highlight Chun-Li and press Right, Down, Down, Down, Down, Left, Up, Up, Up, Up, Right, Right, Down, Down, Left, Left, Down, Down, Right, Right, Up, Up, Up, Up, Left, Left, Up.

PLAY AS LILITH

Highlight Zangief and press Left, Left, Down, Down, Right, Right, Up, Up, Down (x4), Left, Left, Up (x4), Right, Left, Down (x4), Right, Right, Up (x4), Left, Left, Down (x4), Right, Down.

PLAY AS ORANGE HULK

Highlight Chun-Li and press Right, Right, Down, Down, Left, Left, Right, Right, Down, Down, Left, Left, Up (x4), Down, Down, Right, Right, Up, Up, Down (x4), Up (x4), Left, Up.

PLAY AS ROLL

Highlight Zangief and press Left, Left, Down, Down, Right, Right, Down, Down, Left, Left, Up, Right, Up, Up, Right, Right.

PLAY AS SHADOW LADY

Highlight Morrigan and press Up, Right, Right, Down (x4), Left, Left, Up (x4), Right, Right, Left, Left, Down, Down, Right, Right, Down, Down, Left, Left, Up, Up, Right, Right, Up, Up, Left, Left, Down (x5).

SELECT PARTNER

Select your two characters, then hold Start and the following buttons:

CHARACTER	CODE
Anita	Weak Punch, Medium Punch, High Punch
Arthur	Weak Punch, Medium Punch
Colossus	Weak Punch, Medium Punch, Medium Kick
Cyclops	Weak punch, Weak Kick, Medium Punch
Devilot	Medium Punch
Iceman	Medium Punch, Medium Kick
Jubilee	Weak Kick, Medium Punch, High Punch
Juggernaut	Weak Punch, Medium Kick
Lou	Medium Punch
Magneo	Weak Kick, High Punch
Michelle Hart	Weak Punch, Weak Kick
Psylocke	Medium Kick
Pure and Fur	Weak Kick
Rogue	Weak Punch, Weak Kick, Medium Punch, High Punch
Saki	High Punch
Sentinel	Medium Punch, Medium Kick, High Punch
Shadow	Weak Punch, Medium Kick, High Punch
Storm	Weak Punch, Weak Kick, High Punch
Thor	Weak Kick, Medium Punch
Ton-Pooh	Weak Punch, High Punch
Unknown Soldier	Weak Punch
US Agent	High Punch, Medium Kick

MINECRAFT: XBOX 360 EDITION

AVATAR AWARDS

AVATAR	EARNED BY
The Pork-Chop T-Shirt	Earn a Cooked Porkchop.
A Minecraft Watch	Play the game for 100 day to night cycles.
The Creeper Cap	Kill a Creeper with Arrows.

STEVE GAMER PICTURE

Mine redstone for the first time.

CREEPER GAMER PICTURE

Defeat 10 Creepers.

MINECRAFT XBOX 360 EDITION PREMIUM THEME

Pause the game, press Y to grab a shot, and upload the image to Facebook.

NARUTO SHIPPUDEN: ULTIMATE NINJA STORM GENERATIONS

9 NARUTO: ULTIMATE NINJA STORM CHARACTERS

As long as you have a save game from the original Naruto: Ultimate Ninja Storm on your system, nine bonus characters are unlocked. These include: Ino, Shikamaru, Choji, Neji, Tenten, Rock Lee, Kiba, Shino, Hinata, and 50,000 Ryo.

11 NARUTO SHIPPUDEN: ULTIMATE NINJA STORM 2 CHARACTERS

As long as you have a save game from Naruto Shippuden: Ultimate Ninja Storm 2 on your system, 11 bonus characters are unlocked. These include: Ino, Shikamaru, Choji, Neji, Tenten, Rock Lee, Kiba, Shino, Hinata, Asuma, Guy, and 50,000 Ryo.

NINJA CARD PASSWORDS

Select Enter Password from the Collection Screen and enter the following. Each password unlocks one Ninja Info Card.

00HNWGTFV8	BL770WJT70	MKKJMC7CWF
0B7JLNHXA4	BQ7207JT80	MMD4M2BK7K
0CKC96JGVL	BVKHANGBKR	MSJ1BFU4JB
0LP3WPBQ7B	CODGMFHCCD	MUW7LMT1WG
17769QU0KT	CE8Q9UKG8N	NDD9LG0EV0
1TFLMLP4BE	CJE20EPKWV	PLESLFPVKK
1V8WD29DBJ	CVJVLP6PVS	PQVG0KUCL0
1WQ4WR17VV	D53XB9P4LP	PSA21VB6M2
28G1D0FSBS	DCF515Q8X9	Q8M8P2J295
2DRA0BDFAR	DS1BXA13LD	QCS5D53XBA
2LM5CHLVX1	DX0L0382NT	QEB22X9LNP
2MFFXGNKWL	E23G24EB0B	QTBT1W97M2
39PXPFXEDW	EL52EVS00X	R4C43XB8PD
3ET93PHNNM	ENE5N43M9L	R8JE3QS6QT
3J6R2NS6B4	ERCKGKSN1P	RE6KE7GPCC
3USV86L2HM	F515Q009CE	S5JVSL6DDC
4HB5ELA91R	F6DTQBCXCF	S85PRDRU1T
4LTP2Q6U26	F7T1103JNS	SAUFE2T72U
4RTCRU4BWD	FMBB22KR0J	SKJERP5K15
53HXEB6EQ1	G12P36C5QW	TEP2FTPH4A
5DFQ45CJF0	GB7FS2G8EV	TH9NGBKRFF
5FUU285P1D	GR56DKG1CP	TVQ7HC2PQ5
6PF63C1C35	GWQ8EKCNEG	U3GQH7R65P
6QDPEHOHQL	H3D14HNF2X	U59BHXUEF3
6RQD5KD6GN	HH88SX6Q4P	UCM26NV9TW

6UB06B8FS2	HWR9FKDPFH	UFG3GKQJ5B
794L5RFD5J	HX3CS22CEG	UL4KS3Q2SU
7DEDGW26R1	J22C572J3P	UMK7SHU2QQ
7KXC71MSTS	JFXC608F44	UTG4GWQ65P
8CTCJFSQ6L	JMV3HRHBR7	V9TW64S2JJ
8EJ57XFMJ3	JSB8UFKXHL	VG63VA3W6D
8JPPVC8TUG	JXF97FR2F7	VLGL6FEQSU
8Q1VK79N7B	K1C6VJKXHL	VML7SHV3RR
96XD609G54	KE84GXKREE	W1X6BJWX5C
9FP7L7N1H1	KF4RT7RU4B	W57HWX4B7S
9P8BLJ6FXX	KTS46B3JUP	WH0BJBA5HF
ADUMLGTR7M	L3PAK7BPUM	WV72WQ4B7R
ALNQK2L6VS	L6N0B1XT65	XH5G7ASAHD
AQU0KTTFCB	LMTA6QSEJV	XVN2VPX5TT
B7JHWCTWU3	MB3GA4DK88	XXPF0EMWKV

NASCAR THE GAME 2011

MARK MARTIN PAINT SCHEMES

At the garage main menu, press Down, Down, Up, Up, Right, Left, Right, Left. Enter godaddy.com.

KYLE BUSH NOS ENERGY DRINK CAR

At the garage main menu, press Down, Down, Up, Up, Right, Left, Right, Left. Enter drinknos.

NBA 2K11

MJ: CREATING A LEGEND

In Features, select Codes from the Extras menu. Choose Enter Code and enter icanbe23.

2K CHINA TEAM

In Features, select Codes from the Extras menu. Choose Enter Code and enter 2kchina.

2K SPORTS TEAM

In Features, select Codes from the Extras menu. Choose Enter Code and enter 2Ksports.

NBA 2K TEAM

In Features, select Codes from the Extras menu. Choose Enter Code and enter nba2k.

VC TEAM

In Features, select Codes from the Extras menu. Choose Enter Code and enter vcteam.

ABA BALL

In Features, select Codes from the Extras menu. Choose Enter Code and enter payrespect.

2011 ALL-STAR UNIFORMS

In Features, select Codes from the Extras menu. Choose Enter Code and enter wydololoh.

SECONDARY ROAD UNIFORM

In Features, select Codes from the Extras menu. Choose Enter Code and enter ronoilnm. This unlocks the secondary road uniform for the Hornets, Magic, and Timberwolves.

ORANGE SPLIT DUNK

In Features, select Codes from the Extras menu. Choose Enter Code and enter SPRITEDUNK1. Go to Sprite Slam Dunk Showdown and use the help menu to find out more.

SPIN TOMMY DUNK

In Features, select Codes from the Extras menu. Choose Enter Code and enter SPRITEDUNK2. Go to Sprite Slam Dunk Showdown and use the help menu to find out more.

THE VILLAIN DUNK

In Features, select Codes from the Extras menu. Choose Enter Code and enter SPRITEDUNK3. Go to Sprite Slam Dunk Showdown and use the help menu to find out more.

NBA 2K12

ABA BALL

Select Extras from the Features menu. Choose Codes and enter payrespect. This can be toggled on and off from this Codes menu.

2K CHINA TEAM

Select Extras from the Features menu. Choose Codes and enter 2kchina.

2K SPORTS TEAM

Select Extras from the Features menu. Choose Codes and enter 2ksports.

UNLOCK NBA 2K TEAM

Select Extras from the Features menu. Choose Codes and enter nba2k.

VC TEAM

Select Extras from the Features menu. Choose Codes and enter vcteam.

JORDAN RETRO COLLECTION

Select Extras from the Features menu. Choose Codes and enter 23.

SECONDARY ROAD UNIFORMS

Select Extras from the Features menu. Choose Codes and enter hcsilapadatu. This unlocks uniforms for 76ers, Jazz, Kings, and Mavericks.

CHRISTMAS UNIFORMS

Select Extras from the Features menu. Choose Codes and enter ibyasmliancbhlald. This unlocks uniforms for Bulls, Celtics, Heat, Knicks, Lakers, and Mavericks.

HEAT BACK IN BLACK UNIFORM

Select Extras from the Features menu. Choose Codes and enter albkbinkcca.

RAPTORS MILITARY NIGHT UNIFORM

Select Extras from the Features menu. Choose Codes and enter liyrimta.

NBA 2K13

ABA BALL

Select Features from the main menu and then go to Codes. Enter payrespect.

UA TORCH SHOE

Select Features from the main menu and then go to Codes. Enter underarmour.

SPRITE EFFECT BONUS

Select Features from the main menu and then go to Codes. Enter spriteeffect.

BEASTIE BOYS

At the title screen, press Up, Up, Down, Down, Left, Right, Left, Right, **B**, **A**. This team includes Ad Rock, MCA, and Mike D.

J. COLE AND 9TH WONDER

At the title screen, press Up, Left, Down, Right, Up, Left, Down, Right, Circle, **A**.

DEMOCRATS TEAM

At the title screen, press Left (x13), **A**. This team includes Barack Obama, Joe Biden, Bill Clinton, and Hillary Clinton.

REPUBLICANS TEAM

At the title screen, press Right (x13), **A**. The team includes George W. Bush, Sarah Palin, Dick Cheney, and John McCain.

ESPN'S SPORTSNATION

Select Play Now. When entering the initials, enter ESP for P1 and NSN for P2. Advance to the Choose Teams screen to find the team. This team includes the hosts of the show; Colin Cowherd and Michelle Beadle.

NBA MASCOTS

Select Play Now. When entering the initials, enter MAS for P1 and COT for P2.

ORIGINAL GENERATION JAM

Select Play Now. When entering the initials, enter MJT for P1. Advance to the Choose Teams screen to find the team. This team includes Mark Turmell and Tim Kitzrow.

NFL BLITZ

Select Cheats from the Blitz Store to purchase the following cheats. They are entered with X, Y, and B. Press these buttons until the three given icons are shown. The number indicates how many times each button is pressed. X is the first number, Y the second, and B is the third.

GAMEPLAY CHEATS

Buy these cheats to change the game to your advantage.

CHEAT	CODE
Tournament Mode	Goalpost, Goalpost, Goalpost (4 4 4)
Faster Passes	Helmet, NFL, NFL (5 1 1)
Speedster	Goalpost, NFL, EA Sports (4 1 0)
Fast Turbo Drain	Helmet, Headset, NFL (5 3 1)
More Fumbles	Helmet, Goalpost, NFL (5 4 1)
No First Downs	Goalpost, Headset, Goalpost (4 3 4)
No Fumbles	Helmet, EA Sports, Headset (5 0 3)
No Interceptions	Helmet, Helmet, EA Sports (5 5 0)
No Onside Kicks	Goalpost, Foam Finger, Foam Finger (4 2 2)
No Punting	Goalpost, Goalpost, EA Sports (4 4 0)
Power Defense	Goalpost, Whistle, Goalpost (4 8 4)

CHEAT	CODE
Power Offense	Helmet, Foam Finger, Helmet (5 2 5)
No Stepping out of Bounds	Helmet, EA Sports, EA Sports (5 0 0)
Unlimited Turbo	Helmet, NFL, Goalpost (5 1 4)

VISUAL CHEATS

Your team will get a Blitz makeover after you buy these cheats.

CHEAT	CODE
Big Head Player	Foam Finger, Helmet, EA Sports (2 5 0)
Big Head Team	Foam Finger, NFL, Foam Finger (2 1 2)
Tiny Head Team	Foam Finger, Goalpost, Headset (2 4 3)
Tiny Head Player	Headset, EA Sports, Foam Finger (3 0 2)
Huge Head Team	Headset, NFL, Foam Finger (3 1 2)
Huge Head Player	Foam Finger, EA Sports, NFL (2 0 1)
Super Ball Trail	EA Sports, NFL, Football (0 1 6)
Black & Red Ball	EA Sports, EA Sports, Foam Finger (0 0 2)
Camouflage Ball	EA Sports, EA Sports, Helmet (0 0 5)
Chrome Ball	EA Sports, Foam Finger, EA Sports (0 2 0)
Flames Ball	EA Sports, Goalpost, Foam Finger (0 4 2)
Ice Cream Ball	EA Sports, Foam Finger, Marker (0 2 7)
B-52 Ball	NFL, EA Sports, Goalpost (1 0 4)
Beachball	NFL, EA Sports, NFL (1 0 1)
Glow Ball	EA Sports, Marker, EA Sports (0 7 0)
Meat Ball	EA Sports, Football, EA Sports (0 6 0)
Pumpkin Ball	Whistle, Headset, NFL (8 3 1)
Soup Can Ball	Marker, NFL, EA Sports (7 1 0)
Blitz Team Ball	NFL, NFL, NFL (1 1 1)
USA Ball	Headset, NFL, Helmet (3 1 5)
Blitz Stadium	EA Sports, NFL, Goalpost (0 1 4)
Cardinals Stadium	EA Sports, Foam Finger, Foam Finger (0 2 2)
Falcons Stadium	EA Sports, Headset, EA Sports (0 3 0)
Ravens Stadium	EA Sports, Headset, Helmet (0 3 5)
Bills Stadium	EA Sports, Headset, Marker (0 3 7)
Panthers Stadium	EA Sports, Goalpost, Goalpost (0 4 4)
Bears Stadium	EA Sports, Goalpost, Football (0 4 6)
Bengals Stadium	EA Sports, Goalpost, Whistle (0 4 8)
Browns Stadium	EA Sports, Helmet, Headset (0 5 3)
Cowboys Stadium	EA Sports, Helmet, Helmet (0 5 5)
Broncos Stadium	EA Sports, EA Sports, Marker (0 0 7)
Lions Stadium	EA Sports, Helmet, Marker (0 5 7)
Packers Stadium	EA Sports, Football, Foam Finger (0 6 2)
Texans Stadium	EA Sports, Football, Goalpost (0 6 4)
Colts Stadium	EA Sports, Football, Football (0 6 6)
Jaguars Stadium	EA Sports, Marker, Foam Finger (0 7 2)

CHEAT	CODE
Chiefs Stadium	EA Sports, Whistle, EA Sports (0 8 0)
Dolphins Stadium	EA Sports, Marker, Marker (0 7 7)
Vikings Stadium	NFL, EA Sports, Football (1 0 6)
Patriots Stadium	NFL, NFL, Goalpost (1 1 4)
Saints Stadium	NFL, Foam Finger, Headset (1 2 3)
Giants Stadium	NFL, Headset, EA Sports (1 3 0)
Jets Stadium	NFL, EA Sports, Whistle (1 0 8)
Raiders Stadium	NFL, Foam Finger, Helmet (1 2 5)
Eagles Stadium	NFL, Headset, Headset (1 3 3)
Steelers Stadium	NFL, Headset, Helmet (1 3 5)
Chargers Stadium	NFL, Helmet, EA Sports (1 5 0)
Seahawks Stadium	Foam Finger, Foam Finger, EA Sports (2 2 0)
49ers Stadium	Foam Finger, NFL, EA Sports (2 1 0)
Rams Stadium	Foam Finger, Headset, EA Sports (2 3 0)
Bucs Stadium	Foam Finger, Goalpost, EA Sports (2 4 0)
Titans Stadium	Headset, EA Sports, Headset (3 0 3)
Redskins Stadium	Goalpost, EA Sports, NFL (4 0 1)
Day	EA Sports, Whistle, Foam Finger (0 8 2)
Twilight	NFL, NFL, Marker (1 1 7)
Night	NFL, Whistle, Marker (1 8 7)

SETTINGS CHEATS

Change certain game settings when you buy these cheats.

CHEAT	CODE
Hide Player Name	EA Sports, Foam Finger, Goalpost (0 2 4)
Extra Code Time	Helmet, Helmet, Helmet (5 5 5)
No Ball Target	EA Sports, Helmet, NFL (0 5 1)
Wide Camera	NFL, NFL, Foam Finger (1 1 2)
Show Field Goal Percentage	EA Sports, NFL, Foam Finger (0 1 2)
All-Time QB Coop	Headset, Headset, EA Sports (3 3 0)
All-Time WR Coop	EA Sports, Headset, Headset (0 3 3)
Icon Passing	Headset, Helmet, Headset (3 5 3)
No Player Icon	EA Sports, Goalpost, EA Sports (0 4 0)

FANTASY CHARACTERS

Buy these cheats to play as your favorite characters. Characters must be unlocked by defeating them in Blitz Gauntlet first.

UNLOCKABLE CHARACTERS

CHEAT	CODE
Bigfoot	Headset, Headset, Headset (3 3 3)
Bigfoot Team	Marker, EA Logo, EA Logo (7 0 0)
Cowboy	Headset, Foam Finger, Headset (3 2 3)
Cowboy Team	Goalpost, Marker, Goalpost (4 7 4)
Gladiator	Foam Finger, Whistle, Foam Finger (2 8 2)
Gladiator Team	Helmet, NFL, Marker (5 1 7)
Horse	NFL, Marker, NFL (1 7 1)
Horse Team	Foam Finger, Football, Foam Finger (2 6 2)
Hot Dog	NFL, Football, NFL (1 6 1)
Hot Dog Team	Foam Finger, Headset, Foam Finger (2 3 2)
Lion	Foam Finger, EA Sports, Foam Finger (2 0 2)
Lion Team	Headset, Goalpost, Headset (3 4 3)
Ninja	Foam Finger, Marker, Foam Finger (2 7 2)
Ninja Team	Football, NFL, Football (6 1 6)
Pirate	NFL, Foam Finger, NFL (1 2 1)
Pirate Team	Helmet, Headset, Helmet (5 3 5)

NHL 12

3RD JERSEYS

Select NHL 12 Code Entry from My NHL 12 and enter 2wg3gap9mvrth6kq.
This unlocks uniforms for Florida, New York Islanders, Ottawa, and Toronto.

NIGHTS INTO DREAMS

UNLOCK EVERYTHING

At the title screen, press Left, Right, X, B, A, Y, Right Bumper, Right Trigger,
Down, Up, Left Bumper, Left Trigger. Achievements, saving, and posting high
scores are disabled until the game is restarted.

ORCS MUST DIE!

AVATAR AWARDS

AVATAR	EARNED BY
OMD Logo Tee	Complete Act 1 of Orcs Must Die!
OMD Skull Hat	Kill 1,000 enemies in Orcs Must Die!

PHANTOM BREAKER

FIN

Complete Story Mode with each of the original characters.

INFINITY

Complete Arcade Mode.

KURISU

Win 250 matches.

RIMI

Win 200 matches.

PINBALL FX 2

AVATAR AWARDS

AWARD	EARNED BY
Pinball FX 2 T-Shirt	Achieve 5,000 Wizard Score.
Pinball Sorceress Dress (Female)	Achieve 100,000 Wizard Score.
Pinball Wizard Robe (Male)	Achieve 100,000 Wizard Score.

PLANTS VS. ZOMBIES

During a game, press (LB), (RB), (LT), (RT). Now you can enter the following codes. You must be given a code before it can be used.

MUSTACHES FOR ZOMBIE

Enter mustache.

SHADES FOR ZOMBIES

Enter future.

ZOMBIES DANCE

Enter dance.

CANDY WHEN ZOMBIE DIES

Enter piñata.

DEAD ZOMBIES LEAVE DAISIES

Enter daisies.

ALTERNATE LAWN MOWER

Enter trickedout.

PORTAL 2

AVATAR AWARDS

AWARD	EARNED BY
Companion Cube	Complete Portal 2 Single Player.
Love Shirt	Hug three friends in Portal 2 Coop.
Portal 2 Hat	Survive the manual override.
Portal 2 Shirt	Complete Portal 2 Coop
Turret Shirt	Complete Test Chamber 10 in less than 70 seconds.

RENEGADE OPS

AVATAR AWARDS

AVATAR	EARNED BY
Renegade Ops Hoodie	Engage helicopter in Single Player.

ROCK BAND 3

GUILD X-79 GUITAR

At the main menu, press Blue, Orange, Orange, Blue, Orange, Orange, Blue, Blue.

OVATION D-2010 GUITAR

At the main menu, press Orange, Blue, Orange, Orange, Blue, Blue, Orange, Blue.

STOP! GUITAR

At the main menu, press Orange, Orange, Blue, Blue, Orange, Blue, Blue, Orange.

ROCKSMITH

UNLOCKABLE SONGS

As you achieve Double Encores, the following songs are unlocked randomly.

Boss by Chris Lee

Jules by Seth Chapla

Ricochet by Brian Adam McCune

Six AM Salvation by Versus Them

Space Ostrich by Disonaur

The Star Spangled Banner by Seth Chapla

SEGA BASS FISHING

AVATAR AWARDS

AVATAR	EARNED BY
Sega Bass Fishing Tee	Play the game for 5 hours.
Sega Bass Fishing Rod	Play the game for 10 hours.

SEGA VINTAGE COLLECTION: ALEX KIDD & CO.

SUPER HANG-ON

START ARCADE MODE WITH $10,000

Highlight Arcade Mode and press Up, Left, A, B, Start.

THE REVENGE OF SHINOBI

STAGE PRACTICE

At the title screen, hold A + B + C and press Start. This unlocks the mode at the main menu.

SEGA VINTAGE COLLECTION: GOLDEN AXE

A, B, and C refer to the buttons that are mapped to the Sega Genesis A, B, and C.

GOLDEN AXE

27 CREDITS IN ARCADE MODE

At the character select, hold Down-Left + A + C and press Start. At the continue screen, you will have 9 credits instead of 3.

LEVEL SELECT IN ARCADE MODE

At the character select, hold Down-Left + B and press Start. Use the d-pad to change the number in the upper-left corner to the level that you wish to play.

GOLDEN AXE III

LEVEL SELECT

At the character select, press A, A, A, A, Start, C, C, C, C, C, C.

SECRET MESSAGE

At the title screen, press Up, C, Up, C, Up, C, C, C, B, A, Left, Down.

SEGA VINTAGE COLLECTION: STREETS OF RAGE

A, B, and C refer to the buttons that are mapped to the Sega Genesis A, B, and C.

STREETS OF RAGE

EXTRA CONTINUES

At the title screen, press Left, Left, B, B, B, C, C, C, Start.

LEVEL AND LIVES SELECT

At the main menu, hold A + B + C + Right on controller 2 while selecting Options on controller 1.

STREETS OF RAGE 3

9 LIVES

Select Lives from Options, hold Up + A + B + C on controller 2, and press Left or Right on controller 1.

PLAY AS SHIVA

After defeating Shiva, hold B until the next level begins. When you lose your last life and reach a continue screen, Shiva is selectable.

PLAY AS ROO

At the title screen, hold Up + B and press Start.

PLAY AS THE SAME CHARACTER

While select a 2-Player game, hold Down + C on controller 2.

THE SIMPSONS ARCADE GAME

ALL EXTRAS

At the title screen, press Up, Up, Down, Down, Left, Right, Left, Right, B, A.

THE SIMS 3: PETS

CREATION MODE

Pause the game and press Left Trigger + Left Bumper + Right Trigger + Right Bumper. This disables achievements.

SKYLANDERS SPECIFIC QUESTS

Skylanders Giants includes quests specific to each Skylander as a way to improve them. Here we list each Skylander with their quest and tips on how to complete it.

SKYLANDER	QUEST	HOW TO COMPLETE
Bash	On a Roll: Defeat 10 enemies with one roll attack.	If you have trouble completing this quest, opt for the Pulver Dragon upgrade path.
Boomer	On a Troll: Defeat five enemies with one kicked Troll Bomb.	Once you have Troll Bomb Boot, look for a group of tight-knit Chompies. "Chapter 1: Time of the Giants" has several groupings of five Chompies.
Bouncer	Stay on Target!: Target enemies 100 times with laser-guided Shoulder Rockets	You must purchase the Targeting Computer upgrade for Bouncer's Shoulder Rockets.
Camo	Garden Gorger: Eat 10 watermelons.	If you aren't in a rush to complete a level, switch to Camo when a watermelon appears.
Chill	Ice Sore: Defeat six enemies with one Ice Narwhal attack.	Try to find six enemies that are grouped together at a medium distance, such as in an arena.
Chop Chop	Stalwart Defender: Absorb 1,000 damage with your shield.	To complete this quest safely, block attacks from a small group of weaker enemies near a food item (just in case they sneak in some unexpected damage).
Crusher	High Roller: Defeat 100 enemies with boulders.	Use Rockslide defeat enemies until you have completed this quest.
Cynder	On the Haunt: Defeat 50 enemies with your Ghost Ally.	Ghost Ally does not inflict much damage so focus on saving low-health enemies, like Chompies, for the ghost to attack. The Ghost attacks while Cynder is flying, so consider circling an area with Chompies.
Dino-Rang	Fooderang: Pick up 20 food items with boomerangs.	After acquiring Sticky Boomerangs, use it to grab any food found in the area. In the Arena Challenges on Flynn's Ship, the audience throws food items into the arena between rounds.
Double Trouble	Big Bomb Trouble: Defeat 10 enemies with one Magic Bomb attack.	Find a group of 10 or more Chompies and set off a bomb. A good place to earn this is any of of Brock's Arena Challenges with regular Chompies.
Drill Sergeant	Drill Skill: Defeat Drill-X without changing Skylanders.	Drill Sergeant must defeat Drill-X (the final boss in Chapter 11: Drill-X's Big Rig) solo. Use Adventure items (like Healing Potion) to survive the battle. You can complete it on Easy difficulty with a fully-upgraded Drill Sergeant.
Drobot	Feed the Burn: Defeat 50 enemies with Afterburners.	It's easiest to hit enemies with Afterburners when Drobot first takes off.
Eruptor	Pizza Burp: Eat 10 Pizzas.	If you want to have a greater chance of encountering a pizza, equip Lucky Wheel of Health in the Luck-O-Tron.
Eye Brawl	Gold Search: Collect 5,000 gold with the eyeball detached	Remember to detach Eye-Brawl's eye before collecting any treasure from chests or enemies.
Flameslinger	Circular Combustion: Defeat 10 enemies with one column of Fire Flame Dash.	There are two upgrades you can get to help you on this quest. The first is Column of Fire. The second is Supernova in the Pyromancer Path.

SKYLANDER	QUEST	HOW TO COMPLETE
Flashwing	Let It Shine: Defeat 20 enemies with one Crystal Lighthouse.	Since Crystal Lighthouse is stationary, this is a tricky quest. The best candidate for this is one of the arena maps, particularly Kaos' Royal Flush (the second challenge, Birthday Bash). Set up the Lighthouse in the middle of the birthday cake.
Fright Rider	Delving Throw: Toss 50 enemies into the air	The power to use for this quest is Burrow Bomber. Hit any medium or small enemy with the attack to pop them up in the air and register a toss.
Ghost Roaster	Grave Circumstances: Defeat 100 enemies with Skull Charge.	Repeatedly use Skull Charge to attack enemies and you should complete this quest in no time.
Gill Grunt	Anchors Away!: Defeat six enemies with one Anchor Attack.	Line up a group of Chompies with your Anchor Cannon and let loose to complete the quest. If you have Series 2 Gill Grunt, Anchor's Away! makes completing the quest easier.
Hex	Noggin Knocker: Knock away 100 enemies with your Skull Rain.	Once Hex has Skull Shield, allow enemies to get within melee range while Hex is charging that attack. If they get too close, they get knocked back, tallying a point for this quest.
Hot Dog	Animal Aggravator: Scare away 20 birds.	Look for the small birds pecking at the ground in each level. These birds are the ones you need to scare with Hot Dog for this achievement. Chapter 13: The Oracle and Chapter 1: Time of Giants both have plenty of birds.
Hot Head	Buggy Breakthrough: Destroy 20 walls in Hot Rod mode.	The walls this quest is referring to are the walls that can only be crushed by a Giant or a bomb. Whenever you encounter one of these walls, switch to Hot Head. A good spot with plenty of these types of walls is Chapter 2: Junkyard Isles.
Ignitor	Tinder Trekker: Travel 26,000 feet in Flame Form.	Use Flame Form often and this number will accumulate quickly.
Jet-Vac	Bird Cleaner: Suck up 50 birds in your Suction Gun.	Look for tiny birds on the ground throughout most levels with green grass. Chapter 13: The Oracle and Chapter 1: Time of Giants both have plenty of birds.
Lightning Rod	Current Event: Defeat 10 enemies with one Grand Lightning strike.	You need to find a group of 10 Chompies in one area and use the Grand Lightning to blast them all. Choosing the Lord of Lightning Path makes this easier since the Grand Lightning attack lasts longer.
Ninjini	Bottle Beatdown: Defeat 5 enemies within five seconds of exiting your bottle.	Transform Ninjini into the bottle and move into a large group of small enemies. Follow up the bottle attack with her swords.
Pop Fizz	Rampage: Do 200 HP of damage in a single run in Beast Form.	Transform into Beast Form in a large group of enemies and destroy everything in sight to complete the quest.
Prism Break	Bifurcation Sensation: Defeat 100 enemies with double refraction.	A beam must pass through two Shards before hitting an enemy to count. Unlock the Chained Refractions upgrade and place plenty of Crystal Shards. Fire an Energy Beam through them to indirectly take out nearby enemies.
Shroomboom	Lunching Launch: Eat a watermelon while performing a Self-Slingshot!	When you find a watermelon, blast Shroomboom through it with the Self-Slingshot power to complete the quest.
Slam Bam	Ice to Meet You: Trap 100 enemies in your Ice Blocks.	You do not need to damage or freeze enemies with Ice Block; it counts if you just hit them with the Ice Block.
Sonic Boom	Sonic Squeak: Babies defeat 50 enemies.	Upgrade Sonic Boom's egg attack powers and keep babies summoned at all times.

SKYLANDER	QUEST	HOW TO COMPLETE
Sprocket	Mined Your Step: Defeat 50 enemies using the Landmine Golf attack.	Once you unlock the Landmine Golf ability, use it often. A quick way to complete this quest is to load up one of the easier Arena levels.
Spyro	Full Charge: Collect 3 gold, eat 1 food item, and defeat 2 enemies in 1 Sprint Charge.	Look for two low-health enemies (Chompies are a good choice) as well as some food and gold on the screen. Purchase the Sprint Charge upgrade to increase the distance of Spyro's sprint.
Stealth Elf	Stealth Health: Gain 1,000 HP while stealthed.	You need to first purchase Sylvan Regeneration. Once you do, you get credit towards the 1,000 HP every time you heal while Stealth Elf is in the Stealthier Decoy mode.
Stump Smash	Meganut Bowling: Defeat five enemies with one Meganut.	Meganuts are powerful, and bowling over five Chompies with one is no problem. The upgrade Acorn Croquet makes this much easier to achieve since you can wack the acorn directly at enemies.
Sunburn	Immolation Itinerant: Travel 1 mile using Immolation Teleport	Use Immolation Teleport regularly to tally up the distance towards one full mile. The quickest way to complete this quest is to unlock the Flight of the Phoenix and the Guided Teleportation upgrades.
Swarm	Swarm Feelings: Defeat 100 enemies in Swarm Form.	While you can complete this quest without pursuing the Wasp Stormer Path, it's extremely difficult, and you must focus on weaker enemies.
Terrafin	Land Lubber: Eat 20 food items while burrowing.	Once you have Surface Feeder, stay underground and collect Food Items as they drop.
Thumpback	Beached Whale: Defeat 8 enemies with one Belly Flop.	Upgrade Thumpback's Belly Flop attack with Slippery Belly. If you are having trouble getting this quest, invest in the Up Close and Personal path to further increase the strength of the Belly Flop attack.
Tree Rex	Timberrrrr!: Defeat 50 enemies by landing on them. Chompies don't count!	Unfortunately, Elbow Drop doesn't work for this quest. Tree Rex must crush enemies by landing on them. The best way to do this is to find a bounce pad in an area with plenty of Chompies.
Trigger Happy	Holding Gold: Save up 50,000 Gold	This is one of the hardest quests any character has in the game. Not because it's difficult, but because it will take some time to collect 50,000 Gold.
Voodood	Trickwire: Defeat six enemies at once with your tripwire.	Find a group of six or more low-health enemies, like Bone Chompies, and set up the Tripwire near them. Chapter 1: Time of the Giants has several good spots to try for this quest.
Warnado	Chompy Catcher: Catch 100 Chompies in tornadoes.	The best place to do this is in the Arena Challenges. Head to any of the early challenges and there are plenty of Chompies. High Winds also helps gather up more Chompies at once.
Wham-Shell	Irate Invertebrate: Defeat 6 enemies with one Poseidon Strike.	To get the most out of Poseidon Strike, invest in the Captain Crustacean path. Once you have unlocked Mace of the Deep, go for this quest by finding a group of Chompies and blasting them.
Whirlwind	What does it mean?: Create 50 double rainbows.	Unlock the Dual Rainbows ability, then fire out a Tempest cloud and following up with a Rainbow of Doom. Rainbows made via the Double Dose of Doom power don't count unless they hit a Tempest Cloud. Triple rainbows created via Triple Tempest count as one double rainbow.

SKYLANDER	QUEST	HOW TO COMPLETE
Wrecking Ball	Competitive Eater: Swallow 100 Enemies	Purchase Enemy Slurp and swallow as many enemies as you can. Any medium-sized and smaller enemy can be eaten.
Zap	In the Slimelight: Defeat 50 enemies by electrifying them in Sea Slime	Use Sea Slime to electrify enemies regularly and you'll complete this quest in no time.
Zook	Spore It On: Absorb 1,000 points of damage with a Foliage Barrier	Use Foliage Barrier often and you will complete this quest quickly.

SMOOTH OPERATORS

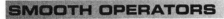

$1,000,000

After loading a call center, select Enter Code and enter dante.

EVERYONE IS HAPPY

After loading a call center, select Enter Code and enter becca.

MAXIMUM BUILD HEIGHT

After loading a call center, select Enter Code and enter gustafsson.

EVERYTHING IS UPGRADABLE

After loading a call center, select Enter Code and enter bengan.

INCREASED WORKLOADS

After loading a call center, select Enter Code and enter kyrksten.

SONIC ADVENTURE 2

AVATAR AWARDS

AVATAR	EARNED BY
2G Vintage Sonic Tee	5 Hours game time in any game mode.
Sonic's 2G Hi-Speed Shoes	10 hours game time in any game mode.

SONIC FREE RIDERS

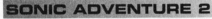

AVATAR AWARDS

AWARD	EARNED BY
Sonic Free Riders Shirt	Watch the credits in their entirety.
E-10000 G Shirt	Place 1st on every course with E-10000 G.
Jet Shirt	Place 1st on every course with Jet.
Sonic Shirt	Place 1st on every course with Sonic.

CHAOS EMERALD BOARD

Get S-rank on all Story Missions.

PROFESSIONAL BOARD

Complete all Trial Missions.

SECRET STATUE ROOM

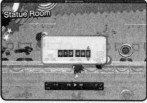

In the Collection Room, hold Back for a few seconds. Sonic jumps into the statue room below. Once there, press Back and enter the following.

STATUE	CODE	STATUE	CODE
Aero-Cannon	329 494	Egg Pawn	125 817
Amy Rose	863 358	Eggrobo	360 031
Big the Cat	353 012	Espio the Chameleon	894 526
Blaze the Cat	544 873	Goal Plate	933 391
Booster	495 497	Goal Ring	283 015
Buzz Bomber	852 363	Grabber	275 843
Capsule	777 921	Gun Beetle	975 073
Chao	629 893	Gun Hunter	668 250
Chaos Emerald	008 140	Hero Chao	507 376
Charmy Bee	226 454	Iblis Biter	872 910
Chip	309 511	Iblis Taker	513 929
Chopper	639 402	Iblis Worm	711 268
Classic Eggman	103 729	Item Box	209 005
Classic Sonic	171 045	Jet the Hawk	383 870
Classic Tails	359 236	Knuckles the Echidna	679 417
Cop Speeder	640 456	Metal Sonic	277 087
Crabmeat	363 911	Miles "Tails" Prower	632 951
Cream the Rabbit	332 955	Moto Bug	483 990
Cucky/Picky/Flicky/Pecky	249 651	Omochao	870 580
Dark Chao	869 292	Ring	390 884
Dr. Eggman	613 482	Rouge the Bat	888 200
E-123 Omega	601 409	Sandworm	548 986
Egg Chaser	200 078	Shadow the Hedgehog	262 416
Egg Fighter	851 426	Silver the Hedgehog	688 187
Egg Launcher	973 433	Sonic the Hedgehog	204 390

STATUE	CODE
Spinner	530 741
Spiny	466 913
Spring – Star	537 070

STATUE	CODE
Spring	070 178
Vector the Crocodile	868 377

AVATAR AWARDS

AVATAR	EARNED BY
Classic Eggman Suit (Head)	Defeat the final boss on Hard Mode.
Classic Eggman Suit (Tops)	Defeat all bosses on Hard Mode.
Classic Eggman Suit (Bottoms)	Defeat all rivals on Hard Mode.

SONIC THE HEDGEHOG 4: EPISODE II

AVATAR AWARDS

AVATAR	EARNED BY
Dr. Eggman Modern Costume (Body)	Defeat the last boss without taking damage.
Dr. Eggman Modern Costume (Legs)	Defeat the "Sylvania Castle Zone" boss without taking damage.

SOULCALIBUR V

ALGOL FEAR AND TOWER OF GLORY: MOST HOLY DICHOTOMY STAGE

Defeat Algol Fear in Legendary Souls or Quick Battle

α PATROKLOS AND ASTRAL CHAOS: PATHWAY STAGE

Defeat Patrolklos in Quick Battle.

EDGE MASTER AND TOWER OF GLORY: SPIRAL OF GOOD AND EVIL

Complete chapter 17 of story mode to unlock Edge Master and his stage. You can also be obtained by defeating him in Arcade, Legendary Souls, or Quick Battle.

ELYSIUM AND UTOPIA OF THE BLESSED

Complete the final chapter of story mode.

KILIK AND THE PENITENTIARY OF DESTINY STAGE

Defeat Kilik in Arcade or Legendary Souls.

PYRRHA Ω AND DENEVER CASTLE: EYE OF CHAOS

Complete chapter 19 of story mode.

DEVIL JIN STYLE

Defeat Harada in Quick Battle or Legendary Souls. Go to Customization and then to Original Characters. At the style select at the bottom of the list is Devil Jin (Tekken).

SPACE CHANNEL 5 PART 2

AVATAR AWARDS

AVATAR	EARNED BY
Vintage Space Channel 5 Tee	Play the game for 5 hours.
Morolian's Costume	Play the game for 10 hours.
Ulala's Costume	Play the game for 10 hours.

LET CPU TAKE OVER

Pause the game, hold Left Bumper + Right Bumper and press B, B, Up, Left, A, Left, A, Left, A. The CPU takes over, but achievements are disabled.

SPELUNKY

AVATAR AWARDS

AVATAR	EARNED BY
Spelunky T-Shirt	Play a game of deathmatch to at least 10 wins.
Pith Helmet	Unlock the first shortcut.
Fedora	Beat the first level of the game.

SPIDER-MAN: EDGE OF TIME

SHATTERED DIMENSIONS BONUS SUITS

If you have a saved game data for Spider-Man: Shattered Dimensions on your system, eight new Alternate Suits become available in the Bonus Gallery.

AMAZING SPIDER-MAN #500 SUIT (AMAZING)

Select Enter Code from VIP Unlock Code and enter laststand. Go to the Bonus Gallery to access the alternate suits.

POISON SUIT (2099)

Select Enter Code from VIP Unlock Code and enter innerspider. Go to the Bonus Gallery to access the alternate suits.

SPIDEY VS WOLVERINE SUIT (AMAZING) — WHAT IF? SPIDERMAN

Select Enter Code from VIP Unlock Code and enter coldhearted. Go to the Bonus Gallery to access the alternate suits.

2099 ARENA CHALLENGE AND AMAZING ARENA CHALLENGE

Select Enter Code from VIP Unlock Code and enter twospidersenter. Select Arenas from the Main Menu.

BIG TIME SUIT (2099)

At the main menu, press Right, Down, Down, Up, Left, Down, Down, Right.

FUTURE FOUNDATION SUIT (AMAZING)

At the main menu, press Up, Down, Left, Up, Down, Left, Right, Left.

THE SPLATTERS

AVATAR AWARDS

AVATAR	EARNED BY
"Die With Style" T-Shirt	Unlock the Air-Strike move to receive this shirt.
"The Splatters" T-Shirt	Unlock the Flip move to receive this shirt.
Splatter-Head	Unlock the Ballistic move to earn this award!

STAR TREK: D-A-C

KOBAYASHI MARU SECRET ACHIEVEMENT

At the start of a solo Death Match, press Start. Then enter Left Trigger, Y, X, X, Y, Right Trigger. This gives you the achievement and improves your ship.

SUPER STREET FIGHTER IV

BARREL BUSTER AND CAR CRUSHER BONUS STAGES

Beat Arcade Mode in any difficulty

COLORS AND TAUNTS

Colors 1 and 2 plus the first taunt for each fighter are available from the start. For colors 11 & 12, start a game with a Street Fighter IV save game on your system. To earn the rest of the colors and taunts, you need to fight a certain number of matches with that character.

COLOR	# OF MATCHES
3	2
4	4
5	6
6	8
7	10
8	12
9	14
10	16

TAUNT	# OF MATCHES
2	1
3	3
4	5
5	7
6	9
7	11
8	13
9	15
10	16

TONY HAWK'S PRO SKATER HD

ALL CHEATS

At the skater select, hold Left Trigger and press A, B, Y.

ALL GAME MODES

At the skater select, hold Left Trigger and press A, Y, B.

ALL LEVELS

At the skater select, hold Left Trigger and press Y, X, B.

ALL SKATERS

At the skater select, hold Left Trigger and press Y, B, X.

ALL TRICKS

At the skater select, hold Left Trigger and press A, X, Y.

MAX ALL STATS

At the skater select, hold Left Trigger and press Y, X, A.

MAX MONEY

At the skater select, hold Left Trigger and press Y, B, A. This gives you $999,999,999.

TOY SOLDIERS: COLD WAR

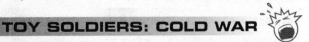

AVATAR AWARDS

AVATAR	EARNED BY
Flight Jacket	Complete the first section of Basic Training.
Mullet	Survive until Wave 9 in Basic Training.
T-Shirt	Play a survival match to Round 5.

COMMANDO GAMER PICTURE

Buy the full game.

RUSSIAN COMMANDO GAMER PICTURE

Complete the game.

TRANSFORMERS: DARK OF THE MOON

RATCHET IN MULTIPLAYER

Select Unlockables from the Extras and enter Up, Right, Down, Left, Up, Start.

TRANSFORMERS: FALL OF CYBERTRON

AVATAR AWARDS

AVATAR	EARNED BY
High Moon T-Shirt	Complete Chapter I.
Optimus Prime Helmet	Complete Chapter XIII as Optimus.
Megatron Helmet	Complete Chapter XIII as Megatron.

ELECTRO BOLTER

Complete the campaign.

GLASS GAS CANNON

Complete the campaign.

TRENCHED

AVATAR AWARDS

AVATAR	EARNED BY
Trenched T-Shirt	Complete Mobile Trench certification.
Trenchie	Wrest control of Europe back from the Northern Pylon.

UFC PERSONAL TRAINER: THE ULTIMATE FITNESS SYSTEM

AVATAR AWARDS

AVATAR	EARNED BY
UFC Trainer Gloves	Earn 10 Medals.
UFC Trainer Shorts	Earn 50 Medals.
UFC Trainer Shirt	Earn 150 Medals.

VIRTUA TENNIS 4

THERON TENNIEL

At the player select, select Load to access Custom Players. Next, press Left Bumper.

VICKY BARNEY

At the player select, select Load to access Custom Players. Next, press Right Bumper.

VOLTRON

AVATAR AWARDS

AVATAR	EARNED BY
Voltron Unlock T-Shirt	Purchase the game to unlock.

WARLORDS

AVATAR AWARDS

AVATAR	EARNED BY
Warlords Classic Tee	Complete the Single Player Campaign.
Snoot Fez	Earn 22 coins in the Single Player Campaign's Time Attack Mode.

WIPEOUT 2

AVATAR AWARDS

AVATAR	EARNED BY
Winter Vest	Complete episode 6 to unlock this sweet avatar item.
Ice Helmet	Complete episode 8 to unlock this stylish avatar item.
Snow Helmet	Complete episode 8 to unlock this stylish avatar item.

WIPEOUT: IN THE ZONE

AVATAR AWARDS

AWARD	EARNED BY
Wipeout Life Jacket	At the main menu, press Left, B, Down, Y, A, B, Right, Up.
Wipeout Safety Helmet	At the main menu, press Y, A, B, Up, Down, Left, Y, Right.

WORMS ULTIMATE MAYHEM

AVATAR AWARDS

AVATAR	EARNED BY
Ultimate Mayhem Tee	Earn any Achievement in Worms: Ultimate Mayhem.
Worm Tee	Locate the five hidden Easter Eggs in Worms: Ultimate Mayhem.

A WORLD OF KEFLINGS

AVATAR AWARDS

AWARD	EARNED BY
Baby Dragon	Make friends with the baby dragon released from an egg in the Ice Kingdom.
Winged Hat Of Kefkimo	Talk to the Chief at the great Hall in the Ice Kingdom.

WRECKATEER

AVATAR AWARDS

AVATAR	EARNED BY
Wreckateer T-Shirt	Compelte the Tutorials to unlock this Avatar Award.
Wreckateer Hoodie	Complete half the levels to unlock this Avatar Award.
Goblin Hoodie	Beat the game to unlock this Avatar Award.

WWE '12

WWE ATTITUDE ERA HEAVYWEIGHT CHAMPIONSHIP

Select Options from My WWE. Next, choose Cheat Codes and enter OhHellYeah!.

WWE ALL STARS

UNLOCK ARENAS, WRESTLERS, AND ATTIRE

At the main menu, press Left, ✪, Down, Left, ✪, ✪, Left, ✪, ✪, Down, Right, ✪, Left, Up, ✪, Right.

AUSTIN AND PUNK ATTIRES

At the main menu, press Left, Left, Right, Right, Up, Down, Up, Down.

ROBERTS AND ORTON ATTIRES

At the main menu, press Up, Down, Left, Right, Up, Up, Down, Down.

SAVAGE AND MORRISON ATTIRES

At the main menu, press Down, Left, Up, Right, Right, Up, Left, Down.

WWE SMACKDOWN VS. RAW 2011

JOHN CENA (ENTRANCE/CIVILIAN)

In My WWE, select Cheat Codes from the Options and enter SLURPEE.

ALL OF RANDY ORTON'S COSTUMES

In My WWE, select Cheat Codes from the Options and enter apexpredator.

TRIBUTE TO THE TROOPS ARENA

In My WWE, select Cheat Codes from the Options and enter 8thannualtribute.

CRUISERWEIGHT TITLE, HARDCORE TITLE, AND MILLION DOLLAR TITLE

In My WWE, select Cheat Codes from the Options and enter Historicalbelts.

X-MEN DESTINY

JUGGERNAUT SUIT

At the title screen, hold Left Bumper + Right Bumper and press Down, Right, Up, Left, Y, B.

EMMA FROST SUIT

At the title screen, hold Left Bumper + Right Bumper and press Up, Down, Right, Left, B, Y.

ZUMBA FITNESS RUSH

QUEBRO EXCLUSIVE

At the Song Select, press Left Trigger, X, Right Bumper.

A NOTE TO PARENTS

This book is an exclusive Scholastic edition that has been edited to remove all Mature-rated codes, as well as games that include excessive violence, sexual content, and inappropriate codes for children.

This book includes only E, E+, and T-rated games.

EARLY CHILDHOOD

Titles rated EC (Early Childhood) have content that may be suitable for ages 3 and older. Contains no material that parents would find inappropriate.

EVERYONE

Titles rated E (Everyone) have content that may be suitable for ages 6 and older. Titles in this category may contain minimal cartoon, fantasy or mild violence and/or infrequent use of mild language.

EVERYONE 10+

Titles rated E10+ (Everyone 10 and older) have content that may be suitable for ages 10 and older. Titles in this category may contain more cartoon, fantasy or mild violence, mild language, and/or minimal suggestive themes.

TEEN

Titles rated T (Teen) have content that may be suitable for ages 13 and older. Titles in this category may contain violence, suggestive themes, crude humor, minimal blood and/or infrequent use of strong language.

MATURE

Titles rated M (Mature) have content that may be suitable for persons ages 17 and older. Titles in this category may contain intense violence, blood and gore, sexual content, and/or strong language.

ADULTS ONLY

Titles rated AO (Adults Only) have content that should only be played by persons 18 years and older. Titles in this category may include prolonged scenes of intense violence and/or graphic sexual content and nudity.

MOBILE GAMES

ANGRY BIRDS

GOLDEN EGGS

#	LOCATION	DESCRIPTION
1	World Select	At the world select, tap the sun until another Golden Egg pops out.
2	Credits	Select i from the Options and scroll up to find the Golden Egg.
3	Help Screen	This Golden Egg becomes available once you unlock the white bird. Then, during any level, pause the game and select the question mark. At the white bird help screen, touch the Golden Egg.
4	Poached Eggs	Earn three stars on all of the Poached Eggs levels.
5	Poached Eggs 1-8	Simply tap the treasure chest until you get the egg.
6	Poached Eggs 2-2	Destroy the beach ball that sits among the ice cubes.
7	Mighty Hoax	Earn three stars on all of the Mighty Hoax levels.
8	Mighty Hoax 4-7	Zoom out to spot the egg on the right cliff. Launch the yellow bird into a high arc and tap when it lines up with the egg.
9	Mighty Hoax 5-19	The egg is located above the rocket ship. Zoom out and use a yellow or white bird to get it. Fire the yellow bird almost straight up and then tap when it reaches the clouds. If done correctly, the bird will get the egg as it comes back down.
10	Danger Above Level Select	Select Danger Above and scroll the level select screens as far as you can to the right to find this egg.
11	Danger Above	Earn three stars on all of the Danger Above levels.

#	LOCATION	DESCRIPTION
12	Danger Above 6-14	Pop the yellow balloon floating below the structure on the right to get this one. Send the boomerang bird over the house and tap to have it come back to the balloon. This requires very good timing with the boomerang.
13	Danger Above 8-15	The Golden Egg is located behind the two boxes below the slingshot. Zoom out to see it. Bounce a yellow bird off the pink cushion located to the right.
14	The Big Setup	Earn three stars on all of The Big Setup levels.
15	The Big Setup 9-14	This egg hides under a hard hat on the far side of the area. Send a bird over or through the structure to get it.
16	The Big Setup 10-3	Destroy the rubber duck located below the bridge to get another Golden Egg.
17	The Big Setup 11-15	Zoom out to spot an egg below and to the left of your location. Fire the boomerang bird to the left and tap the screen to bring it back to the egg.
18	Ham 'Em High	Earn three stars on all of the Ham 'Em High levels.
19	Ham 'Em High 12-12	Destroy the cup that sits on the small platform below the big structure. Destroy the building and send a bird through the opening to get it.
20	Ham 'Em High 13-10	Zoom out to see the egg hanging on the far side of the map. Send the white bird toward the middle of the structure, just above the two concrete bars on top. At this time, tap the screen to send the bird into the egg.
21	Ham 'Em High 13-12	You cannot see this egg until you get it. Zoom out so that you see the entire hill that you sit upon. Send a white bird to the left and quickly drop an explosive egg to reveal the Golden Egg.
22	Ham 'Em High 14-4	Zoom out so that you can see the Golden Egg that sits high on the mountain in the upper-right corner. Launch the yellow bird at about a 60 degree angle and then tap the screen to send it toward the egg.
23	Mine and Dine 15-12	Zoom out and an egg becomes visible in the top-right corner. Getting this one is very similar to 20. Send the yellow bird up and tap when it lines up with the egg.
24	Mine and Dine 16-9	Zoom out to spot the egg on the rock formation to the right. Aim a yellow bird just to the left of the first platform above the slingshot. Immediately tap the screen and if done correctly, the bird will reach the egg on the descent.
25	Mine and Dine	Earn three stars on all Mine and Dine levels.
26	Mine and Dine 17-12	Zoom out and a treasure chest can be seen on a rock high above. The first two birds cannot reach it, so use them up. Then fire the yellow bird at about a sixty degree angle up and to the right. As it lines up with the chest, tap the screen to get it.

ANGRY BIRDS HD

UNLOCKING WORLDS THE EASY WAY

At the world select, center on a locked world. Back out all the way out of the game. Go back into Angry Birds. At the Play button, tap it very quickly. Pass the first level to unlock the world.

SOUND BOARD

Earn three stars for all levels on worlds 1 through 3.

ANGRY BIRDS SPACE

GOLDEN EGGSTEROID

Golden Eggsteroids are hidden in six levels. These unlock bonus levels that are based on classic video games.

EGGSTEROID #	WORLD	LEVEL	LOCATION
1	Pig Bang	1-9	In brush below two pigs in bubbles.
2	Pig Bang	1-20	In brush on top of the planet.
3	Cold Cuts	2-13	In brush on planet below slingshot.
4	Cold Cuts	2-25	Under slingshot.
5	Cold Cuts	2-28	Hidden in snow, being pointed out by arrow.
6	Fry Me to the Moon	3-10	In bush on west side of planet.

BAG IT!

COMBOS

There are combos that get you extra rewards when bagging the groceries. Place the following items next to each other to create the combo. The characters names are as follows: Lucky is the cereal, Spilt is the milk, Sunshine is juice, Crusteau is the

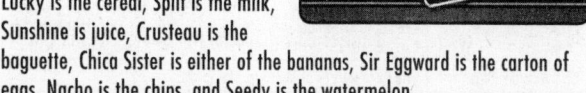

baguette, Chica Sister is either of the bananas, Sir Eggward is the carton of eggs, Nacho is the chips, and Seedy is the watermelon.

COMBO NAME	REQUIRED ITEMS
Balanced Breakfast	Spilt + Sunshine + Lucky + Sir Eggward
Banana Split	Both Chica Sisters
Breakfast Club	Lucky (x3)
Crusty Rivals	Sir Eggward + Crusteau
Double Date	Spilt (x2) + Sunshine (x2)
Eggcelent	Sir Eggward (x4)
Fiesta of Flavor	Nacho (x6)
Milky Way	Spilt (x4)
Mutiny!	Seedy (x5)
Nice Melons	Seedy (x2)
Scallywags	Seedy (x4)
Slumber Party	Sunshine (x3)
Sweethearts	Spilt + Sunshine
Three Amigos	Nacho (x3)
Well Bread	Crusteau (x4)

BATTLESHIP CRAFT

MIKASA

Go to options, select Code, and enter Jmsdf.

CHU CHU ROCKET HD

HARD PUZZLES

Complete all 25 Normal puzzles.

SPECIAL PUZZLES

Complete all 25 Hard puzzles.

MANIA PUZZLES

Complete all 25 Special puzzles.

CRAZY TAXI

EXPERT MODE

In Crazy Box, complete 1-x stages. Select Special from Help & Options to access this option.

TOGGLE ARROW AND DESTINATION MARK ON AND OFF

In Crazy Box, complete 2-x stages. Select Special from Help & Options to access this option.

ANOTHER DAY MODE AND RICKSHAW BIKE

In Crazy Box, complete 3-x stages. Select Special from Help & Options to access this option.

THE CREEPS! HD

DOODLER FROM DOODLE JUMP TOWER

Look at the Credits and click on the word AWESOME 100 times. Doodler shows up on the right side. Tap him to enable the secret. Now you can toggle Doodler on and off in the help menu.

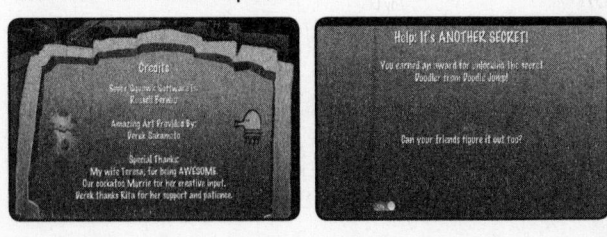

PYGMIES FROM POCKET GOD ENEMIES

Look at the Credits and click on the egg on the left side to enable this secret. Now you can toggle the Pygmies on and off in the help menu.

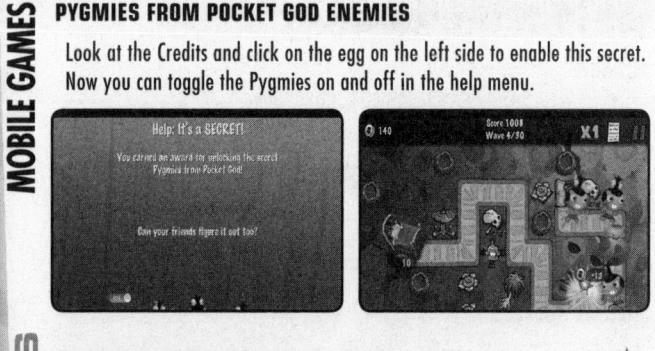

CRIMSON DRAGON: SIDE STORY

WINDOWS PHONE AVATAR AWARDS

AVATAR	EARNED BY
White T-Shirt	Clear the First Level.
Dragon Head	Clear the Second Level.

CUT THE ROPE (IOS)

OM NOM'S DRAWINGS

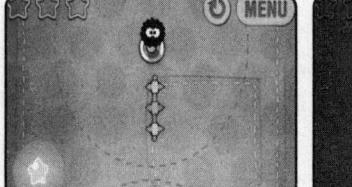

In 12 levels, if you tap on a certain spot of the background a drawing will be revealed. This spot can be something like a caution exclamation point or peeling wallpaper. Just look for something that looks a little off in the following levels: 1-16, 2-18, 3-3, 3-20, 4-14, 5-1, 5-15, 6-7, 7-3, 7-21, 8-17, and 9-21. Select Om Nom's Drawings to look at your collection.

DOODLE JUMP (IOS)

OOG FROM POCKET GOD

After falling, enter Ooga, Klik, or Klak as your name. This only works with version 1.2.1 or later.

MONSTERS FROM THE CREEPS

After falling, enter Creeps as a name.

EASTER LEVEL

After falling, enter E.B., HOP, or Bunny as your name.

SNOW THEME

After falling, enter Snow as a name.

HALLOWEEN THEME

After falling, enter Boo as a name.

FLIGHT CONTROL

ACHIEVEMENTS

ACHIEVEMENT	DESCRIPTION
Safety Card	Read the Game Tutorial.
First Flights	Land an aircraft on each airfield.
Jet Power	Land 20 jets in a game.
Centurion	Reach 100 Total Aircraft Landed.
Helicopter Love	Land five helicopters in a row.
Rush Hour	Land seven aircraft within 12 seconds.
Holding Pattern	Keep the same aircraft in the sky for 5 minutes.
Restrainer	Land no aircraft for 1.5/2 minutes.
Perfect Timing	Land three aircraft at the same time.
Crowded Sky	Reach 15/20 Most Aircraft on Screen.
Veteran	Play 250 games in total.
Wings	Land 200 aircraft in a game.

FRUIT NINJA

BLADES

Unlock the following blades by completing the task. These can be found in Sensei's Swag in the Dojo.

BLADE	EARNED BY
Disco Blade	Slice 50 bananas.
Mr. Sparkle	Slice three pineapples in a row in Classic Mode.
Old Glory	Finish a game with a score matching the number of stars on the U.S. Flag.
Butterfly Knife	Get a combo with a strawberry 40 times.
Flame Blade	Slice a combo after the timer ends in Zen Mode.
Ice Blade	Slice 20 freeze bananas in Arcade Mode to unlock.
The Shadow	Get a score of exactly 234 in Arcade Mode.
Pixel Love	Get 50 combos in classic mode.
Piano Blade	Slice 100 criticals to unlock.
Party Time	Slice every strawberry (and nothing else) in a game of Arcade Mode!
The Firecracker	Get the same score as the year of the Battle of Red Cliffs (208).
Bamboo Shoot	Play a full game of Zen Mode every day, five days in a row.

BACKGROUNDS

Unlock the following backgrounds by completing the task. These can be found in Sensei's Swag in the Dojo.

BACKGROUND	EARNED BY
Fruit Ninja	Get 125 points without dropping a fruit in Classic Mode.
I Heart Sensei	Read three of Sensei's Fruit Facts that are about strawberries.
Great Wave	Slice 250 watermelons.
Yin Yang	Slice 75 passion fruit.
Chinese Zodiac	Slice 384 peaches.

HEAD SOCCER

CAMEROON TEAM

In Arcade mode, defeat 12 characters. Alternatively, you can purchase it for 100,000 points.

NIGERIA TEAM

Win 30 times in a tournament. Alternatively, you can purchase it for 200,000 points.

INFINITY BLADE

NEGATIVE BLOODLINE

After starting Bloodline 3, lose to anyone except the God King. Restart from Bloodline 1 to be taken to the tutorial. Lose to the Dark Knight by tapping the shield instead of holding. After you die, select Save and Restart Castle. This takes you to Bloodlines -1 with Dark Mech gear equipped. If you have enough money, this is a good time to purchase some great equipment. When you return to Bloodline 1, you keep anything in your inventory but the Dark gear is gone.

NEW GAME +

After unlocking the Infinity Blade, defeat each monster behind the three doors at the bottom of the castle followed by the final two high-level enemies. Select New Game + to restart from Bloodline 1 with all of your stats intact. You do lose your inventory, but much better items wait in the Store.

KINGDOM RUSH

ACHIEVEMENTS

ACHIEVEMENT	DESCRIPTION
First Blood	Kill one Enemy.
Daring	Call 10 early waves.
Constructor	Build 30 Towers.
Bloodlust	Kill 500 Enemies.
Armaggedon [sic]	Use Rain of Fire 5 times in a single stage.
Home Improvement	Upgrade all basic Tower types to level 3.
Starry	Earn 15 Stars.
Whats That?	Open 10 Enemy information cards.
Supermario	Earn 30 Stars.
Nuts and Bolts	Defeat The Juggernaut.
Engineer	Build 100 Towers.
Is He Dead Yeti?	Defeat J.T.
Slayer	Kill 2500 Enemies.
Death From Above	Kill 100 Enemies with Meteor Shower.

ACHIEVEMENT	DESCRIPTION
Tactician	Change Soldiers rally point 200 times.
Superstar	Earn 45 Stars.
The architect	Build 150 Towers.
This is the End!	Defeat Vez'nan.
Terminator	Kill 10,000 Enemies.
Die Hard	Have your Soldiers regenerate a total of 50,000 life.
G.I. Joe	Train 1,000 Soldiers.
Cannon Fodder	Send 1,000 Soldiers to their deaths.
Fearless	Call all waves early in a single mission.
Real Estate	Sell 30 Towers.
Indecisive	Sell five Towers in a single mission.
Impatient	Call an early wave within three seconds of the icon showing up.
Forest Diplomacy	Recruit max Elves at The Silveroak Outpost.
Like a Henderson	Free the Sasquatch on the Icewind Pass.
Sunburner!	Fire the Sunray 20 times.
Imperial Saviour	Complete The Citadel with at least three surviving Imperial Guards.
Specialist	Build all 8 Tower specializations.
50 Shots 50 Kills	Snipe 50 Enemies.
Toxicity	Kill 50 Enemies by poison damage.
Entangled	Hold 500 or more Enemies with Wrath of the Forest.
Dust to Dust	Desintegrate [sic] 50 or more Enemies.
Beam Me Up Scotty	Teleport 250 or more Enemies.
Shepherd	Polymorph 50 Enemies into sheeps [sic].
Elementalist	Summon five rock elementals in any one stage.
Axe Rain	Throw 500 or more axes.
Are You Not Entertained?	Have a single Barbarian kill 10 Enemies.
Medic	Have your Paladins heal a total of 7,000 life.
Holy Chorus	Have your Paladins perform 100 Holy Strike.
Rocketeer	Shoot 100 Missiles.
Clustered	Drop 1,000 or more bomblets with the cluster bomb.
Energy Network	Build four Tesla towers in any stage.
AC/DC	Kill 300 Enemies with electricity.
Ovinophobia	Kill 10 or more Sheep with your hands
Twin Rivers Angler	Catch a Fish.
Great Defender	Complete all Campaign stages in Normal difficulty.
Heroic Defender	Complete all Heroic stages in Normal difficulty.
Iron Defender	Complete all Iron stages in Normal difficulty.

LET'S GOLF 2 HD

WIZZY THE WIZARD IN INSTANT PLAY

Select Profile from the Options and then tap Edit. Enter Wizzy10.

MAGIC: THE GATHERING— DUELS OF THE PLANESWALKERS 2013

PROMO UNLOCK 01

At the Player Status screen, select Promotional Unlocks. Click Enter Code and enter WMKFGC.

PROMO UNLOCK 02

At the Player Status screen, select Promotional Unlocks. Click Enter Code and enter KWPMZW.

PROMO UNLOCK 03

At the Player Status screen, select Promotional Unlocks. Click Enter Code and enter FNMDGP.

PROMO UNLOCK 04

At the Player Status screen, select Promotional Unlocks. Click Enter Code and enter MWTMJP.

PROMO UNLOCK 05

At the Player Status screen, select Promotional Unlocks. Click Enter Code and enter FXGJDW.

PROMO UNLOCK 06

At the Player Status screen, select Promotional Unlocks. Click Enter Code and enter GDZDJC.

PROMO UNLOCK 07

At the Player Status screen, select Promotional Unlocks. Click Enter Code and enter HTRNPW.

PROMO UNLOCK 08

At the Player Status screen, select Promotional Unlocks. Click Enter Code and enter NCTFJN.

PROMO UNLOCK 09

At the Player Status screen, select Promotional Unlocks. Click Enter Code and enter PCNKGR.

PROMO UNLOCK 10

At the Player Status screen, select Promotional Unlocks. Click Enter Code and enter GPCRSX.

MIRROR'S EDGE

ALL WALLPAPERS

Earn all 28 Badges.

PEWPEW 2

AMALGAM STAGE

Complete 50% of Campaign.

CHROMATIC CONFLICT

Complete 100% of Campaign.

PLANTS VS. ZOMBIES

ZOMBIE YETI

Complete Adventure Mode. Then, play the mode again to 4-10.

QUICK PLAY

Complete Adventure Mode.

ACHIEVEMENTS

All achievements are not available on all platforms.

ACHIEVEMENT	DESCRIPTION
Home Lawn Security	Complete Adventure Mode.
Spudow!	Blow up a zombie using a Potato Mine.
Explodonator	Take out 10 full-sized zombies with a single Cherry Bomb.
Morticulturalist	Collect all 49 plants (including plants from Crazy Dave's Shop).
Don't Pea in the Pool	Complete a daytime pool level without using Pea Shooters of any kind.
Roll Some Heads	Bowl over five Zombies with a single Wall-nut.
Grounded	Defeat a normal Roof level without using any catapult plants.
Zombologist	Discover the Yeti Zombie.
Penny Pincher	Pick up 30 coins in a row on a single level without letting any disappear.
Sunny Days	Accumulate 8,000 sun during a single level
Popcorn Party	Defeat two Gargantuars with Corn Cob missiles in a single level
Good Morning	Complete daytime level by planting only Mushrooms and Coffee Beans.
No Fungus Among Us	Complete a nighttime Level without planting any Mushrooms.
Last Mown Standing	Defeat the last zombie in a level with a lawn mower.
20 Below Zero	Immobilize 20 full-sized zombies with a single Ice-shroom.
Flower Power	Keep 10 Twin Sunflowers alive in a single level.
Pyromaniac	Complete a level using only explosive plants to kill zombies.
Lawn Mower Man	Kill 10 zombies with a single lawn mower.
Chill Out	Feel the rhythm, feel the rhyme, you've one level to destroy three bobsleds, its jalapeno time!
Defcorn 5	Build five Cob Cannons in a single level.
Monster Mash	Crush five zombies with a single Squash.
Blind Faith	Complete an extremely foggy level without using Planterns or Blovers.
Pool's Closed	Complete a pool level without using water plants.
Melon-y Lane	Plant a Winter Melon on every lane.
Second Life	Complete Adventure Mode a second time.
Lucky Spin	Get three diamonds in Slot Machine.
Chilli Free	Complete Column Like You See 'Em without using Jalapenos.
Enlighted	Collect all Zen Garden, Mushroom Garden, and Aquarium Garden plants.
Diamond Beghouler	Upgrade all your plants in Beghouled.
Sultan of Spin	Upgrade all your plants in Beghouled Twist.
Green Fingers	Grow 10 Zen Garden plants to full size.
Wall-Not-Attack	Complete ZomBotany with no Wall-Nuts, Tall-Nuts, or Pumpkins.
Beyond the Grave	Beat all 18 mini-games.
Down the Hole!	Dig your way to see the Chinese Zombies.
Thrilling the Zombies	Hypnotize the lead Dancer Zombie.
Alive and Planting	Survive 40 waves of pure zombie ferocity.

POCKET GOD

OOGA JUMP JET PACK BONUS

At an island, click the arrow in the upper-left corner and then select the 3-star graphic. Tap the star and then Pocket God Comic Pre-Order Bonus. Enter journey to Uranus. You can participate in the promotion and get the jet pack otherwise you need to score 6000 in Ooga Jump.

QUELL

ACHIEVEMENTS

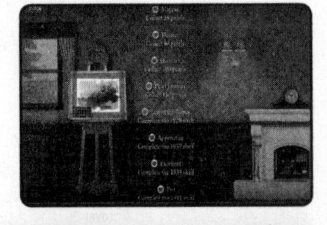

ACHIEVEMENT	DESCRIPTION
Magpie	Collect 25 pearls
Hunter	Collect 50 pearls
Hoarder	Collect 100 pearls
Pearl Jammer	Collect 150 pearls
Pearl Harboring	Collect 200 pearls
Learnt the Ropes	Complete the 1928 shelf
Apprentice	Complete the 1937 shelf
Excellent	Complete the 1939 shelf
Pro	Complete the 1941 shelf
Expert	Complete the 1943 shelf
Champion	Complete the 1945 shelf
Complete	Complete every Quell level
Minimalist	Complete three levels perfectly
Accomplished	Complete 10 levels perfectly
Flawless	Complete 20 levels perfectly
Impeccable	Complete 40 levels perfectly
Precise	Complete a stage in perfect moves
Meticulous	Complete a shelf in perfect moves
Perfect	Complete every Quell level in perfect moves
Keep Going!	Play for 10 minutes
Time Flies	Play for 30 minutes
High Stamina	Play for 1 hour
Suicidal	Die on a first move
Ouch!	Spiked three times
Fearless	Spiked 10 times
Funeral Bill	Spiked 20 times

ACHIEVEMENT	DESCRIPTION
Road to Nowhere	Get stuck in a loop five times
Groundhog Day	Retry a level 20 times
Matchmaker	Push two sets of blocks together
Tired	Push 10 blocks
Ring Leader	Use the ring five times
Quick Thinking	Complete a level in under five seconds
Defiant	Take over 10 minutes to complete a level
Scenic Route	Take twice as many moves as necessary

RPG ALPHADIA

CHEAT MODE

Defeat the game to unlock cheat mode. This gives you the ability to double experience, gold, and skill points and skip enemy encounters.

THE SIMPSONS: TAPPED OUT

10 Extra Doughnuts and Jebediah Springfield Statue

During a game, select Homer to get his task menu. Tap Homer ten times to get a message for performing the code correctly.

SPIDER-MAN: TOTAL MAYHEM HD

ULTIMATE DIFFICULTY

Defeat the game.

BLACK SUIT

Defeat the game. Access the suit on the level select with an icon in upper-left corner.

SUPER STICKMAN GOLF

ACHIEVEMENTS

ACHIEVEMENTS	DESCRIPTION	POINTS
Sticky Ball	Unlocked the Sticky Ball	10
Ice Ball	Unlocked the Ice Ball	10
Hazard Swap	Unlock the Hazard Swap	20
Air Brakes	Unlock the Air Brakes	20
Super Ball	Unlock the Super Ball	30
Nitro Ball	Unlock the Nitro Ball – Get 30 Achievements	30
Thats A Bingo	Get a hole in one	10
Eagle	Get an eagle	10
Nothing But Net	Get a hole in one without touching the green	20
500 Strokes	Reach a combined 500 shots	10
Lunar Lander	Get a hole in one on the first hole in The Moon Base	10
Funky Dry	Score under par on Funky Town without getting wet	10
The Slew Sniper	Score under par on The Slew without hitting a sand trap	10
Parnage	Beat Dapper Dunes without getting a single bogey	10
1000 Strokes	Take a combined 1000 shots	20
Jacob's Cabin	Can you find Jacob's Cabin? (Dapper Dunes – Hole 1)	10
The Tire Swing	Can you find The Tire Swing? (Lofstrom Links – Hole 8)	10
The Locksmith	Unlock all the courses	20
Cool It Down	Shoot a superball into a water hazard	10
The Trio	Bag three hole in one's in a row	10
2000 Strokes	Take a combined 2000 shots	30
3000 Strokes, Hardcore	Take a combined 3000 shots	50
The Impossible Shot	Get a hole in one on the second hole in The Ice Flows	20
Nil Score	Score a zero on a hole	20

ACHIEVEMENTS	DESCRIPTION	POINTS
Negative Score	Score a negative number on a hole	20
Purple Passion	Score a hole in one on hole 6 in Purple Haze	10
Purple Zero	Score a zero or less on hole 7 in Purple Haze	10
The Woodsman	Score a hole in one on hole 8 in The Woods	10
10 Clean Balls	Score under par on 10 courses without powerups	10
The Long One	Sink a super long putt	10
Look Up	Get a negative score on hole 3 in The Graveyard	10
Iced Temple	Freeze all the hazards on hole 3 in The Temple	10
Parkland Dry	Score under par on Parkland without getting wet	10
Freeze, Bounce, Drop	Beat hole 2 in Parkland In 3 strokes	10
Tropical Slide	Score a hole in one on hole 4 in The Tropics	10
Ride The Boundary	Score a hole in one on hole 3 in Key Lime Links	10
1 Multiplayer Win	Win 1 multiplayer game	10
5 Multiplayer Wins	Win 5 multiplayer games	10
10 Multiplayer Wins	Win 10 multiplayer games	20
10 Multiplayer Points	Reach a combined 10 awarded multiplayer points	10
50 Multiplayer Points	Reach a combined 50 awarded multiplayer points	10
100 Multiplayer Points	Reach a combined 100 awarded multiplayer points	20
200 Multiplayer Points	Reach a combined 200 awarded multiplayer points	50
Haunted Hazards	Score under par on Haunted Hills, without getting wet	10
Haunted Drop-in	Score a hole-in-one on hole 7 in the Haunted Hills	10
All Aces	Score all hole-in-one's in Parkland without powerups	50
Cinnamon Bounce	Score a hole-in-one on hole 7 in the Cinnamon Bluffs	20
Nitro Master	Score a hole-in-one on hole 7 on the Pipes	30
Food For Thought	Score a hole-in-one on hole 6 in the Belts	20
Belts Nil	Beat Belts hole 7 in zero or less strokes	20
Cinnamon Nil	Beat Cinnamon Bluffs hole 2 in zero or less strokes	20

TEMPLE RUN

These codes do not work if you have updated to 1.4. You need the ability to bring up the keyboard to enter them.

EXTRA CHARACTERS

At the title screen, enter rxh7nigh.

INVINCIBILITY

At the title screen, enter samhines86.

PURCHASABLE CHARACTERS

As of version 1.4.1, you can purchase the following characters with the given amount of coins from the store.

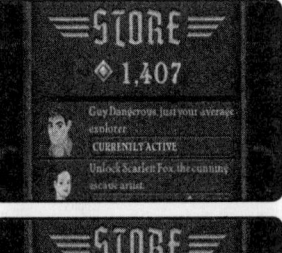

CHARACTER	COST
Scarlett Fox	10,000
Barry Bones	10,000
Karma Lee	25,000
Montana Smith	25,000
Francisco Montoya	25,000
Zack Wonder	25,000

PURCHASABLE WALLPAPERS

The following wallpapers can also be purchased at the store.

WALLPAPER	COST
Temple Wall	5000
Guy Dangerous	5000
Evil Demon Monkeys	5000

OBJECTIVES

OBJECTIVE	DESCRIPTION
Novice Runner	Run 500 meters
Pocket Change	Collect 100 coins
Adventurer	Scored 25,000 points
Sprinter	Ran 1000 meters
Miser Run	500 m collecting no coins
Piggy Bank	Collect 250 coins
Treasure Hunter	Scored 50,000 points
Mega Bonus	Fill the bonus meter 4x
Athlete	Ran 2500 meters
Lump Sum	Collected 500 coins
Resurrection	Resurrected after dying

OBJECTIVE	DESCRIPTION
Basic Powers	All level 1 Powerups
High Roller	Scored 100,000 points
Payday	Collected 750 coins
Head Start	Used a Head Start
Steady Feet	Ran 2500 m without tripping
Allergic to Gold	1000 m collecting no coins
5k Runner	Ran 5000 meters
No Trip Runner	Ran 5000 meters without tripping
1/4 Million Club	Scored 250,000 points
Double Resurrection	Resurrected twice in one run
Money Bags	Collected 1000 coins
1/2 Million Club	Scored 500,000 points
Super Powers	All level 5 powerups
Dynamic Duo	Unlocked two characters
Million Club	Scored 1,000,000 points
Money Bin	Collected 2,500 coins
Fantastic Four	Unlocked Four Characters
Sexy Six	Unlocked six characters
Interior Decorator	Unlocked three wallpapers
10k Runner	Run 10,000 meters
Fort Knox	Collect 5,000 coins
2.5 Million Club	Scored 2,500,000 points
5 Million Club	Scored 5,000,000 points
The Spartan	1 million without power ups
10 Million Club	Score 10,000,000 points

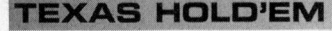

TEXAS HOLD'EM

CHEAT MENU

Select New Player from the Options menu and enter YOUCHEAT as the player name. Hold down the center button until you get confirmation. This gives you a cheat menu with the following five options: Unlock All Tournaments, Start with $100,000, Show Tells and/or Down Cards, and Adjust AI Folding frequency.

APPLE CONFERENCE ROOM TOURNAMENT

Select New Player from the Options menu and enter THREEAMI as the player name. Hold down the center button until you get confirmation.

DOG TOURNAMENT

Select New Player from the Options menu and enter PLAYDOGS as the player name. Hold down the center button until you get confirmation.

FUTURISTIC TOURNAMENT

Select New Player from the Options menu and enter SPACEACE as the player name. Hold down the center button until you get confirmation.

ITUNES BAR TOURNAMENT

Select New Player from the Options menu and enter BARTUNES as the player name. Hold down the center button until you get confirmation.

STONEHENGE TOURNAMENT

Select New Player from the Options menu and enter BIGROCKS as the player name. Hold down the center button until you get confirmation.

SEE SECRET CHARACTERS

Select New Player from the Options menu and enter ALLCHARS as the player name. Hold down the center button until you get confirmation.

WHERE'S MY WATER?

HIDDEN PLANETARIUM LEVEL

Go to the Achievements screen and scroll all the way to the top. Continue to scroll up until you see a drawing of a planet. Tap it to enter the level.

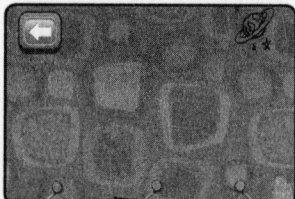 

JELLY CAR BONUS LEVEL

If Jelly Car is installed on your device, view the credits. When a Jelly Car goes by, tap it to unlock this level.

COLLECTION SCREEN EASTER EGG

Go to the Collection screen and scroll all the way to the bottom. Continue to scroll and you will see someone carved a message into the wall.

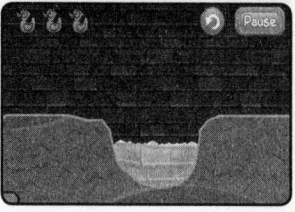

EMBARASSED ACHIEVEMENT

Clicking on Swampy during a level causes him to perform a random action. If he hides behind the curtain, this achievement is earned.

WORLD OF GOO

WHISTLE ITEM

Complete Leap Hole level.

WORLD OF GOO CORPORATION MINI GAME

Complete Hang Low level.

NINTENDO DS™/3DS™

3D CLASSICS: TWINBEE

10 LIVES

When starting a game, hold Up + Right and press A.

ADVANCE WARS: DAYS OF RUIN

UNLOCK COS

Complete the following missions to unlock the corresponding CO.

COMPLETE MISSION	CO UNLOCKED
12	Tasha
13	Gage
14	Forthsythe
20	Waylon
21	Greyfield
24	Penny
25	Tabitha
26	Caulder

ALICE IN WONDERLAND

BIG PLAYING CARD

Enter the Bonus door, click the padlock, and enter 2273.

DORMOUSE COAT FOR DGAMER AVATAR

Enter the Bonus door, click the padlock, and enter 3676.

DORMOUSE MASK FOR DGAMER AVATAR

Enter the Bonus door, click the padlock, and enter 3675.

DRINK ME BOTTLE FOR DGAMER AVATAR

Enter the Bonus door, click the padlock, and enter 7493.

GREEN ALICE BOOK FOR DGAMER AVATAR

Enter the Bonus door, click the padlock, and enter 4625.

IMPOSSIBLE IDEAS T-SHIRT FOR DGAMER AVATAR

Enter the Bonus door, click the padlock, and enter 4332.

KEYHOLE T-SHIRT FOR DGAMER AVATAR

Enter the Bonus door, click the padlock, and enter 5398.

MAD HATTER COAT FOR DGAMER AVATAR

Enter the Bonus door, click the padlock, and enter 2628.

MAD HATTER T-SHIRT FOR DGAMER AVATAR

Enter the Bonus door, click the padlock, and enter 4288.

MARCH HARE MASK FOR DGAMER AVATAR

Enter the Bonus door, click the padlock, and enter 2675.

RED GUARD SHIELD FOR DGAMER AVATAR

Enter the Bonus door, click the padlock, and enter 7453.

RED QUEEN DRESS FOR DGAMER AVATAR

Enter the Bonus door, click the padlock, and enter 7483.

RED QUEEN MASK FOR DGAMER AVATAR

Enter the Bonus door, click the padlock, and enter 7675.

TAN ALICE BOOK FOR DGAMER AVATAR

Enter the Bonus door, click the padlock, and enter 2625.

TEA CUP FOR DGAMER AVATAR

Enter the Bonus door, click the padlock, and enter 8328.

TWEEDLE OUTFIT FOR DGAMER AVATAR

Enter the Bonus door, click the padlock, and enter 8946.

WHITE QUEEN DRESS FOR DGAMER AVATAR

Enter the Bonus door, click the padlock, and enter 9483.

WHITE RABBIT MASK FOR DGAMER AVATAR

Enter the Bonus door, click the padlock, and enter 9675.

WHITE RABBIT WATCH FOR DGAMER AVATAR

Enter the Bonus door, click the padlock, and enter 8463.

THE AMAZING SPIDER-MAN

BLACK SPIDER-MAN SUIT

Complete Vigilante Mode.

CLASSIC SPIDER-MAN SUIT

Complete all petty crimes.

BAKUGAN BATTLE BRAWLERS

1000 BP

Start a new game and enter the name as 180978772269.

5000 BP

Start a new game and enter the name as 332044292925.

10,000 BP

Start a new game and enter the name as 423482942968.

BRONZE WARIUS

Start a new game and enter the name as 449824934071.

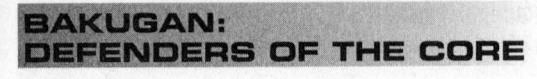

BAKUGAN: DEFENDERS OF THE CORE

UNLOCK CODES

Select Unlock Codes from the Collection menu. Enter the verification code, HXV6Y7BF. Now you can enter the following:

EFFECT	PASSWORD
10 Vexos Passes	YQLHBBSMDC
10,000 Core Energy	QY8CLD5NJE
Earthen Armor Ability Card	JJUZDEACXX
Fire Spirit Ability Card	YJ7RGG7WGZ

EFFECT	PASSWORD
Tornado Vortex Ability Card	2FKRRMNCDQ
Water Pillar Ability Card	HUUH8ST7AR
Zorch Thunder Ability Card	82D77YK6P8

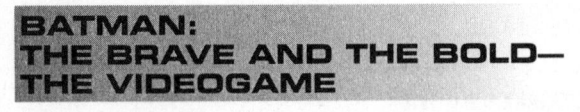

BATMAN: THE BRAVE AND THE BOLD— THE VIDEOGAME

BATMAN COSTUMES

Access the terminal on the left side of the Batcave and enter the following:

COSTUME	CODE
Dark Batsuit	3756448
Medieval Batsuit	5644863

COSTUME	CODE
Rainbow Suit	7629863

CHALLENGE MAPS

CHALLENGE MAP	CODE
Gotham 1 & 2	4846348
Proto Sparring	6677686
Science Island 1 & 2	7262348

WEAPONS

WEAPON	CODE
Barrier	2525655
Belt Sword	2587973
Flashbangs	3527463
Smoke Pellets	7665336

BATTLE OF GIANTS— DRAGONS

Select Unlock Gold Gems from the Extras Menu and enter the following passwords:

BREATH ATTACK GOLD GEMS

LEVEL	ATTACK	PASSWORD
1	NAMGILIMA	ISAM SKNF DKTD
2	NIGHHALAMA	ZNBN QOKS THGO
3	KUGDIM	AWBF CRSL HGAT
4	KUZEN	ACLC SCRS VOSK
5	SUGZAG	XSPC LLSL KJLP

CLAW ATTACK GOLD GEMS

LEVEL	ATTACK	PASSWORD
1	USUD	NAKF HLAP SDSP
2	ULUH	SAPO RLNM VUSD
3	NIGHZU	POZX MJDR GJSA
4	GHIDRU	GPGE SMEC TDTB
5	MUDRU	ABLP CGPG SGAM

HEAD ATTACK GOLD GEMS

LEVEL	ATTACK	PASSWORD
1	MEN	PQTM AONV UTNA
2	SAGHMEN	TNAP CTJS LDUF
3	KINGAL	FHSK EUFV KALP
4	DALLA	EPWB MPOR TRTA
5	AGA	GPKT BBWT SGNR

TAIL ATTACK GOLD GEMS

LEVEL	ATTACK	PASSWORD
1	A'ASH	LSSN GOAJ READ
2	ASH	FUTY HVNS LNVS
3	ASH SAR	LPAQ KOYH TGDS
4	AHS BALA	VLQL QELB IYDS
5	NAMTAGTAG	VLDB DDSL NCJA

WING ATTACK GOLD GEMS

LEVEL	ATTACK	PASSWORD
1	NIM	SGHJ VLPO QEIK
2	NIMSAHARA	QPLA OKFC NBUS
3	BARASH	IQUW ENPC SRGA
4	A'SHUM	LRYV LCJC MEBT
5	ATUKU	ALVN HRSF MSEP

BATTLE OF GIANTS: MUTANT INSECTS

UNLOCK REWARDS

Select Unlock Rewards from the Options and enter the following passwords:

REWARD	PASSWORD	REWARD	PASSWORD
500 Golden Gems	SRKC RDZR KZAE	Head Upgrade	TDFS ZITF BKYE
500 Golden Gems	HDTQ JCLO SSUU	Ice upgrade	PLAL TALG JPZV
750 Golden Gems	OAZN CEYQ XRDT	Mutant Wasp	CHYV UEMJ QVGM
750 Golden Gems	FBRY CMTR KXUQ	Red Color	QODI LHGH HNBN
Claw Upgrade	PLQO ILQJ YKEQ	Shock Upgrade	WLUA DZCN ZNKE
Cyan Color	LYYD UAXR IPRT	Yellow Color	TZCK AXZJ VSTW
Green Color	LCYH FVQZ XEVB		

BEN 10 GALACTIC RACING

KINECELARATOR

Select Enter Code from Extras and enter Ben, Spidermonkey, Kevin Levin, Ultimate Echo Echo.

BEN 10: PROTECTOR OF EARTH

GALACTIC ENFORCER SKINS

At the level select, press A, B, X, Y, L, R, Select.

GWEN 10 SKINS

At the level select, press Left, Right, Left, Right, L, R, Select.

ULTRA BEN SKINS

At the level select, press Up, Right, Down, Left, A, B, Select.

UPCHUCK

At the level select, press A, Left, Y, Right, X, Up, B, Down, Select.

BONUS MISSION

At the level select, press Left, L, Right, R, Up, Down, Select.

BRAIN AGE EXPRESS: ARTS & LETTERS

ELIMINATE ENEMIES IN WORD ATTACK

In Word Attack, during the Space mode, press A, Y, X, B. You can use this once each training session.

BRAIN QUEST GRADES 5 & 6

MAD COW STICKER

Select Cheats from the Options and enter MADCOW.

BRAIN VOYAGE

ALL GOLD MEDALS

At the World Map, press A, B, Up, L, L, Y.

INFINITE COINS

At the World Tour Mode, press L, Up, X, Up, R, Y.

BUBBLE BOBBLE REVOLUTION

BONUS LEVELS IN CLASSIC MODE

At the Classic mode Title screen, press L, R, L, R, L, R, Right, Select. Touch the door at Level 20.

POWER UP! MODE IN CLASSIC VERSION

At the Classic mode Title screen, press Select, R, L, Left, Right, R, Select, Right.

SUPER BUBBLE BOBBLE IN CLASSIC VERSION

You must first defeat the boss with two players. At the Classic mode Title screen, press Left, R, Left, Select, Left, L, Left, Select.

BUILD-A-BEAR WORKSHOP

At the Select a Slot screen, press Up, Up, Down, Down, Left, Right, Left, Right, B, A. Now you can enter the following codes:

ALL LEVELS

At the level select, hold L + R.

ALL ACTIVITIES

At the workshop screen, press R.

ALL MOVES

At the garden screen, press L.

CARTOON NETWORK: PUNCH TIME EXPLOSION

BATTLE MODE CHARACTERS

In Battle Mode, win the following number of matches to unlock the corresponding characters.

CHARACTER	# OF MATCHES	CHARACTER	# OF MATCHES
Captain Knuckles	3	Samurai Jack	33
Bubbles	7	Father	42
Blossom	12	Vilgax	52
Monkey	18	Mojo Jojo	63
Grim	25	Captain Planet	75

CAVE STORY

TITLE SCREEN MUSIC AND CURSOR

Complete the Sanctuary Time Attack under the following times to get new music and cursor on the title screen.

MUSIC/CURSOR	FINISH UNDER (MINUTES)
Safety / Sue	3
White / King	4
Toroko's Theme / Toroko	5
Running Hell / Curly	6

CENTIPEDE: INFESTATION

PLAY AS RIVET WITH RIVETER GUN

Select Code Entry from Extras and enter 121213.

CITY LIFE DS

1,000,000

Pause the game and press A, B, Y, L, R.

ALL BUILDINGS

Pause the game and hold B + Y + X + R for 2 seconds.

CLUB PENGUIN: ELITE PENGUIN FORCE

FLOWER HUNT MISSION

Change your system's date to April 1st.

APRIL ITEMS IN CATALOG

Change your system's date to April 1st.

SUMMER PARTY MISSION

Change your system's date to June 21st.

FIESTA HAT ON FROZEN POND

Change your system's date to June 21st.

JUNE ITEMS IN CATALOG

Change your system's date to June 21st.

HALLOWEEN PARTY MISSION

Change your system's date to October 31st.

FISH COSTUME IN LODGE ATTIC

Change your system's date to October 31st.

DELIVER THE PRESENTS MISSION

Change your system's date to December 25th.

ICE SKATES ON THE ICEBERG

Change your system's date to December 25th.

CODE OF PRINCESS

TRUE UNICORN

Win a Versus Match.

GOLD HOOP

Win 100 Versus Matches.

PEGASUS WEAPON

Complete 100 Quests.

ALL CHARACTERS FOR ONLINE CO-OP

Complete 100 quests.

BONUS CHARACTERS

SILVER HOOP MIND ACCESSORY

Complete 500 Quests.

TRUE MARS WEAPON

Clear 1000 Quests.

TRUE SERAPH

Complete 100 Co-op Quests.

BONUS CHARACTERS IN FREE MISSIONS AND BONUS QUESTS

Defeat the Campaign.

CHARACTER	COMPLETE FOLLOWING QUEST OR CAMPAIGN
Alchemia	Little Witch
Distille	Fallen Angel
General Jupponogi	Return of the Ninja
Joe the Liongate	Eclipse Calibur
Marco Neko	Epic Mandrake
Boss Jupponogi	All Free Missions and Bonus Quests
King Golgius	Complete Campaign and Watch Thousand Years with Allegro
Schwartz	Complete Campaign and Watch Thousand Years with Solange
The Guardian	Complete Campaign and Watch Thousand Years with Zozo

STONE CIRCLE PASSWORDS

Defeat the game to unlock the Stone Circle in South Euro. Now you can enter the following passwords to unlock dinosaurs. Find the level 1 dinosaur in a chest at the shrine.

009 DASPLETEOSARUS

Enter Grass, Water, Ligthning, Lightning, Earth, Earth, Water, Wind.

012 SIAMOTYRRANUS

Enter Fire, Wind, Fire, Water, Wind, Grass, Fire, Water.

025 JOBARIA

Enter Water, Lightning, Lightning, Earth, Fire, Earth, Fire, Wind.

029 TRICERATOPS

Enter Lightning, Fire, Lightning, Fire, Water, Lightning, Grass, Earth.

038 MONOCLONIUS

Enter Lightning, Earth, Water, Water, Grass, Fire, Earth, Wind.

046 EUOPLOCEPHALUS

Enter Earth, Earth, Grass, Water, Wind, Earth, Wind, Fire.

058 ALTIRHINUS

Enter Wind, Fire, Fire, Fire, Lightning, Earth, Water, Grass.

061 CARNOTAURUS

Enter Earth, Wind, Water, Lightning, Fire, Wind, Wind, Water.

EX ACE/EX CHOMP

Enter Lightning, Grass, Fire, Earth, Water, Water, Lightning, Fire. This gives you Ace if you are playing as Rex and Chomp as Max.

EX MINI-KING

Enter Lightning, Wind, Earth, Lightning, Grass, Wind, Fire, Water.

EX PARIS

Enter Grass, Water, Water, Earth, Wind, Grass, Lightning, Lightning.

EX Saurophaganax

Enter Fire, Water, Earth, Grass, Wind, Lightning, Fire, Water.

EX SPINY

Enter Water, Earth, Fire, Water, Fire, Grass, Wind, Earth.

EX TANK

Enter Earth, Grass, Earth, Water, Wind, Water, Grass, Fire.

EX TERRY

Enter Fire, Lightning, Wind, Wind, Water, Fire, Fire, Earth.

DISNEY FAIRIES: TINKER BELL

TINKERBELL MAGIC BOOK CODES

Talk to Queen Clarion about the Magic Book and enter the following codes.

EFFECCT	CODE
Augustus	5318 3479 7972
Baden	1199 2780 8802
Blair	6899 6003 4480
Cera	1297 0195 5747
Chipper	7980 9298 9818
Dewberry	0241 4491 0630
Elwood	3527 5660 3684
Fawn	9556 0047 1043
Idalia	2998 8832 2673
Iridessa	0724 0213 6136
Luminaria	8046 5868 5678
Magnolia	1697 4780 6430
Mariana	5138 8216 9240
Minister Autumn	2294 0281 6332
Minister Spring	2492 1155 4907
Minister Summer	2582 7972 6926
Minister Winter	2618 8587 2083
Nollie	5905 2346 9329
Olwen	7629 0545 7105
One Black Shell	1234 5678 9012
One Blue Dewdrop	0987 6543 2109

EFFECCT	CODE
One Fairy Medal	1111 1111 1111
One Green Leaf	4444 4444 4444
One Pink Petal	2222 2222 2222
One Red Leaf	5555 5555 5555
One Snow Grain	7777 7777 7777
One Weak Thread	9999 9999 9999
One White Feather	8888 8888 8888
One Yellow Leaf	6666 6666 6666
One Yellow Petal	3333 3333 3333
Party Shoes	1390 5107 4096
Party Skirt	6572 4809 6680
Party Tiara	8469 7886 7938
Party Top	0977 4584 3869
Queen Clarion	1486 4214 8147
Rosetta	8610 2523 6122
Rune	3020 5768 5351
Silvermist	0513 4563 6800
Terence	8606 6039 6383
Tinkerbell	2495 7761 9313
Vidia	3294 3220 0349

DRAGLADE

CHARACTERS

CHARACTER	TO UNLOCK
Asuka	Defeat Daichi's story
Gyamon	Defeat Guy's story
Koki	Defeat Hibito's story
Shura	Defeat Kairu's story

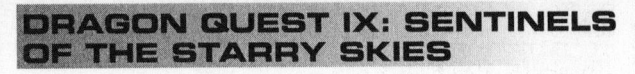

DRAGON QUEST IX: SENTINELS OF THE STARRY SKIES

MINI MEDAL REWARDS

Trade your mini medals with Cap'N Max Meddlin in Dourbridge. These are cumulative, so giving him 80 medals gets all of the rewards.

# MINI MEDALS	REWARD	# MINI MEDALS	REWARD
4	Thief's Key	32	Miracle Sword
8	Mercury Bandanna	40	Sacred Armor
13	Bunny Suit	50	Meteorite Bracer
18	Jolly Roger Jumper	62	Rusty Helmet
25	Transparent Tights	80	Dragon Robe

After you have given him 80 mini medals, he sells items for mini medals.

# MINI MEDALS	ITEM	# MINI MEDALS	ITEM
3	Prayer Ring	10	Reset Stone
5	Elfin Elixir	15	Orichalcum
8	Saint's Ashes	20	Pixie Boots

DOURBRIDGE SECRET SHOP

In Dourbridge, you can find a secret shop located behind the Dourbridge Item Shop. You need the Ultimate Key to access the shop.

DRAGON QUEST HEROES: ROCKET SLIME

KNIGHTRO TANK IN MULTIPLAYER

While in the church, press Y, L, L, Y, R, R, Y, Up, Down, Select.

THE NEMESIS TANK IN MULTIPLAYER

While in the church, press Y, R, R, up, L, L, Y, Down, Down, Down, Y, Select.

DRAGON QUEST MONSTERS: JOKER

CAPTAIN CROW

As you travel between the islands on the sea scooters, you are occasionally attacked by pirates. Discover the route on which the pirates are located at the bulletin board in any scoutpost den. When you face them between Infant Isle and Celeste Isle, Captain Crow makes an appearance. Defeat him and he forces himself into your team.

SOLITAIRE'S CHALLENGE

After completing the main game, load your game again for a new endeavor. The hero is in Solitaire's office, where she proposes a new nonstop challenge known as Solitaire's Challenge.

DRAGON QUEST MONSTERS: JOKER 2

UNLOCK MONSTERS

MONSTER	OWN THIS MANY DIFFERENT MONSTERS
Great Argon Lizard	50
Drakularge	100
Metal King Slime	150
Grandpa Slime	200

MONSTERS FROM DRAGON QUEST VI: REALMS OF REVELATION

Activate Dreamsharing on Dragon Quest VI and then turn on Tag Mode on Dragon Quest Monsters: Joker 2. This unlocks Malevolamp, Mottle Slime, Noble Gasbagon, and Overkilling Machine.

MONSTERS FROM DRAGON QUEST IX: SENTINELS OF THE STARRY SKIES

Activate Tag Mode on Dragon Quest IX and then turn on Tag Mode on Dragon Quest Monsters: Joker 2. This unlocks Shogum, Slime Stack, and Teeny Sanguini.

DRAWN TO LIFE: THE NEXT CHAPTER

TEMPLATES

At the Creation Hall, hold L and press X, Y, B, A, A to unlock the following Templates.

Astronaut Template

Knight Template

Ninja Girl Template

Spartan Template

Super Girl Template

DRAWN TO LIFE: SPONGEBOB SQUAREPANTS EDITION

EXTRA REWARD COINS

Select Cheat Entry and enter Down, Down, B, B, Down, Left, Up, Right, A.

ED, EDD N EDDY: SCAM OF THE CENTURY

INVINCIBILITY

During a game, press Select + A, Up, Select + R, Down, Up.

RESTORE HALF HEALTH

During a game, press A, A, Select + A, Down, Down, Down.

RESTORE HEALTH

During a game, press B, B, Select + X, A + R, Select.

HALF SPECIAL ATTACK GAUGE

During a game, press Down, Down, Left, Right, Select + X.

CAMERA

During a game, press Down, Up, Right, Right, Select + B.

MARSHMALLOW

During a game, press Down, Down, Left, Left, Select + A.

ELEBITS: THE ADVENTURES OF KAI & ZERO

BIG RED BONUS OMEGA

Select Download Additional Omegas from the Extra menu. Choose Download Data and press B, Y, Up, L, Right, R, Down, Left, X, A.

GODZILLA UNLEASHED: DOUBLE SMASH

ANGUIRUS

Defeat Hedorah Terrorizes San Francisco.

DESTOROYAH

Defeat Monster Island, The Final Battle.

FIRE RODAN

Defeat Biollante Attacks Paris.

KING GHIDORAH

Defeat Mecha King Ghidorah Ravages Bangkok.

GRID

UNLOCK ALL

Select Cheat Codes from the Options and enter 233558.

INVULNERABILITY

Select Cheat Codes from the Options and enter 161650.

DRIFT MASTER

Select Cheat Codes from the Options and enter 789520.

PERFECT GRIP

Select Cheat Codes from the Options and enter 831782.

HIGH ROLLER

Select Cheat Codes from the Options and enter 401134.

GHOST CAR

Select Cheat Codes from the Options and enter 657346.

TOY CARS

Select Cheat Codes from the Options and enter 592014.

MM MODE

Select Cheat Codes from the Options and enter 800813.

INFINITE SPACE

NEW GAME+ AND EXTRA MODE

Complete the game. New Game+ gives you additional blue prints. Extra Mode is another game mode with limited resources.

IZUNA: LEGEND OF THE UNEMPLOYED NINJA

PATH OF TRAILS BONUS DUNGEON

After completing the game, touch the crystal from the beginning.

JAKE HUNTER: DETECTIVE CHRONICLES

PASSWORDS

Select Password from the main menu and enter the following:

UNLOCKABLE	PASSWORD
1 Password Info	AAAA
2 Visuals	LEET
3 Visuals	GONG
4 Visuals	CARS

UNLOCKABLE	PASSWORD
5 Movies	ROSE
6 Jukebox	BIKE
7 Hints	HINT

JAKE HUNTER DETECTIVE STORY: MEMORIES OF THE PAST

JAKE HUNTER QUIZ

Select Password and enter NEET.

JAKE HUNTER SERIES

Select Password and enter MISS.

JAKE HUNTER UNLEASHED 01 BONUS

Select Password and enter NONE.

JAKE HUNTER UNLEASHED 02 BONUS

Select Password and enter ANGL.

JAKE HUNTER UNLEASHED 03 BONUS

Select Password and enter SNAP.

JAKE HUNTER UNLEASHED 04 BONUS

Select Password and enter DOOR.

JAKE HUNTER UNLEASHED 05 BONUS

Select Password and enter STOP.

JAKE HUNTER UNLEASHED DS1 BONUS

Select Password and enter KING.

JAKE HUNTER VISUALS 1

Select Password and enter LEET.

JAKE HUNTER VISUALS 2

Select Password and enter GONG.

JAKE HUNTER VISUALS 3

Select Password and enter CARS.

JAKE HUNTER VISUALS 4

Select Password and enter TREE.

JAKE HUNTER VISUALS 5

Select Password and enter PAPA.

JUKEBOX

Select Password and enter BIKE.

MOVIE GALLERY

Select Password and enter ROSE.

PASSWORD HINTS

Select Password and enter HINT.

SIDE CHARACTER'S BONUS STORY

Select Password and enter MINU.

STAFF COMMENTS 1

Select Password and enter AQUA.

STAFF COMMENTS 2

Select Password and enter MOTO.

WHAT IS A PASSWORD?

Select Password and enter AAAA.

JUMBLE MADNESS

FEBRUARY 31 PUZZLE

For Daily Jumble and Jumble Crosswords, select the square under February 28, 2009.

KID ICARUS: UPRISING

BOSS RUSH MODE

Defeat the Final Boss. Boss Rush Mode can be accessed next to Chapter 25.

DIALOGUE

Complete Solo Mode. Select Other from Options and then Hidden Options to toggle Dialogue on and off.

PALUTENA OR VIRIDI LOOKS OVER MENU

Complete Chapter 21. Select Other from Options and then Hidden Options to access Palutena and Viridi.

KINGDOM HEARTS 3D: DREAM DROP DISTANCE

CRITICAL MODE

Complete the game.

NEW GAME+

Complete the game and create a new game when asked.

KONAMI CLASSICS SERIES: ARCADE HITS

GRADIUS

ALL POWER-UPS EXCEPT SPEED

At the Gradius title screen, press Up, Up, Down, Down, Left, Right, Left, Right, B, A. After starting a game, press Start to get every power-up except Speed. This code can be entered only once.

THE LAST AIRBENDER

FOCUS UPGRADE

Select Cheats from the Options and enter Earth, Earth, Water, Earth.

HEAVY HITTER

Select Cheats from the Options and enter Water, Earth, Fire, Fire.

HEALTH UPGRADE

Select Cheats from the Options and enter Air, Water, Fire, Fire.

ALFRED PENNYWORTH

Use the computer in the Batcave, select Enter Code and enter ZAQ637.

BATGIRL

Use the computer in the Batcave, select Enter Code and enter JKR331.

BRUCE WAYNE

Use the computer in the Batcave, select Enter Code and enter BDJ327.

CLASSIC CATWOMAN

Use the computer in the Batcave, select Enter Code and enter M1AAWW.

CLOWN GOON

Use the computer in the Batcave, select Enter Code and enter HJK327.

COMMISSIONER GORDON

Use the computer in the Batcave, select Enter Code and enter DDP967.

FISHMONGER

Use the computer in the Batcave, select Enter Code and enter HGY748.

FREEZE GIRL

Use the computer in the Batcave, select Enter Code and enter XVK541.

FREEZE HENCHMAN

Use the computer in the Batcave, select Enter Code and enter NJL412.

JOKER GOON

Use the computer in the Batcave, select Enter Code and enter UTF782.

JOKER HENCHMAN

Use the computer in the Batcave, select Enter Code and enter YUN924.

NIGHTWING

Use the computer in the Batcave, select Enter Code and enter MVY759.

TROPICAL JOKER

Use the computer in the Batcave, select Enter Code and enter CCB199.

1 MILLION STUDS

At the main menu, press X, Y, B, B, Y, X, L, L, R, R, Up, Down, Left, Right, Start, Select.

3 MILLION STUDS

At the main menu, press Up, Up, B, Down, Down, X, Left, Left, Y, L, R, L, R, B, Y, X, Start, Select.

LEGO BATMAN 2: DC SUPER HEROES

STUDS X2

Pause the game, select Extras, and then choose Enter Code. Enter 74EZUT.

SUPER BUILD

Pause the game, select Extras, and then choose Enter Code. Enter JN2J6V.

CHARACTERS

In the Batcave, access the characters screen and select Cheats. These cheats still need to be purchased.

CHEAT	CODE
Clown Goon	9ZZZBP
LexBot	W49CSJ
Mime Goon	ZQA8MK

CHEAT	CODE
Poison Ivy Goon	M9CP6L
Riddler Goon	Q285LK
Two-Face Goon	95KPYJ

LEGO BATTLES

INVINCIBLE HERO

At the Lego Store, tap the Red Brick and enter HJCRAWK.

REGENERATING HEALTH

At the Lego Store, tap the Red Brick and enter ABABLRX.

ONE HIT KILL (HEROES)

At the Lego Store, tap the Red Brick and enter AVMPWHK.

LONG RANGE MAGIC

At the Lego Store, tap the Red Brick and enter ZPWJFUQ.

SUPER MAGIC

At the Lego Store, tap the Red Brick and enter DWFTBNS.

DOUBLE LEGO BRICKS

At the Lego Store, tap the Red Brick and enter BGQOYRT.

FAST BUILDING

At the Lego Store, tap the Red Brick and enter QMSLPOE.

FAST HARVESTING

At the Lego Store, tap the Red Brick and enter PQZLJOB.

FAST MAGIC

At the Lego Store, tap the Red Brick and enter JRTPASX.

FAST MINING

At the Lego Store, tap the Red Brick and enter KVBPQRJ.

FULL UNIT CAP

At the Lego Store, tap the Red Brick and enter UMSXIRQ.

SUPER EXPLOSIONS

At the Lego Store, tap the Red Brick and enter THNBGRE.

UPGRADED TOWERS

At the Lego Store, tap the Red Brick and enter EDRFTGY.

SHOW ENEMIES

At the Lego Store, tap the Red Brick and enter IBGOFWX.

SHOW LEGO STUDS

At the Lego Store, tap the Red Brick and enter CPLYREK.

SHOW MINIKIT

At the Lego Store, tap the Red Brick and enter LJYQRAC.

SHOW RED BRICKS

At the Lego Store, tap the Red Brick and enter RTGYPKC.

REVEAL MAP

At the Lego Store, tap the Red Brick and enter SKQMXPL.

UNLOCK ISLANDER

At the Lego Store, tap the Red Brick and enter UGDRSQP.

UNLOCK NINJA MASTER

At the Lego Store, tap the Red Brick and enter SHWSDGU.

UNLOCK SPACE CRIMINAL LEADER

At the Lego Store, tap the Red Brick and enter ZVDNJSU.

UNLOCK TROLL KING

At the Lego Store, tap the Red Brick and enter XRCTVYB.

LEGO BATTLES: NINJAGO

PASSWORDS

Select Cheat Codes from the LEGO shop and enter the following:

EFFECT	PASSWORD
Kruncha	HJEKTPU
Spaceman	TSDYHBZ

EFFECT	PASSWORD
Show Enemies on Minimap	KMRWLSS

PASSWORDS FOR STUDS

Select Cheat Codes from the LEGO shop and enter the following:

# OF STUDS	PASSWORD
5000	GQBAUJP
10000	GALNAFE
15000	LQMZPBX
20000	PPMSUGS
25000	SLBQFSW
30000	MXQNVQP
35000	SJVPMAA
40000	WZURMZM

# OF STUDS	PASSWORD
45000	UABBMZQ
55000	BGCHKHA
60000	JXULZZW
65000	FBMRSWG
70000	ZZXWUZJ
75000	HXMVRZP
80000	NYUXUZF

LEGO INDIANA JONES: THE ORIGINAL ADVENTURES

You should hear a confirmation sound after the following codes are entered.

ALL CHARACTERS

At the title screen, press X, Up, B, Down, Y, Left, Start, Right, R, R, L, R, R, Down, Down, Up, Y, Y, Y, Start, Select.

ALL EPISODES AND FREE PLAY MODE

Right, Up, R, L, X, Y, Right, Left, B, L, R, L, Down, Down, Up, Y, Y, X, X, B, B, Up, Up, L, R, Start, Select.

ALL EXTRAS

Up, Down, L, R, L, R, L, Left, Right, X, X, Y, Y, B, B, L, Up, Down, L, R, L, R, Up, Up, Down, Start, Select.

1,000,000 STUDS

At the title screen, press X, Y, B, B, Y, X, L, L, R, R, Up, Down, Left, Right, Start, Select.

3,000,000 STUDS

At the title screen, press Up, Up, B, Down, Down, X, Left, Left, Y, L, R, L, R, B, Y, X, Start, Select.

LEGO PIRATES OF THE CARIBBEAN: THE VIDEO GAME

CHARACTER CODES

Pause the game and select Extras. Choose Enter Code and enter the following codes:

CHARACTER	PASSWORD	CHARACTER	PASSWORD
Ammand the Corsair	EW8T6T	Jacoby	BWO656
Blackbeard	D3DWOD	Jimmy Legs	13GLW5
Clubba	644THF	Koehler	RT093G
Davy Jones	4DJLKR	Mistress Ching	GDETDE
Governor Weath-erby Swann	LD9454	Philip	WEV040
Gunner	Y611WB	Quartermaster	RX58HU
Hungry Cannibal	64BNHG	The Spaniard	P861JO
Jack Sparrow	VDJSPW	Twigg	KDLFKD

LEGO ROCK BAND

BLUR

In Tour Mode, complete Song 2.

DAVID BOWIE

In Tour Mode, complete Let's Dance.

IGGY POP

In Tour Mode, complete The Passenger.

QUEEN

In Tour Mode, complete We Are the Champions.

LEGO STAR WARS: THE COMPLETE SAGA

3,000,000 STUDS

At the main menu, press Start, Start, Down, Down, Left, Left, Up, Up, Select. This cheat can only be used once.

DEBUG MENUS

At the main menu, press Up, Left, Down, Right, Up, Left, Down, Right, Up, Left, Down, Right, R, L, Start, Select.

BONUS TOUCH GAME 1

At the main menu, press Up, Up, Down, L, L, R, R.

LEGO STAR WARS II: THE ORIGINAL TRILOGY

10 STUDS

At the Mos Eisley cantina, enter 4PR28U.

OBI WAN GHOST

At the Mos Eisley cantina, enter BEN917.

LEGO STAR WARS III: THE CLONE WARS

RED BRICK CHEATS

Each level has a Red Brick that when found unlocks a cheat for purchase at the shop.

CHEAT	COST (STUDS)
Auto Pickup	500,000
Fast Build	500,000
Flight Weapon Power Up	2,000,000
Funny Jump	250,000
Infinite Missiles	150,000
Invincibility	4,000,000

CHEAT	COST (STUDS)
Minigames	50,000
Regenerate Hearts	400,000
Score x2	100,000
Score x4	250,000
Score x6	500,000
Score x8	1,000,000
Score x10	2,500,000

LITTLEST PET SHOP: GARDEN

GIRAFFE PET

Select Passwords from the Options and enter LPSTRU. It is available in the Meow Market.

LITTLEST PET SHOP: JUNGLE

GIRAFFE PET

Select Passwords from the Options and enter LPSTRU. It is available in the Meow Market.

LOCK'S QUEST

REPLACE CLOCKWORKS WITH KINGDOM FORCE

After completing the game, hold R and select your profile.

ENDING STORY

After completing the game, hold L and select your profile.

MARIO KART 7

CHARACTERS

CHARACTER	FINISH 1ST IN...
Daisy	Mushroom Cup 150cc
Honey Queen	Banana Cup 150cc
Lakitu	Lightning Cup 150cc
Metal Mario	Special Cup 150cc
Rosalina	Star Cup 150cc
Shy Guy	Shell Cup 150cc
Wario	Flower Cup 150cc
Wiggler	Leaf Cup 150cc

MII

Place in all cups in one of the CC levels.

MARIO & LUIGI: BOWSER'S INSIDE STORY

LUMBAR NOOK ALARM

In the Lumbar Nook, when you dig into the bone, press A, B, X, Y, L, R, Y, X, B, A to set off the alarm. Otherwise, you have to wait awhile for it.

MARIO PARTY DS

BOSS BASH

Complete Story Mode.

EXPERT CPU DIFFICULTY LEVEL

Complete Story Mode.

MUSIC AND VOICE ROOM

Complete Story Mode.

SCORE SCUFFLE

Complete Story Mode.

TRIANGLE TWISTER PUZZLE MODE

Complete Story Mode.

MARIO TENNIS OPEN

BABY MARIO

In the Super Mario Tennis Special Game, complete 1-3.

BABY PEACH

In the Ring Shot Special Game, complete the Pro Rings.

DRY BOWSER

In the Ink Showdown Special Game, complete Inksplosion.

LUMA

In the Galaxy Rally Special Game, complete Superstar.

STAR CHARACTER

Winning the Champions Cup of the World Open gives the character you used a star. This improves the character.

FIRE MARIO

Give two characters a star.

PRO DIFFICULTY IN EXHIBITION

Complete the Champions Cup.

ACE DIFFICULTY IN EXHIBITION

Complete the Final Cup.

HIDDEN GOODIES

At the Select a File screen, hold Up and press Start. This turns on the camera. If you have found one of the QR Codes online that unlocks something for Mario Tennis Open, scan it with the camera.

MARVEL SUPER HERO SQUAD

APOCALYPSE MODE

Select Cheats from the Settings and enter Wolverine, Wolverine, Dr Doom, Abomination, Wolverine. This gives everyone one hit kills.

MEGA MAN STAR FORCE 3: BLACK ACE

STARS ON NEW GAME/CONTINUE SCREEN

Do the following to earn each star on the New Game/Continue screen.

STAR	HOW TO EARN
Black Ace	Defeat the game
G Comp	Collect all Giga cards
M Comp	Collect all Mega cards
S Comp	Collect all Standard cards
SS	Defeat Sirius

RANDOM SIGMA BOSSES

At the New Game/Continue screen, hold L and tap S Comp Star, G Comp Star, S Comp Star, M Comp Star, SS Star, SS Star, Black Ace Star.

FIGHT ROGUEZZ

At the New Game/Continue screen, hold L and tap G Comp Star, M Comp Star, M Comp Star, SS Star, G Comp Star, S Comp Star, Black Ace Star. RogueZZ appears in Meteor G Control CC.

MEGA MAN STAR FORCE 3: RED JOKER

STARS ON NEW GAME/CONTINUE SCREEN

DO THE FOLLOWING TO EARN EACH STAR ON THE NEW GAME/CONTINUE SCREEN.	
Star	How to earn
Red Joker	Defeat the game
G Comp	Collect all Giga cards
M Comp	Collect all Mega cards
S Comp	Collect all Standard cards
SS	Defeat Sirius

RANDOM SIGMA BOSSES

At the New Game/Continue screen, hold L and tap S Comp Star, G Comp Star, S Comp Star, M Comp Star, SS Star, SS Star, Red Joker Star.

FIGHT ROGUEZZ

At the New Game/Continue screen, hold L and tap G Comp Star, M Comp Star, M Comp Star, SS Star, G Comp Star, S Comp Star, Red Joker Star. RogueZZ appears in Meteor G Control CC.

METROID PRIME PINBALL

PHAZON MINES

Complete Omega Pirate in Multi Mission mode.

PHENDRANA DRIFTS

Complete Thardus in Multi Mission mode.

MIGHT & MAGIC: CLASH OF HEROES

UNLOCK CHARACTERS IN QUICK BATTLE AND MULTIPLAYER

Unlock new characters in Quick Battle and Multiplayer modes as you complete the chapters.

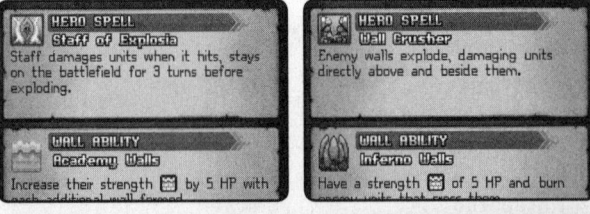

CHARACTER UNLOCKED	CHAPTER COMPLETED
Findan	1 - Anwen
Varkas	2 - Godric
Markal	3 - Fiona
Jezebeth	4 - Aidan
Cyrus	5 – Nadia

MONSTER TALE

YELLOW CLOTHES FOR ELLIE AND 5% OFF ITEMS

At the title screen, press Up, Up, Down, Down, Left, Right, Left, Right, Select.

MUTANT MUDDS

PLAY AS GRANNIE

After collecting all 200 Diamonds and 40 Water Sprites, press L at the title screen to switch to Grannie.

MY JAPANESE COACH

UNLOCK LESSONS

Look up the word cheat in the dictionary. Touch the V next to the verb to open the conjugation chart. Hold L + R for a few seconds. You should hear the word cheat in Japanese. Return to the main menu, go to Options, then Sound. Pressing R will advance you 1 lesson, and pressing L will advance you to the beginning of the next lesson group.

MY WORD COACH

WORD POPPERS MINIGAME

After reaching 200 word successes, at the options menu, press A, B, X, Y, A, B.

MYSIMS KINGDOM

COW COSTUME

Pause the game and press R, X, L, Y, Up, Right, Left, Down.

COW HEADGEAR

Pause the game and press L, R, Y, X, Left, Down, Left, Right.

PATCHWORK CLOTHES

Pause the game and press Right, Down, Left, Up, L, R, L, R.

PATCHWORK PANTS

Pause the game and press Down, L, Left, R, Up, Y, Right, X.

PUNK BOTTOM

Pause the game and press Left, R, L, Right, Y, Y, X, X.

PUNK TOP

Pause the game and press Up, X, Down, Y, Left, L, Right, R.

SAMURAI ARMOR

Pause the game and press Y, X, Right, Left, L, R, Down, Up.

SAMURAI HELMET

Pause the game and press X, Y, R, L, X, Y, R, L.

N+

ATARI BONUS LEVELS

Select Unlockables from the main menu, hold L + R and press A, B, A, B, A, A, B.

NAMCO MUSEUM DS

DIG-DUG 2 OLD VERSION

From the Dig Dug 2 menu, select Hardcore Options from the Settings. Change New Version to Old.

SECRET GAME: SUPER XEVIOUS

From the Xevious menu, select Hardcore Options from the Settings. Change the version to Super Xevious.

NARUTO: PATH OF THE NINJA

After defeating the game, talk to Knohamaru on the roof of the Ninja Academy. He allows you go get certain cheats by tapping four successive spots on the touch screen in order. There are 12 different spots on the screen. We have numbered them from left to right, top to bottom, as follows:

1	2	3	4
5	6	7	8
9	10	11	12

Enter the following codes by touching the four spots in the order listed.

UNLOCK	CODE	UNLOCK	CODE
4th Hokage's Sword	4, 7, 11, 5	Rajin's Sword	7, 6, 5, 11
Fuji Fan	8, 11, 2, 5	Rasengan	9, 2, 12, 7
Jiraiya	11, 3, 1, 6		

NARUTO: PATH OF THE NINJA 2

CHARACTER PASSWORDS

Talk to Konohamaru at the school to enter the following passwords. You must first complete the game for the passwords to work.

CHARACTER	PASSWORD	CHARACTER	PASSWORD
Gaara	DKFIABJL	Kankuro	ALJKBEDG
Gai	IKAGDEFL	Kyuubi Naruto	GJHLBFDE
Iruka	JGDLKAIB	Orochimaru	AHFBLEJG
Itachi Uchiha	GBEIDALF	Temari	HFICLKBG
Jiraiya	EBJDAGFL	The Third Hokage	CGHAJBEL

MISSION PASSWORDS

Talk to Konohamaru at the school to enter the following passwords. You must first complete the game for the passwords to work.

MISSION	PASSWORD	MISSION	PASSWORD
An Extreme Battle!	HLBAKGCD	The Legendary Sannin!	BCEGKFHL
The Legendary Haze Ninja!	FGEHIDAL		

NEW SUPER MARIO BROS.

PLAY AS LUIGI IN SINGLE PLAYER

At the Select a File screen, hold L + R while selecting a saved game.

SECRET CHALLENGE MODE

On the map, pause the game and press L, R, L, R, X, X, Y, Y.

NEW SUPER MARIO BROS. 2

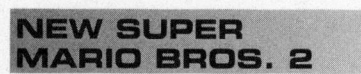

PLAY AS LUIGI IN SINGLE PLAYER

Defeat Bowser in World 6. Then, at the file select, hold L + R as you select a file with A.

ALTERNATE TITLE SCREEN

Collect 1,000,000 coins to get a Gold Mario title screen.

ANOTHER ALTERNATE TITLE SCREEN

Collect 9,999,999 coins to get a Tanooki Mario title screen.

NICKTOONS: ATTACK OF THE TOYBOTS

DANNY PHANTOM 2

Select Unlock Code from the Options and enter Tak, Jimmy, Zim, El Tigre.

SPONGEBOB 2

Select Unlock Code from the Options and enter Patrick, Jenny, Timmy, Tak.

NICKTOONS: BATTLE FOR VOLCANO ISLAND

FRUIT BECOMES TOYS IN FRUIT COLLECTING MINI-GAME

Select Unlock Codes from the Options and enter Spongebob, Danny, Timmy, Cosmo.

NIGHT AT THE MUSEUM: BATTLE OF THE SMITHSONIAN

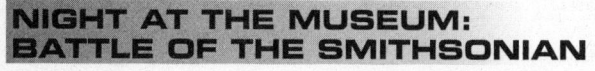

SUPER LARRY

During a game, hold L + R, and press Left, A, Right, Right, Y.

NINTENDOGS + CATS: GOLDEN RETRIEVER & NEW FRIENDS

DOG BREEDS

Unlock the following breeds with the given amount of trainer points.

DOG BREED	TRAINER POINTS REQUIRED
Basset Hound	9800
Boxer	5800
Bull Terrier	3400
Cavalier King Charles Spaniel	5800
Chihuahua	600
Dalmatian	3400
French Bulldog	9800
German Shepherd	2100
Jack Russell Terrier	600

DOG BREED	TRAINER POINTS REQUIRED
Labrador Retriever	3400
Miniature Poodle	9800
Miniature Schnauzer	2100
Pembroke Welsh Corgi	7400
Pomeranian	2100
Shetland Sheepdog	600
Shih Tzu	7400
Siberian Husky	5800
Yorkshire Terrier	7400

NINTENDOGS + CATS: FRENCH BULLDOG & NEW FRIENDS

DOG BREEDS

Unlock the following breeds with the given amount of trainer points.

DOG BREED	TRAINER POINTS REQUIRED
Beagle	3400
Boxer	3400
Bull Terrier	600
Cocker Spaniel	2100
Golden Retriever	9800
Great Dane	5800
Jack Russell Terrier	7400
Labrador Retriever	5800
Maltese	3400

DOG BREED	TRAINER POINTS REQUIRED
Miniature Dachshund	600
Miniature Pinscher	2100
Miniature Poodle	9800
Miniature Schnauzer	5800
Pembroke Welsh Corgi	2100
Pomeranian	5800
Pug	5800
Shiba Inu	9800
Shih Tzu	600

NINTENDOGS + CATS: TOY POODLE & NEW FRIENDS

DOG BREEDS

Unlock the following breeds with the given amount of trainer points.

DOG BREED	TRAINER POINTS REQUIRED	DOG BREED	TRAINER POINTS REQUIRED
Basset Hound	3600	German Shepherd	7400
Beagle	3600	Dachshund	5800
Cavalier King Charles	2000	Dalmatian	7400
Chihuahua	5800	Cocker Spaniel	3600
Great Dane	600	Yorkshire	600
Husky	2000	Shetland	5800
Maltese	2000	Pug	600
Mini Pinscher	7400		

THE OREGON TRAIL

HEIRLOOMS

HEIRLOOMS	HOW TO OBTAIN
Banjo	Finish the Gold Rush storyline.
Birch Pole	Catch 60 pounds of fish in one day.
Bugle	Bring the piano as your heirloom and complete the journey to Oregon.
Doctor's Bag	Get to the end of the trail without losing any family members.
Evil Eye	Score more than 150,000 points in a chapter.
Fine Suit	Score more than 120,000 points in a chapter.
Fine Whip Heirloom	Complete a trail segment without hitting an obstacle.
Fur Hat	Finish the Three Brave Brothers storyline.
Henry Rifle	Finish the Stuck in the Middle storyline.
Horseshoe	Get robbed 10 total times in one trip down the trail.
Piano	Finish the Family Affair storyline.

PEGGLE: DUAL SHOT

A LEVEL 10

Send the trial game to another DS.

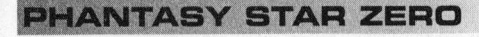

PHANTASY STAR ZERO

PASSWORD MACHINE

Check out the vending machine on the far right side of the sewers. Type in special passwords here to find free items.

ITEM	PASSWORD
Selvaria's Spear	5703-8252
Selvaria's Shield	4294-2273
Blade Cannon	7839-3594
Caduceus's Rod	5139-6877
Game Master (Ge-maga)	7162-5792
CONSOLES+ (Famitsu)	9185-6189

ITEM	PASSWORD
INGame: Greg&Kiri (Nintendo Dream)	5531-0215
Nintendo Power (Dengeki DS)	3171-0109
Puyo Soul	3470-1424
Taupy Soul	9475-6843
Lassie Soul	4775-7197

PHINEAS AND FERB

STOP CANDACE

At the title screen, press X, Y, L, R, Select.

DOUBLE SPEED

At the title screen, press A, B, L, R, Select.

PHOTO DOJO

FAST FIGHTERS

At the title screen, hold Select and choose Head into Battle. Continue to hold Select and choose Vs. Mode.

POKÉMON BLACK/WHITE VERSION 2

LEGENDARY POKÉMON

POKÉMON	LOCATION	HOW TO FIND
Cobalion	Route 13	Defeat when found on Route 13. Return after defeating the Elite Four to find it at a higher level.
Terrakion	Route 22	Defeat when found on Route 22 on a small platform. Return after defeating the Elite Four to find it at a higher level.
Virizion	Route 11	Defeat when found on Route 11. Return after defeating the Elite Four to find it at a higher level.
Reshiram (White version)/ Zekrom (Black version)	Dragonspiral Tower	After defeating the game, defeat N to get a stone. Take that to the top of Dragonspiral Tower.
Kyurem	Giant Chasm	After catching Resiram/Zekrom, return to Giant Chasm.
Cresselia	Marvelous Bridge near Nimbasa City	Visit Marvelous Bridge with the Lunar Wing.

POKÉMON	LOCATION	HOW TO FIND
Regirock	Clay Tunnel	After defeating the game, go to the back of Clay Tunnel and find a hidden switch in an empty room. Activate the switch to find Regirock. This rewards you with an Iceberg Key (White version) or an Iron Key (Black version).
Registeel	Clay Tunnel	Use the Iron Key in the same room as before.
Regice	Clay Tunnel	Use the Iceberg Key in the same room as before.
Regigigas	Twist Mountain	With Regirock, Registeel, and Regice caught, go to the lower level of Twist Mountain.
Latias (White version)/Latios (Black version)	Dreamyard	Chase down Latias/Latios for the chance to battle.
Heatran	Reversal Mountain	Return to Reversal Mountain with Magma Stone.
Azelf	Route 23	Return to Route 23 from Victory Road, head west, cut down a shrub, and up some steps.
Mesprit	Celestial Tower	Climb to top of tower and wander around until Mesprit appears.
Uxie	Nacrene City	Walk around just outside the museum.

PERMIT

See all Pokémon in Unova Pokedex. Receive the Permit from Professor Juniper.

ROUND CHARM

Catch all Pokémon in Unova Pokedex. Receive the Round Charm from Professor Juniper.

SHINY CHARM

Catch all Pokémon in the National Pokedex. Receive from the Shiny Charm from Professor Juniper.

POKÉMON CONQUEST

PASSWORDS FOR RARE POKÉMON

Select Password from the main menu and enter the following. They appear the next month.

EFFECT	PASSWORD	EFFECT	PASSWORD
Axew	BqWxXEK3xg	Gyarados	mq2xRVNgRL
Beldum	CMqkZRRSRX	Lapras	GfV33RVN3F
Chimchar	DNB3x2gCgk	Larvitar	Lpu3ggCYk8
Cincinno	vVALFrGTXX	Musharna	iMYXwqtHgL
Croagunk	LKpk8FRQR8	Oshawott	frCLRpXG88
Darmanitan	pK5RgzqLG8	Panpour	CNZF3wpq3x
Deino	PKSRGpCPZJ	Pansage	6xSG8UCAZR
Dratini	Sr5Z5GqAgR	Pansear	niE33w9rwM
Drifloon	eqCgRvXwXX	Pikachu	FZP8GqRZRR
Eevee	2rz3XFCKmR	Riolu	Shw8mxRAJR
Emolga	Jnm3kqgN8X	Scyther	8GV3LMGrnM
Gible	LTb3n3RYJ8	Sneasel	Rc338MpqLx

KEIJI SPECIAL MISSION

Select Password and enter
EDw8w2HaRn.

MOTONARI & MOTOCHIKA

Select Password and enter
J2TRZXPUm3.

OKUNI SPECIAL MISSION

Select Password and enter
gauRnak2nR.

RANMARU SPECIAL MISSION

Select Password and enter
2aL38Ek2Rx.

RESHIRAM EVENT

Select Password and enter
2rz3XFEKxR.

POKÉMON DREAM RADAR

#249 LUGIA

After you have earned the 3,000 points necessary to get Landorous, insert
Pokémon SoulSilver into the 3DS. A new level will become available. Diving
Extension becomes available and gives you Lugia.

#250 HO-OH

After you have earned the 3,000 points necessary to get Landorous, insert
Pokémon HeartGold. A new level will become available. Rainbow Extension
becomes available and gives you Ho-oh.

#483 DIALGA

After you have earned the 3,000 points necessary to get Landorous, insert
Pokémon Diamond. A new level will become available. Time Extension
becomes available and gives you Dialga.

#484 PALKIA

After you have earned the 3,000 points necessary to get Landorous, insert
Pokémon Pearl. A new level will become available. Space Extension becomes
available and gives you Palkia.

#487 GIRATINA

After you have earned the 3,000 points necessary to get Landorous, insert
Pokémon Platinum. Renegade Extension becomes available and gives you
Giratina.

POKÉMON RUMBLE BLAST

The following passwords give you Pokémon that have special abilities. After the code has been entered, go to the indicated location to fight them.

EMBOAR IN ECHO VALLEY

Speak to Munna in Easterly Town and enter 8902-7356.

GALLADE IN EVERSPRING VALLEY

Speak to Munna in Easterly Town and enter 3535-6928.

GLISCOR IN SUNNY SEASHORE

Speak to Munna in Easterly Town and enter 9625-7845.

OSHAWOTT IN SHIMMERING LAKE

Speak to Munna in Easterly Town and enter 7403-2240.

PIKACHU IN VOLCANIC SLOPE

Speak to Munna in Easterly Town and enter 7746-3878.

TORNADUS IN VOLCANIC SLOPE

Speak to Munna in Easterly Town and enter 0250-7321.

LEGACY MODE

Complete the game and then at the title screen, hold L + R + Left and press A. Continue holding the buttons until you hear a sound.

POP CUTIE! STREET FASHION SIMULATION

LAYERED DRESS

At a phone, enter 7247.

POODLE OUTFIT

At a phone, enter 3107.

HOTEL PATAGONIA/EDDIE RETURNS

At a phone, enter 9901.

CALL GIBSONS

At a phone, enter 9801.

FASHION HOTLINE

At a phone enter 0000, 1111, 2222, 3333, 4444, 5555, 6666.

RAYMAN (DSIWARE)

Re-enter the code to toggle it off.

LEVEL SELECT (PAUSED ON THE WORLD MAP)

On the world map, enter R, Up, Left, Right, Down, Right, L.

INVINCIBILITY

Pause the game and enter L, Right, Up, Right, Left, Right, R.

99 LIVES

Pause the game and enter L Left, Right, Down, Right, Left, R.

ALL OF RAYMAN'S POWERS

Pause the game and enter R, Down, Left, Right, Left, Up, L.

10 HITPOINTS

Pause the game and enter L, Down, Up, Down, R.

25 BLUE TINGS

Pause the game and enter L, Up, Left, Right, Left, L.

RETRO GAME CHALLENGE

COSMIC GATE

HARD MODE

At the title screen, press Down, Down, B, B, A, A, Start.

POWERED-UP INFINITY

Pause the game and press Up, Up, A, B. This cheat can only be used once per game.

SHIP POWER-UP

Pause the game and press Up, Up, A, A, B, B.

CONTINUE GAME

At the Game Over screen, press Left + Start. You will continue the game with a score of 000.

HAGGLE MAN CODES

FULL HEALTH

Pause the game and press Down, Right, Up, Left, B, B, B, B, A, A, A, A.

SCROLLS APPEAR

Pause the game and press Up Right Down Left A A A A B B B B.

INFINITE TIME

Before a level, hold Up/Left and press A + B.

HAGGLE MAN 2

STAGE SELECT

At the title screen, hold A and press Up, Up, Right, Right, Right, Down, Down, Left, Left, Left.

FULL POWER

Pause the game and press Up, Down, Up, Down, B, B, A, A.

SCROLLS APPEAR

Pause the game and press Down, Up, Down, Up, A, A, B, B.

CONTINUE

At the Game Over screen

HAGGLE MAN 3

99 LIVES

Pause the game and press A, B, A, B, Left, Right, Left, Right.

9999 GEARS

Pause the game and press B, A, B, A, Right, Left, Right, Left.

WARP TO BOSS

Pause the game and press B, B, A, A, Left, Left, Right, Right.

RALLY KING

INVINCIBILITY

At the title screen, press Select + Left.

CARS DISAPPEAR

At the title screen, hold Select and press Down/Right.

START AT COURSE 2

At the title screen, press A, B, A, B, Up + Select.

START AT COURSE 3

At the title screen, press A, B, A, B, Left + Select.

START AT COURSE 4

At the title screen, press A, B, A, B, Down + Select.

STAR PRINCE

INVINCIBILITY

At the title screen, hold Up and press A, A, A. Then, hold Down and press B, B, B.

CONTINUE

At the Game Over screen, hold Left and press Start.

RHYTHM HEAVEN

RHYTHM TOYS - TELEPHONE NUMBERS

Enter the following numbers into the telephone in Rhythm Toys to unlock sounds from Rhythm Tengoku:

5553282338

5557325937

5557268724

5557625688

RIDGE RACER 3D

CATEGORY 3 MACHINES

Complete Beginner Grand Prix Event No. 08

CATEGORY 2 MACHINES & ADVANCED GRAND PRIX

Complete Beginner Grand Prix Event No. 18

CATEGORY 1 MACHINES

Complete Advanced Grand Prix Event No. 26

EXPERT GRAND PRIX

Complete Advanced Grand Prix Event No. 36

KAMATA ANGL CONCEPT (SPECIAL CAT. 1 MACHINE)

Complete Expert Grand Prix Event No. 42

SOLDAT CRINALE (SPECIAL CAT. 1 MACHINE)

Complete Expert Grand Prix Event No. 43

AGE SOLO PETIT500 (SPECIAL CAT. 1 MACHINE)

Complete Expert Grand Prix Event No. 44

LUCKY & WILD MADBULL (SPECIAL CAT. 1 MACHINE)

Complete Expert Grand Prix Event No. 45

NAMCO PACMAN (SPECIAL CAT. 1 MACHINE) & PACMAN MUSIC CD

Complete Expert Grand Prix Event No. 46

NAMCO NEW RALLY-X (SPECIAL CAT. 1 MACHINE)

Complete Expert Grand Prix Event No. 47

MIRRORED & MIRRORED REVERSE COURSES

Complete Expert Grand Prix Event No. 48

RUBIK'S PUZZLE WORLD

ALL LEVELS AND CUBIES

At the main menu, press X, Y, Y, X, X.

SCOOBY-DOO! FIRST FRIGHTS

DAPHNE'S SECRET COSTUME

Select Codes from the Extras menu and enter 2839.

FRED'S SECRET COSTUME

Select Codes from the Extras menu and enter 4826.

SCOOBY DOO'S SECRET COSTUME

Select Codes from the Extras menu and enter 1585.

SHAGGY'S SECRET COSTUME

Select Codes from the Extras menu and enter 3726.

VELMA'S SECRET COSTUME

Select Codes from the Extras menu and enter 6588.

SIMCITY CREATOR

99999999 MONEY

Enter MONEYBAGS as a password.

AMERICAN PROSPERITY AGE MAP

Enter NEWWORLD as a password.

ASIA AGE MAP

Enter SAMURAI as a password.

ASIA AGE BONUS MAP

Enter FEUDAL as a password.

DAWN OF CIVILIZATION MAP

Enter ANCIENT as a password.

GLOBAL WARMING MAP

Enter MODERN as a password.

GLOBAL WARMING BONUS MAP

Enter BEYOND as a password.

RENAISSANCE BONUS MAP

Enter HEREANDNOW as a password.

THE SIMS 2 APARTMENT PETS

$10,000

From the PDA screen, select the disk icon. Then choose Unlockable from the Options and enter Cash.

SONIC CLASSIC COLLECTION

SONIC THE HEDGEHOG

DEBUG MODE

At the title screen, press A, A, Up, Down, Left, Right, hold Y and press Start.

LEVEL SELECT

At the title screen press Up, Down, Left, Right, hold Y and press Start.

SONIC THE HEDGEHOG 2

LEVEL SELECT

At the title screen, press Up, Up, Up, Down, Down, Down, Left, Right, Left, Right, hold Y and press Start.

SONIC THE HEDGEHOG 3

LEVEL SELECT

As the SEGA logo fades, quickly press Up, Up, Down, Down, Up, Up, Up, Up. Highlight Sound Test and press Start.

SONIC KNUCKLES

LEVEL SELECT WITH SONIC THE HEDGEHOG 2

At the title screen, press Up, Up, Up, Down, Down, Down, Left, Right, Left, Right, hold A and press Start.

SOUL BUBBLES

REVEAL ALL CALABASH LOCATIONS

Pause the game and press A, L, L, R, A, Down, A, R.

ALL LEVELS

At the World Select, press L, Up, X, Up, R, Y.

ALL GALLERY ITEMS

At the Gallery, press B, Up, B, B, L, Y.

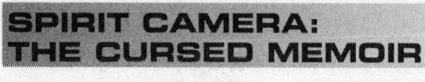

SPIRIT CAMERA: THE CURSED MEMOIR

GOTHIC LOLITA COSTUME FOR MAYA

Complete the story mode.

PRINCESS PEACH COSTUME FOR MAYA

Complete all Battle Mode missions on Nightmare difficulty.

GOTHIC LOLITA COSTUME FOR PHOTO-OP

Complete the story mode on Nightmare difficulty.

BOY IN THE BOOK CURSED PAGES MINI-GAME

Complete all Four Strange Masks levels.

SPIRIT HOUSE CURSED PAGES MINI-GAME

Complete the first level of Boy in the Book.

SPONGEBOB SQUAREPANTS FEATURING NICKTOONS: GLOBS OF DOOM

INFINITE HEALTH

Select Unlock Codes from the Options and enter Tak, Tlaloc, Jimmy Neutron, Beautiful Gorgeous.

INSTANT KO

Select Unlock Codes from the Options and enter Dib, Tak, Beautiful Gorgeous, Plankton.

EXTRA ATTACK

Select Unlock Codes from the Options and enter Dib, Plankton, Technus, Jimmy Neutron.

EXTRA DEFENSE

Select Unlock Codes from the Options and enter Zim, Danny Phantom, Plankton, Beautiful Gorgeous.

MAX DEFENSE

Select Unlock Codes from the Options and enter Plankton, Dib, Beautiful Gorgeous, Plankton.

ITEMS +

Select Unlock Codes from the Options and enter Danny Phantom, Beautiful Gorgeous, Jimmy Neutron, Technus.

ITEMS ++

Select Unlock Codes from the Options and enter SpongeBob, Tlaloc, SpongeBob, Danny Phantom.

NO HEALTH ITEMS

Select Unlock Codes from the Options and enter Tak, SpongeBob, Technus, Danny Phantom.

LOWER PRICES

Select Unlock Codes from the Options and enter Tlaloc, Zim, Beautiful Gorgeous, SpongeBob.

STAR WARS:
THE FORCE UNLEASHED

INCREASED HEALTH

Select Unleashed Codes from the Extras menu and enter QSSPVENXO.

MAX OUT FORCE POWERS

Select Unleashed Codes from the Extras menu and enter CPLOOLKBF.

UNLIMITED FORCE ENERGY

Select Unleashed Codes from the Extras menu and enter TVENCVMJZ.

MORE POWERFUL LIGHTSABER

Select Unleashed Codes from the Extras menu and enter lightsaber.

UBER LIGHTSABER

Select Unleashed Codes from the Extras menu and enter MOMIROXIW.

ROM KOTA

Select Unleashed Codes from the Extras menu and enter mandalore.

CEREMONIAL JEDI ROBES

Select Unleashed Codes from the Extras menu and enter CURSEZRUX.

DAD'S ROBES

Select Unleashed Codes from the Extras menu and enter wookiee.

DARTH VADER'S COSTUME

Select Unleashed Codes from the Extras menu and enter HRMXRKVEN.

KENTO'S ROBE

Select Unleashed Codes from the Extras menu and enter KBVMSEVNM.

KOTA'S OUTFIT

Select Unleashed Codes from the Extras menu and enter EEDOPVENG.

SITH ROBE

Select Unleashed Codes from the Extras menu and enter ZWSFVENXA.

SITH ROBES

Select Unleashed Codes from the Extras menu and enter holocron.

SITH STALKER ARMOR

Select Unleashed Codes from the Extras menu and enter CPLZKMZTD.

STAR WARS EPISODE III: REVENGE OF THE SITH

MASTER DIFFICULTY

Defeat the game.

ANAKIN'S STARFIGHTER

Beat the Anakin bot in multiplayer.

DARTH VADER'S TIE FIGHTER

Defeat the Darth Vader bot in multiplayer.

GENERAL GREVIOUS'S STARFIGHTER

Defeat the General Grevious bot in multiplayer.

MILLENIUM FALCON

Defeat the Solo bot in multiplayer.

SLAVE I

Defeat the Fett bot in multiplayer.

X-WING

Defeat the Luke bot in multiplayer.

SUPER MARIO 3D LAND

SPECIAL WORLD

Complete World 8.

PLAY AS LUIGI

Complete the castle in Special World 1. Touch the L icon to switch to Luigi.

SUPER MONKEY BALL 3D

MONKEY FIGHT CHARACTERS

Complete the following series to unlock the characters in Monkey Fight

CHARACTER	COMPLETE THIS SERIES
W-MeeMee	Basic
P-YanYan	Super Fight

MONKEY RACE CHARACTERS

Complete the following cups in Grand Prix mode to unlock the characters in Monkey Race

CHARACTER	FINISH GRAND PRIX IN GIVEN POSITION
N-Jam	1st in Sky-Way
A-Baby	2nd in Sky-Way
R-Doctor	3rd in Sky-Way
B-Jet	1st in Mt. Tyrano
P-YanYan	2nd in Mt. Tyrano
F-GonGon	3rd in Mt. Tyrano

MONKEY RACE CARS

To unlock more cars in Monkey Race, enter time trial mode and beat the given record for that track. If you beat it faster than that record, you unlock one car per level.

CAR	BEAT RECORD ON THIS TRACK
Robotron	Track 1 of Sky-Way
Mini Shooter	Track 2 of Sky-Way
Kitana	Track 3 of Sky-Way
6 Caterpillar	Track 1 of Mt. Tyrano
Flying Carpet	Track 2 of Mt. Tyrano
Super Tops	Track 3 of Mt. Tyrano

SUPER ROBOT TAISEN OG SAGA: ENDLESS FRONTIER

NEW GAME +

After you have finished the game and saved, load your save and start again with your items and money.

061 CHOKER

Start a new game or load a saved file with the GBA game Super Robot Taisen: Original Generation in the GBA slot. This item boosts your SP by 100.

062 PENDANT

Start a new game or load a saved file with the GBA game Super Robot Taisen 2: Original Generation in the GBA slot. This item boosts your HP by 250.

SUPER SPEED MACHINES

UNLOCK VEHICLES

WIN GRAND PRIX	UNLOCK THIS VEHICLE
1	Haima (Rally)
2	Sandstrom (4x4)
3	Striker (Sports)
4	Copperhead (Muscle)
6	Gold Digger (Custom)
7	Blue Flame (Classic)

SUPER STREET FIGHTER IV: 3D EDITION

FIGURINES

Select Password from the Figurine Collection and enter the following:

FIGURINE	PASSWORD	FIGURINE	PASSWORD
Silver Rose	GkKKXxibSe	Silver Akuma	RYSsPxSbTh
Silver Sakura	uzISxzibKn	Silver Balrog	PqUsWOobWG
Golden Blanka	DmdkeRvbxc	Silver Chun-Li	rtWKWvrbIz
Golden Chun-Li	zAAkcHYbHK	Silver Cody	naMKEQbgDG
Golden Guile	qeJKznbDkE	Silver Dan	rDKKsIsbqS
Golden M.Bison	CgISQNWbHu	Silver Dhalsim	JKbSOVHbVC
Golden Ryu	KjckTnSbwK	Silver E. Honda	uUDsTlmbUN
Golden Vega	CgISQNWbHu	Silver Hakan	rLPyIrgbUy
Golden Zangief	hinsVnebTu	Silver Ibuki	ilMsRabpB
Platinum Ryu	DFrkMnybCd	Silver Juri	OfoKARpbJR
Special Akuma	uQHKWgYbJC	Silver Ken	NyosHgYbuW
		Silver Makoto	GhdKWCTbsI

TAMAGOTCHI CONNECTION: CORNER SHOP 3

DOUBLE LAYERED CAKE

Select Enter Code from the Special menu and enter R6194BJD6F.

TAO'S ADVENTURE: CURSE OF THE DEMON SEAL

DEBUG MODE

During a game, press Up, Up, Down, Left, Left, Right, Right, Select, Select, Start, Start, L, R, L, R, A, A, A, A, A, A, A, B.

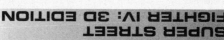

THEATRHYTHM FINAL FANTASY

COLLECTACARDS

Select Collection from the Museum menu and then choose Password. Enter the following to unlock the CollectaCard. Each password can be entered once and if you already own the Collectacard, it adds one level.

COLLECTACARD	PASSWORD	COLLECTACARD	PASSWORD
01 Warrior of Light	Class Change	14 Princess Sarah	Cornelia
01 Warrior of Light	Sarah's Lute	14 Princess Sarah	Hostage
01 Warrior of Light	Warrior of Light	15 Minwu	An urban turban
02 Firion	Cyclone	15 Minwu	Likes canoeing
02 Firion	Wild Rose	15 Minwu	White Mage
02 Firion	Wyvern	16 Cid	Always around?
03 Onion Knight	Pintsized Powerhouse	16 Cid	The Enterprise
03 Onion Knight	Unreleased	17 Rydia	Early bloomer
04 Cecil	Brothers	17 Rydia	Pyrophobia
04 Cecil	Dark Knight	17 Rydia	We're all the same
04 Cecil	Holy Paladin	18 Faris	Beautiful pirate
05 Bartz	Boko loves Koko	18 Faris	Friend to Syldra
05 Bartz	I am Bartz	18 Faris	Princess of Tycoon
05 Bartz	Rides Boko	19 Locke	Bandana man
06 Terra	Flowered tights	19 Locke	Hates mushrooms
06 Terra	Magitek Armor	20 Aerith	A the-TE!
06 Terra	Slave Crown	20 Aerith	Cetra
07 Cloud	Former SOLDIER	20 Aerith	Mother's Materia
07 Cloud	Hardy-Daytona	21 Seifer	Another gunblade
07 Cloud	Lifestream	21 Seifer	Disciplinary Committee
08 Squall	I'm going to pass	21 Seifer	Twin Scars
08 Squall	Lionheart	22 Vivi	Black Mage
08 Squall	Tall, dark, and silent	22 Vivi	Doesn't like heights
09 Zidane	Beloved Dagger	22 Vivi	Master Vivi
09 Zidane	Tantalus	23 Yuna	.R.P.
09 Zidane	Zidane Tribal	23 Yuna	Eternal Calm
10 Tidus	Final Summoning	23 Yuna	The Gullwings
10 Tidus	Jecht Shot	24 Prishe	Detestable Child
10 Tidus	Zanarkand Abes	24 Prishe	Feed me
11 Shantotto	Ohoho!	24 Prishe	I looo...ve lobster
11 Shantotto	Pain 101	25 Ashe	Amalia?
11 Shantotto	Unmarried	25 Ashe	Dawn Shard
12 Vaan	Alone in the world	25 Ashe	Then steal me.
12 Vaan	Denser than lead	26 Snow	Do-rag
12 Vaan	Sky Pirate wannabe	26 Snow	Serah!
13 Lightning	Guardian Corps	26 Snow	Sis!
13 Lightning	Serah's sister	27 Kain	Cecil's best friend
13 Lightning	The White Knight	27 Kain	Son of Richard
14 Princess Sarah	Beloved princess	28 Sephiroth	Black Materia

COLLECTACARD	PASSWORD	COLLECTACARD	PASSWORD
28 Sephiroth	Masamune	48 Scarmiglione	Undead minions
28 Sephiroth	One-winged angel	49 Cagnazzo	Drowned King
29 Cosmos	Asteraceae	49 Cagnazzo	Second life
29 Cosmos	Goddess of Harmony	50 Barbariccia	Lord of Wind
29 Cosmos	The Great Will	50 Barbariccia	Maelstrom
30 Chocobo	Fat Chocobo	50 Barbariccia	The lone female
30 Chocobo	Gysahl Greens	51 Rubicante	Autarch of Flame
30 Chocobo	Kweh! KWEH!	51 Rubicante	Awesome cloak
31 Moogle	Bat wings	52 Magic Pot	Miss!
31 Moogle	Kupo KUPO! Kupo?	52 Magic Pot	What's in the pot?
31 Moogle	Red pompom	53 Tonberry	Everyone's Grudge
32 Shiva	Diamond Dust	53 Tonberry	Knife and lantern
32 Shiva	Heavenly Strike	53 Tonberry	Voodoo
32 Shiva	Ice Queen	54 Gilgamesh	Bartz's rival
33 Ramuh	Judgment Bolt	54 Gilgamesh	Big Bridge
33 Ramuh	Love the beard	55 Enkidu	Vampire
34 Ifrit	Hellfire	55 Enkidu	White Wind
34 Ifrit	Infernal Blaze	56 Omega	Superboss
35 Odin	Sleipnir's rider	56 Omega	Wave Cannon
35 Odin	Zantetsuken	57 Shinryu	Ragnarok
36 Bahamut	Mega Flare	57 Shinryu	Tidal Wave
36 Bahamut	Rat tail	58 Cactaur	1000 Needles
37 Goblin	Goblin Punch	58 Cactaur	10000 Needles
38 Bomb	BOOM!	58 Cactaur	Gigantuar
38 Bomb	Three strikes	59 Hill Gigas	Magnitude 8
39 Green Dragon	Another tail?	59 Hill Gigas	Once a Giant
39 Green Dragon	Dangerous breath	60 Ultros	I AM an octopus!
39 Green Dragon	Not just green	60 Ultros	Mr. Typhon
40 Malboro	Bad breath	61 Deathgaze	Level 5 Death
40 Malboro	Darkness, Silence, Poison	62 Kefka	Heartless Angel
40 Malboro	Drooling Daisy	62 Kefka	I just can't believe it!
41 Behemoth	Surprisingly regular	62 Kefka	Life... Dreams... Hope....
41 Behemoth	What a meathead	63 Ultima Weapon	Bribes welcome
42 Black Knight	Sun Blade	63 Ultima Weapon	Shadow Flare
42 Black Knight	Unbeatable?	64 Jenova Synthesis	Calamity from the Skies
42 Black Knight	Yoichi Bow	64 Jenova Synthesis	Countdown to Ultima
43 Iron Giant	Reaper	64 Jenova Synthesis	Mother
43 Iron Giant	Strongest small fry	65 Safer Sephiroth	I am the chosen one!
43 Iron Giant	What's under the armor?	65 Safer Sephiroth	Pale Horse
44 Hein	Barrier Shift	65 Safer Sephiroth	Super Nova
44 Hein	Elemental weakness	66 Esthar Soldier	Bodysuit
45 Ahriman	Good at magic	66 Esthar Soldier	Shotgun
46 Xande	Libra!	66 Esthar Soldier	Terminator
46 Xande	Mortality	67 Gesper	Black Hole
47 Flan	Weak against Mages	67 Gesper	Defective weapon
48 Scarmiglione	Blighted Despot	67 Gesper	Degenerator
48 Scarmiglione	Sssrrr...	68 Pupu	Elixir please!

COLLECTACARD	PASSWORD
68 Pupu	UFO?
69 Black Waltz No. 3	Best of the Black Mages
69 Black Waltz No. 3	triple time
70 Ozma	Curse, Meteor, Doomsday
70 Ozma	The round guy
71 Anima	Pain
71 Anima	Seymour's mother
72 Seymour Natus	One of the Guado
73 Gigas	Loves rocks
73 Gigas	Qu'lhm Island
74 Shadow Lord	Implosion
74 Shadow Lord	The Crystal War
74 Shadow Lord	Xarcabard
75 Bangaa Thief	Hates water
75 Bangaa Thief	One of the Bangaa
76 Mandragoras	Rogue Tomato
76 Mandragoras	Sochen Cave Palace

COLLECTACARD	PASSWORD
76 Mandragoras	Too cute to hate
77 Judge	Basch's younger twin
77 Judge	Gabranth
77 Judge	Judge Magister
78 Psicom Enforcer	The Hanging Edge
78 Psicom Enforcer	The Purge
79 Manasvin Warmech	Annihilator
79 Manasvin Warmech	Crystal Rain
79 Manasvin Warmech	Targeting
80 Adamantoise	Earth Shaker
80 Adamantoise	Platinum Ingot
80 Adamantoise	Trapezohedron
81 Chaos	Demonsdance
81 Chaos	God of Discord
81 Chaos	Know despair!

UNLOCK CHARACTERS

The following characters are unlocked by collecting 8 Crystal Fragments in the given color.

CHARACTER	CRYSTAL FRAGMENT COLOR
Aerith (Final Fantasy VII)	Pink
Ashe (Final Fantasy XII)	Crimson
Cid (Final Fantasy III)	Yellow
(Cosmos) (Dissidia)	Rainbow
Faris (Final Fantasy V)	Red
Kain (Final Fantasy IV)	Navy Blue
Locke (Final Fantasy VI)	Blue
Minwu (Final Fantasy II)	Silver
Princess Sarah (Final Fantasy I)	Gold

CHARACTER	CRYSTAL FRAGMENT COLOR
Prish (Final Fantasy XI)	Purple
Rydia (Final Fantasy IV)	Emerald
Seifer (Final Fantasy VIII)	Grey
Sephiroth (Final Fantasy VII)	Black
Snow (Final Fantasy XIII)	White
Vivi (Final Fantasy IX)	Orange
Yuna (Final Fantasy X)	Sapphire

TRANSFORMERS: WAR FOR CYBERTRON - AUTOBOTS

AUTOBOT SILVERBOLT IN STORY & ARENA

Select Cheats from the main menu and enter 10141.

DECEPTICON RAMJET IN ARENA

Select Cheats from the main menu and enter 99871.

TRANSFORMERS: WAR FOR CYBERTRON - DECEPTICONS

DECEPTICON RAMJET IN STORY & ARENA

Select Cheats from the main menu and enter 99871.

AUTOBOT SILVERBOLT IN ARENA

Select Cheats from the main menu and enter 10141.

TRON: EVOLUTION

THE ISLAND, TANK AND DISC BATTLE MAP

At the cheat menu, enter 25E0DE6B.

QUORRA COSTUME

At the cheat menu, enter c74f395f.

UP

INVINCIBILITY

After completing the game, enter B, Y, B, Y, X, Y, X, Y, B, A at the title screen. This cheat disables saving.

YU-GI-OH!
NIGHTMARE TROUBADOUR

CREDITS

Unlock the Password Machine by defeating the Expert Cup. Enter the Duel Shop and select the
Slot maching. Enter 00000375.

SOUND TEST

Unlock the Password Machine by defeating the Expert Cup. Enter the Duel Shop and select the
Slot maching. Enter 57300000.

YU-GI-OH! WORLD
CHAMPIONSHIP 2008

CARD PASSWORDS

Enter the following in the password machine to receive the corresponding card. You must already have the card to use the password.

PASSWORD EFFECT

CARD	PASSWORD	CARD	PASSWORD
7	67048711	Amazoness Blowpiper	73574678
7 Colored Fish	23771716	Amazoness Chain Master	29654737
7 Completed	86198326	Amazoness Fighter	55821894
A Feint Plan	68170903	Amazoness Paladin	47480070
A Hero Emerges	21597117	Amazoness Spellcaster	81325903
Abyss Soldier	18318842	Amazoness Swords Woman	94004268
Acid Rain	21323861	Amazoness Tiger	10979723
Acid Trap Hole	41356845	Amphibian Beast	67371383
Adhesive Explosive	53828196	Amplifier	00303660
Agido	16135253	Anti-Spell	53112492
Airknight Parshath	18036057	Aqua Madoor	85639257
Aitsu	48202661	Aqua Spirit	40916023
Alkana Knight Joker	06150044	Archfiend of Gilfer	50287060
Alligator's Sword	64428736	Armed Changer	90374791
Alligator's Sword Dragon	03366982	Armed Ninja	09076207
Alpha the Magnet Warrior	99785935	Armored Glass	21070956
Altar for Tribute	21070956	Armored Zombie	20277860
Amazon Archer	91869203	Array of Revealing Light	69296555
Amazoness Archers	67987611		

CARD	PASSWORD
Arsenal Bug	42364374
Arsenal Robber	55348096
Assault on GHQ	62633180
Asura Priest	02134346
Attack and Receive	63689843
Autonomous Action Unit	71453557
Axe of Despair	40619825
Axe Raider	48305365
B. Skull Dragon	11901678
Baby Dragon	88819587
Back to Square One	47453433
Backfire	82705573
Bad Reaction to Simochi	40633297
Bait Doll	07165085
Ballista of Rampart Smashing	00242146
Banisher of the Light	61528025
Banner of Courage	10012614
Bark of The Dark Ruler	41925941
Baron of the Fiend Sword	86325596
Barrel Behind the Door	78783370
Barrel Dragon	81480460
Battery Charger	61181383
Batteryman AA	63142001
Batteryman C	19733961
Batteryman D	55401221
Battle Ox	05053103
Battle Warrior	55550921
Beast Fangs	46009906
Beast Soul Swap	35149085
Beastking of the Swamps	99426834
Beautiful Head-huntress	16899564
Beckoning Light	16255442
Berfomet	77207191
Berserk Gorilla	39168895
Beta the Magnet Warrior	39256679
Bickuribox	25655502
Big Bang Shot	61127349

CARD	PASSWORD
Big Eye	16768387
Big Shield Gardna	65240384
Birdface	45547649
Black Illusion Ritual	41426869
Black Luster Ritual	55761792
Black Luster Soldier	72989439
Black Magic Ritual	76792184
Black Pendant	65169794
Bladefly	28470714
Blast Held by a Tribute	89041555
Blast Magician	21051146
Blast Sphere	26302522
Blast with Chain	98239899
Blasting the Ruins	21466326
Blessings of the Nile	30653173
Blowback Dragon	25551951
Blue Medicine	20871001
Blue-Eyes Toon Dragon	53183600
Blue-Eyes Ultimate Dragon	23995346
Blue-Eyes White Dragon	80906030
Blue-Eyes White Dragon	80906030
Book of Taiyou	38699854
Bottomless Trap Hole	29401950
Bowganian	52090844
Bracchio-Raidus	16507828
Brain Control	87910978
Breaker the Magical Warrior	71413901
Breath of Light	20101223
Bright Castle	82878489
Burning Land	24294108
Burning Spear	18937875
Burst Return	27191436
Burst Stream of Destruction	17655904
Buster Rancher	84740193
Cannon Soldier	11384280
Cannonball Spear Shellfish	95614612
Card Destruction	72892473

CARD	PASSWORD	CARD	PASSWORD
Card of Sanctity	04266498	Curse of Anubis	66742250
Card Shuffle	12183332	Curse of Darkness	84970821
Castle of Dark Illusions	00062121	Curse of Dragon	28279543
Castle Walls	44209392	Curse of the Masked Beast	94377247
Catapult Turtle	95727991	Cursed Seal of the Forbidden Spell	58851034
Ceasefire	36468556	Cyber Raider	39978267
Celtic Guardian	91152256	Cyber Shield	63224564
Cemetery Bomb	51394546	Cyber-Tech Alligator	48766543
Centrifugal Field	01801154	D.D. Borderline	60912752
Cestus of Dagla	28106077	D.D. Designator	33423043
Chain Destruction	01248895	D.D. Assailant	70074904
Chain Disappearance	57139487	D.D. Dynamite	08628798
Chain Energy	79323590	D.D. Trap Hole	05606466
Chaos Command Magician	72630549	D.D. Warrior	37043180
Chaos End	61044390	D.D. Warrior Lady	07572887
Chaos Greed	97439308	D. Tribe	02833249
Chimera the Flying Mythical Beast	04796100	Dark Artist	72520073
Chiron the Mage	16956455	Dark Deal	65824822
Chorus of Sanctuary	81380218	Dark Dust Spirit	89111398
Chthonian Alliance	46910446	Dark Elf	21417692
Chthonian Blast	18271561	Dark Energy	04614116
Chthonian Polymer	72287557	Dark Factory of Mass Production	90928333
Clay Charge	22479888	Dark Jeroid	90980792
Cocoon of Evolution	40240595	Dark Magic Attack	02314238
Coffin Seller	65830223	Dark Magic Curtain	99789342
Cold Wave	60682203	Dark Magician	46986414
Command Knight	10375182	Dark Magician Girl	38033121
Conscription	31000575	Dark Magician of Chaos	40737112
Continuous Destruction Punch	68057622	Dark Master - Zorc	97642679
Contract with Exodia	33244944	Dark Mimic LV1	74713516
Contract with the Dark Master	96420087	Dark Mimic LV3	01102515
Convulsion of Nature	62966332	Dark Mirror Force	20522190
Copycat	26376390	Dark Necrofear	31829185
Cosmo Queen	38999506	Dark Paladin	98502113
Covering Fire	74458486	Dark Rabbit	99261403
Crass Clown	93889755	Dark Room of Nightmare	85562745
Crawling Dragon #2	38289717	Dark Sage	92377303
Crimson Sunbird	46696593	Dark Snake Syndrome	47233801
Crush Card Virus	57728570	Dark Spirit of the Silent	93599951

CARD	PASSWORD
Dark World Lightning	93554166
Darkness Approaches	80168720
Dark-Piercing Light	45895206
Deck Devastation Virus	35027493
Decoy Dragon	02732323
Dedication through Light and Darkness	69542930
De-Fusion	95286165
Delta Attacker	39719977
Despair from the Dark	71200730
De-Spell	19159413
Destiny Board	94212438
Destruction Ring	21219755
Dian Keto the Cure Master	84257639
Dice Re-Roll	83241722
Different Dimension Capsule	11961740
Different Dimension Dragon	50939127
Different Dimension Gate	56460688
Diffusion Wave-Motion	87880531
Dimension Fusion	23557835
Dimension Wall	67095270
Dimensional Prison	70342110
Dimensionhole	22959079
Disappear	24623598
Disarmament	20727787
Divine Sword - Phoenix Blade	31423101
Divine Wrath	49010598
DNA Surgery	74701381
Doomcaliber Knight	78700060
Double Coston	44436472
Double Snare	03682106
Double Spell	24096228
Dragged Down into the Grave	16435235
Dragon Capture Jar	50045299
Dragon Seeker	28563545
Dragon Treasure	01435851
Dragonic Attack	32437102

CARD	PASSWORD
Dragon's Mirror	71490127
Draining Shield	43250041
Dramatic Rescue	80193355
Dream Clown	13215230
Drill Bug	88733579
Driving Snow	00473469
Drop Off	55773067
Dunames Dark Witch	12493482
Dust Barrier	31476755
Dust Tornado	60082867
Earth Chant	59820352
Earthbound Spirit's Invitation	65743242
Earthquake	82828051
Eatgaboon	42578427
Ectoplasmer	97342942
Ekibyo Drakmord	69954399
Electro-Whip	37820550
Elegant Egotist	90219263
Elemental Hero Avian	21844576
Elemental Hero Burstinatrix	58932615
Elemental Hero Clayman	84327329
Elemental Hero Flame Wingman	35809262
Elemental Hero Rampart Blaster	47737087
Elemental Hero Sparkman	20721928
Elemental Hero Thunder Giant	61204971
Embodiment of Apophis	28649820
Emergency Provisions	53046408
Enchanted Arrow	93260132
Enchanting Fitting Room	30531525
Enemy Controller	98045062
Energy Drain	56916805
Enervating Mist	26022485
Enraged Battle Ox	76909279
Eradicating Aerosol	94716515
Eternal Drought	56606928
Eternal Rest	95051344

CARD	PASSWORD	CARD	PASSWORD
Exarion Universe	63749102	Gaia the Dragon Champion	66889139
Exchange	05556668	Gaia the Fierce Knight	06368038
Exhausting Spell	95451366		
Exodia Necross	12600382	Gamma the Magnet Warrior	11549357
Exodia the Forbidden One	33396948	Garoozis	14977074
Fairy Box	21598948	Garuda the Wind Spirit	12800777
Fairy King Truesdale	45425051	Gazelle the King of Mythical Beasts	05818798
Fairy Meteor Crush	97687912		
Fairy's Hand Mirror	17653779	Gear Golem the Moving Fortress	30190809
Fake Trap	03027001	Gearfried the Iron Knight	00423705
Feather Shot	19394153		
Feather Wind	71060915	Gearfried the Swordmaster	57046845
Fengsheng Mirror	37406863		
Feral Imp	41392891	Gemini Elf	69140098
Fiend Comedian	81172176	Generation Shift	34460239
Fiend Skull Dragon	66235877	Germ Infection	24668830
Fiend's Hand Mirror	58607704	Getsu Fuhma	21887179
Fiend's Sanctuary	24874630	Giant Flea	41762634
Final Countdown	95308449	Giant Germ	95178994
Final Destiny	18591904	Giant Rat	97017120
Firewing Pegasus	27054370	Giant Red Seasnake	58831685
Fissure	66788016	Giant Soldier of Stone	13039848
Flame Cerebrus	60862676		
Flame Manipulator	34460851	Giant Trunade	42703248
Flame Swordsman	40502030	Gigantes	47606319
Flying Kamakiri #1	84834865	Gilasaurus	45894482
Foolish Burial	81439173	Gilford the Legend	69933858
Forced Ceasefire	97806240	Gilford the Lightning	36354007
Forest	87430998	Gil Garth	38445524
Fortress Whale	62337487	Goblin Attack Force	78658564
Fortress Whale's Oath	77454922	Goblin Fan	04149689
		Goblin King	18590133
Frozen Soul	57069605	Goblin Thief	45311864
Fulfillment of the Contract	48206762	Goblin's Secret Remedy	11868825
Full Salvo	70865988		
Fusilier Dragon, the Duel-Mode Beast	51632798	Goddess of Whim	67959180
		Goddess with the Third Eye	53493204
Fusion Gate	24094653		
Fusion Sage	26902560	Gokibore	15367030
Fusion Sword Murasame Blade	37684215	Gorgon's Eye	52648457
		Graceful Dice	74137509
Gaia Power	56594520	Gradius' Option	14291024
		Granadora	13944422

CARD	PASSWORD
Grand Tiki Elder	13676474
Gravedigger Ghoul	82542267
Gravekeeper's Assailant	25262697
Gravekeeper's Cannonholder	99877698
Gravekeeper's Chief	62473983
Gravekeeper's Commandant	17393207
Gravekeeper's Curse	50712728
Gravekeeper's Guard	37101832
Gravekeeper's Servant	16762927
Gravekeeper's Spear Soldier	63695531
Gravekeeper's Spy	24317029
Gravekeeper's Vassal	99690140
Gravekeeper's Watcher	26084285
Gravity Axe - Grarl	32022366
Gravity Bind	85742772
Great Moth	14141448
Greed	89405199
Green Baboon, Defender of the Forest	46668237
Greenkappa	61831093
Ground Collapse	90502999
Gust	73079365
Gust Fan	55321970
Gyaku-Gire Panda	09817927
Hammer Shot	26412047
Hand Collapse	74519184
Hannibal Necromancer	05640330
Harpie Lady	76812113
Harpie Lady 1	91932350
Harpie Lady 2	27927359
Harpie Lady 3	54415063
Harpie Lady Sisters	12206212
Harpies' Hunting Ground	75782277
Harpie's Pet Dragon	52040216
Headless Knight	5434080
Heart of Clear Water	64801562

CARD	PASSWORD
Heart of the Underdog	35762283
Heavy Mech Support Platform	23265594
Heavy Slump	52417194
Heavy Storm	19613556
Helpoemer	76052811
Hercules Beetle	52584282
Hero Kid	32679370
Hero Signal	22020907
Hidden Book of Spell	21840375
Hieroglyph Lithograph	10248192
Hinotama	46130346
Hiro's Shadow Scout	81863068
Hitotsu-Me Giant	76184692
Horn Imp	69669405
Horn of Light	38552107
Horn of the Unicorn	64047146
Hoshiningen	67629977
House of Adhesive Tape	15083728
Human-Wave Tactics	30353551
Illusionist Faceless Mage	28546905
Impenetrable Formation	96631852
Inferno	74823665
Inferno Fire Blast	52684508
Infinite Cards	94163677
Infinite Dismissal	54109233
Injection Fairy Lily	79575620
Insect Armor with Laser Cannon	03492538
Insect Barrier	23615409
Insect Imitation	96965364
Insect Queen	91512835
Inspection	16227556
Interdimensional Matter Transporter	36261276
Invigoration	98374133
Jack's Knight	90876561
Jade Insect Whistle	95214051
Jam Breeding Machine	21770260
Jam Defender	21558682

CARD	PASSWORD
Jar of Greed	83968380
Jigen Bakudan	90020065
Jinzo	77585513
Jinzo #7	77585513
Jowgen the Spiritualist	41855169
Jowls of Dark Demise	05257687
Judge Man	30113682
Judgment of the Pharaoh	55948544
Just Desserts	24068492
Kabazauls	51934376
Kabazauls	51934376
Kanan the Sword-smistress	12829151
Killer Needle	88979991
Kinetic Soldier	79853073
King of the Skull Servants	36021814
King of the Swamp	79109599
King Tiger Wanghu	83986578
King's Knight	64788463
Koitsu	69456283
Krokodilus	76512652
Kryuel	82642348
Kunai with Chain	37390589
Kuriboh	40640057
Kycoo the Ghost Destroyer	88240808
Labyrinth of Nightmare	66526672
Labyrinth Tank	99551425
Larvae Moth	87756343
Laser Cannon Armor	77007920
Last Day of the Witch	90330453
Launcher Spider	87322377
Lava Battleguard	20394040
Lava Golem	00102380
Left Arm of the Forbidden One	07902349
Left Leg of the Forbidden One	44519536
Legacy of Yata-Garasu	30461781
Legendary Sword	61854111

CARD	PASSWORD
Level Conversion Lab	84397023
Level Limit - Area A	54976796
Level Limit - Area B	03136426
Level Modulation	61850482
Level Up!	25290459
Light of Judgment	44595286
Lighten the Load	37231841
Lightforce Sword	49587034
Lightning Vortex	69162969
Little Chimera	68658728
Luminous Soldier	57482479
Luminous Spark	81777047
Luster Dragon	11091375
Machine Duplication	63995093
Machine King	46700124
Mad Sword Beast	79870141
Mage Power	83746708
Magic Cylinder	62279055
Magic Drain	59344077
Magic Formula	67227834
Magic Jammer	77414722
Magical Arm Shield	96008713
Magical Dimension	28553439
Magical Explosion	32723153
Magical Hats	81210420
Magical Stone Excavation	98494543
Magical Thorn	53119267
Magician of Black Chaos	30208479
Magician of Faith	31560081
Magician's Circle	00050755
Magician's Unite	36045450
Magician's Valkyria	80304126
Maha Vailo	93013676
Maharaghi	40695128
Maiden of the Aqua	17214465
Major Riot	09074847
Malevolent Catastrophe	01224927
Malevolent Nuzzler	99597615
Malfunction	06137091
Malice Dispersion	13626450

CARD	PASSWORD
Man-Eater Bug	54652250
Man-Eating Treasure Chest	13723605
Manga Ryu-Ran	38369349
Marauding Captain	02460565
Marie the Fallen One	57579381
Marshmallon	31305911
Marshmallon Glasses	66865880
Mask of Brutality	82432018
Mask of Darkness	28933734
Mask of Dispel	20765952
Mask of Restrict	29549364
Mask of the Accursed	56948373
Mask of Weakness	57882509
Masked Sorcerer	10189126
Mass Driver	34906152
Master Kyonshee	24530661
Mataza the Zapper	22609617
Mausoleum of the Emperor	80921533
Mechanicalchaser	07359741
Mega Ton Magical Cannon	32062913
Megamorph	22046459
Melchid the Four-Faced Beast	86569121
Meltiel, Sage of the Sky	49905576
Mesmeric Control	48642904
Messenger of Peace	44656491
Metal Detector	75646520
Metal Reflect Slime	26905245
Metalmorph	68540058
Metalzoa	50705071
Meteor Black Dragon	90660762
Meteor Dragon	64271667
Michizure	37580756
Micro Ray	18190572
Millennium Shield	32012841
Milus Radiant	07489323
Mind Control	37520316
Mind Crush	15800838

CARD	PASSWORD
Miracle Dig	63434080
Miracle Kids	55985014
Miracle Restoring	68334074
Mirror Force	44095762
Mispolymerization	58392024
Mist body	47529357
Moisture Creature	75285069
Mokey Mokey	27288416
Mokey Mokey King	13803864
Mokey Mokey Smackdown	01965724
Molten Destruction	19384334
Monster Gate	43040603
Monster Recovery	93108433
Monster Reincarnation	74848038
Mooyan Curry	58074572
Morphing Jar	33508719
Morphing Jar #2	79106360
Mother Grizzly	57839750
Mountain	50913601
Muka Muka	46657337
Multiplication of Ants	22493811
Multiply	40703222
Mushroom Man	14181608
My Body as a Shield	69279219
Mysterious Puppeteer	54098121
Mystic Box	25774450
Mystic Horseman	68516705
Mystic Probe	49251811
Mystic Swordsman LV2	47507260
Mystic Swordsman LV4	74591968
Mystic Swordsman LV6	60482781
Mystic Tomato	83011277
Mystical Elf	15025844
Mystical Moon	36607978
Mystical Refpanel	35563539
Mystical Sheep #1	30451366
Mystical Space Typhoon	05318639
Narrow Pass	40172183

CARD	PASSWORD
Necrovalley	47355498
Needle Wall	38299233
Needle Worm	81843628
Negate Attack	14315573
Neo the Magic Swordsman	50930991
Newdoria	04335645
Next to be Lost	07076131
Nightmare Wheel	54704216
Nimble Momonga	22567609
Nitro Unit	23842445
Non Aggression Area	76848240
Non-Fusion Area	27581098
Non-Spellcasting Area	20065549
Numinous Healer	02130625
Nuvia the Wicked	12953226
Obnoxious Celtic Guard	52077741
Ojama Black	79335209
Ojama Delta Hurricane!!	08251996
Ojama Green	12482652
Ojama King	90140980
Ojama Trio	29843091
Ojama Yellow	42941100
Ojamagic	24643836
Ojamuscle	98259197
Ominous Fortune-telling	56995655
Ookazi	19523799
Opti-Camouflage Armor	44762290
Order to Charge	78986941
Order to Smash	39019325
Otohime	39751093
Overpowering Eye	60577362
Panther Warrior	42035044
Paralyzing Potion	50152549
Parasite Paracide	27911549
Parrot Dragon	62762898
Patrician of Darkness	19153634
Pendulum Machine	24433920
Penguin Knight	36039163

CARD	PASSWORD
Penguin Soldier	93920745
Perfectly Ultimate Great Moth	48579379
Petit Moth	58192742
Pharaoh's Treasure	63571750
Pigeonholing Books of Spell	96677818
Pikeru's Second Sight	58015506
Pinch Hopper	26185991
Pitch-Black Power Stone	34029630
Poison Fangs	76539047
Poison of the Old Man	08842266
Polymerization	35550694
Pot of Avarice	67169062
Premature Burial	70828912
Prepare to Strike Back	04483989
Prevent Rat	00549481
Princess of Tsurugi	51371017
Prohibition	43711255
Protector of the Sanctuary	24221739
Pumpking the King of Ghosts	29155212
Queen's Knight	25652259
Rabid Horseman	94905343
Radiant Jeral	84177693
Radiant Mirror Force	21481146
Raigeki Break	04178474
Rapid-Fire Magician	06337436
Ray of Hope	82529174
Ready for Intercepting	31785398
Really Eternal Rest	28121403
Reaper of the Cards	33066139
Reckless Greed	37576645
Recycle	96316857
Red Archery Girl	65570596
Red Medicine	38199696
Red-Eyes B. Chick	36262024
Red-Eyes Black Dragon	74677422
Red-Eyes Black Metal Dragon	64335804

CARD	PASSWORD
Reflect Bounder	02851070
Reinforcement of the Army	32807846
Reinforcements	17814387
Release Restraint	75417459
Relieve Monster	37507488
Relinquished	64631466
Remove Trap	51482758
Respect Play	08951260
Restructer Revolution	99518961
Reversal Quiz	05990062
Reverse Trap	77622396
Revival Jam	31709826
Right Arm of the Forbidden One	70903634
Right Leg of the Forbidden One	08124921
Rigorous Reaver	39180960
Ring of Magnetism	20436034
Riryoku Field	70344351
Rising Energy	78211862
Rite of Spirit	30450531
Ritual Weapon	54351224
Robbin' Goblin	88279736
Robbin' Zombie	83258273
Robotic Knight	44203504
Rock Bombardment	20781762
Rocket Warrior	30860696
Rod of Silence - Kay'est	95515060
Rogue Doll	91939608
Roll Out!	91597389
Royal Command	33950246
Royal Decree	51452091
Royal Magical Library	70791313
Royal Oppression	93016201
Royal Surrender	56058888
Royal Tribute	72405967
Rude Kaiser	26378150
Rush Recklessly	70046172
Ryu Kokki	57281778
Ryu-Kishin	15303296
Ryu-Ran	02964201

CARD	PASSWORD
Sage's Stone	13604200
Saggi the Dark Clown	66602787
Sakuretsu Armor	56120475
Salamandra	32268901
Salvage	96947648
Sangan	26202165
Sasuke Samurai #3	77379481
Sasuke Samurai #4	64538655
Satellite Cannon	50400231
Second Coin Toss	36562627
Sengenjin	76232340
Serial Spell	49398568
Serpentine Princess	71829750
Seven Tools of the Bandit	03819470
Shadow Ghoul	30778711
Shadow of Eyes	58621589
Share the Pain	56830749
Shield & Sword	52097679
Shield Crush	30683373
Shift	59560625
Shifting Shadows	59237154
Shinato, King of a Higher Plane	86327225
Shinato's Ark	60365591
Shining Abyss	87303357
Shining Angel	95956346
Shooting Star Bow - Ceal	95638658
Shrink	55713623
Silver Bow and Arrow	01557499
Simultaneous Loss	92219931
Skilled Dark Magician	73752131
Skilled White Magician	46363422
Skull Dice	00126218
Skull Servant	32274490
Skull-Mark Ladybug	64306248
Skyscraper	63035430
Slate Warrior	78636495
Slot Machine	03797883
Smashing Ground	97169186

CARD	PASSWORD
Smoke Grenade of the Thief	63789924
Snake Fang	00596051
Sogen	86318356
Solar Ray	44472639
Solemn Judgment	41420027
Solemn Wishes	35346968
Sorcerer of the Doomed	49218300
Soul Absorption	68073522
Soul Demolition	76297408
Soul Exchange	68005187
Soul of Purity and Light	77527210
Soul of the Pure	47852924
Soul Release	05758500
Soul Resurrection	92924317
Soul Reversal	78864369
Soul Taker	81510157
Spark Blaster	97362768
Spatial Collapse	20644748
Special Hurricane	42598242
Spell Absorption	51481927
Spell Reproduction	29228529
Spell Vanishing	29735721
Spellbinding Circle	18807108
Spell-stopping Statute	10069180
Spiral Spear Strike	49328340
Spirit Message "A"	94772232
Spirit Message "I"	31893528
Spirit Message "L"	30170981
Spirit Message "N"	67287533
Spirit of Flames	13522325
Spirit of the Pharaoh	25343280
Spirit's Invitation	92394653
Spiritual Earth Art - Kurogane	70156997
Spiritual Energy Settle Machine	99173029
Spiritual Fire Art - Kurenai	42945701
Spiritual Water Art - Aoi	06540606
Spiritual Wind Art - Miyabi	79333300

CARD	PASSWORD
Spiritualism	15866454
St. Joan	21175632
Staunch Defender	92854392
Steel Ogre Grotto #2	90908427
Steel Scorpion	13599884
Stim-Pack	83225447
Stone Statue of the Aztecs	31812496
Stop Defense	63102017
Stray Lambs	60764581
Stumbling	34646691
Swamp Battleguard	40453765
Swift Gaia the Fierce Knight	16589042
Sword of Deep-Seated	98495314
Sword of the Soul-Eater	05371656
Swords of Concealing Light	12923641
Swords of Revealing Light	72302403
Swordsman of Landstar	03573512
System Down	07672244
Tailor of the Fickle	43641473
Terraforming	73628505
The A. Forces	00403847
The Agent of Force - Mars	91123920
The Agent of Judgement - Saturn	91345518
The Big March of Animals	01689516
The Bistro Butcher	71107816
The Cheerful Coffin	41142615
The Creator	61505339
The Creator Incarnate	97093037
The Dark Door	30606547
The Earl of Demise	66989694
The Fiend Megacyber	66362965
The First Sarcophagus	31076103
The Flute of Summoning Kuriboh	20065322

CARD	PASSWORD
The Forgiving Maiden	84080938
The Gross Ghost of Fled Dreams	68049471
The Illusory Gentleman	83764996
The Inexperienced Spy	81820689
The Last Warrior from Another Planet	86099788
The Law of the Normal	66926224
The League of Uni-form Nomenclature	55008284
The Little Swords-man of Aile	25109950
The Masked Beast	49064413
The Portrait's Secret	32541773
The Regulation of Tribe	00296499
The Reliable Guardian	16430187
The Rock Spirit	76305638
The Sanctuary in the Sky	56433456
The Second Sarcophagus	04081094
The Secret of the Bandit	99351431
The Shallow Grave	43434803
The Snake Hair	29491031
The Spell Absorbing Life	99517131
The Statue of Easter Island	10261698
The Third Sarcophagus	78697395
The Unhappy Girl	27618634
The Unhappy Maiden	51275027
The Warrior Return-ing Alive	95281259
The Wicked Worm Beast	06285791
Thestalos the Firestorm Monarch	26205777
Thousand Dragon	41462083
Thousand Energy	05703682
Thousand Knives	63391643
Thousand-Eyes Idol	27125110

CARD	PASSWORD
Threatening Roar	36361633
Three-Headed Geedo	78423643
Thunder Crash	69196160
Thunder Dragon	31786629
Thunder Nyan Nyan	70797118
Time Machine	80987696
Time Wizard	06285791
Token Feastevil	83675475
Toon Alligator	59383041
Toon Cannon Soldier	79875176
Toon Dark Magician Girl	90960358
Toon Defense	43509019
Toon Gemini Elf	42386471
Toon Goblin Attack Force	15270885
Toon Masked Sorcerer	16392422
Toon Mermaid	65458948
Toon Summoned Skull	91842653
Toon Table of Contents	89997728
Toon World	15259703
Tornado	61068510
Tornado Wall	18605135
Torpedo Fish	90337190
Tower of Babel	94256039
Tragedy	35686187
Transcendent Wings	25573054
Trap Hole	04206964
Trap Jammer	19252988
Trap Master	46461247
Tremendous Fire	46918794
Triage	30888983
Triangle Ecstasy Spark	12181376
Triangle Power	32298781
Tribute Doll	02903036
Tribute to the Doomed	79759861
Tri-Horned Dragon	39111158
Twin Swords of Flashing Light - Tryce	21900719

CARD	PASSWORD
Twin-Headed Behemoth	43586926
Twin-Headed Thunder Dragon	54752875
Two-Headed King Rex	94119974
Two-Pronged Attack	83887306
Tyhone	72842870
Type Zero Magic Crusher	35346968
UFO Turtle	60806437
Ultimate Offering	80604091
Ultra Evolution Pill	22431243
Umiiruka	82999629
Union Attack	60399954
United We Stand	56747793
Unity	14731897
Upstart Goblin	70368879
Uraby	01784619
Valkyrion the Magna Warrior	75347539
Versago the Destroyer	50259460
Vile Germs	39774685
Vorse Raider	14898066
Waboku	12607053
Wall of Illusion	13945283
Wall of Revealing Light	17078030
Wall Shadow	63162310
Warrior Elimination	90873992
Warrior Lady of the Wasteland	05438492
Wasteland	98239899

CARD	PASSWORD
Weapon Change	10035717
Weather Report	72053645
Weed Out	28604635
White Magical Hat	15150365
White-Horned Dragon	73891874
Wicked-Breaking Flamberge - Baou	68427465
Widespread Ruin	77754944
Wild Nature's Release	61166988
Winged Dragon, Guardian of the Fortress #1	87796900
Winged Kuriboh	57116033
Winged Kuriboh LV10	98585345
Witch's Apprentice	80741828
Wolf	49417509
Wolf Axwielder	56369281
Woodland Sprite	06979239
World Suppression	12253117
Xing Zhen Hu	76515293
Yamata Dragon	76862289
Yami	59197169
Yellow Luster Shield	04542651
Yu-Jo Friendship	81332143
Zaborg the Thunder Monarch	51945556
Zero Gravity	83133491
Zoa	24311372
Zolga	16268841
Zombie Warrior	31339260

WWE ALL STARS

ALL CHARACTERS AND RING GEAR

At the main menu, press Left, Right, Left, Down, Up, Left, Right, Up.

PLAYSTATION® VITA

BEN 10 GALACTIC RACING

KINECELARATOR KART

Select Enter Code from Extras and enter Ben 10, Spidermonkey, Kevin, and Ultimate Echo Echo.

DISGAEA 3: ABSENCE OF DETENTION

GET ACCESS TO NEW VITA CONTENT

Highlight Continue and press ▲, ■, ●, ▲, ■, ●, ✕. Talk to the Parallel Worlder under the stairs in the lower levels of the base.

EARTH DEFENSE 2017 PORTABLE

PALE WING

Complete the game with Storm 1.

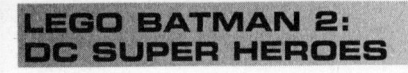

LEGO BATMAN 2: DC SUPER HEROES

STUDS X2

Pause the game, select Extras, and then choose Enter Code. Enter 74EZUT.

SUPER BUILD

Pause the game, select Extras, and then choose Enter Code. Enter JN2J6V.

CHARACTERS

In the Batcave, access the characters screen and select Cheats. These cheats still need to be purchased.

CHEAT	CODE
Clown Goon	9ZZZBP
LexBot	W49CSJ
Mime Goon	ZQA8MK

CHEAT	CODE
Poison Ivy Goon	M9CP6L
Riddler Goon	Q285LK
Two-Face Goon	95KPYJ

LITTLEBIGPLANET PS VITA

GOD COMPLEX SECRET PIN

Spin any of the planets 720 degrees with a single flick.

HOUSE PROUD SECRET PIN

Place 10 stickers or decorations in your pod.

PLATINUM CLUB SECRET PIN

Earn all LittleBigPlanet Vita Trophies.

WHO'S WHO SECRET PIN

Watch the credits all the way through.

The following pins are handpicked.

AWESOMESAUCE SECRET PIN

Congratulations! You are more awesome than awesome!

MASTER OF THE INTERNETS SECRET PIN

Run an awesome LBP Vita fansite!

TARSIER PIN SECRET PIN

Work at Tarsier Studios.

TEAM PICKED SECRET PIN

Have one of your levels featured in Team Picks.

MICHAEL JACKSON: THE EXPERIENCE HD

BLACK ARMGUARD

Draw 50 Perfect Shapes in a Row on Hollywood Tonight on Expert Difficulty.

EMERALD GLOVE

During Smooth Criminal, draw 45 perfect shapes in a row.

GOLDEN GLOVE

For Leave Me Alone, reach the top spot on the leaderboard.

RED RUBY GLOVE

On Ghosts, wear the alternate outfit.

STAR SAPPHIRE GLOVE

On Beat It, score 145,000.

MOTORSTORM RC

THUNDER LIZARD VEHICLE

Spend 1 hour in the Playground.

BEELZEBUGGY BOOM VEHICLE

Spend 2 hours in the Playground.

DUNK VEHICLE

Jump through the basketball hoop in the Playground 10 times.

HEADCASE VEHICLE

Jump through the basketball hoop in the Playground 20 times.

PATRIOT TOUCHDOWN VEHICLE

Score 10 soccer goals in the Playground.

NORD GNITRO VEHICLE

Score 20 soccer goals in the Playground.

PLANTS VS. ZOMBIES

If a code does not work, your Tree of Wisdom may not be tall enough. Try again later.

ALTERNATE LAWN MOWER

During a game, press R1 + R2 + L1 + L2 and enter trickedout.

ZOMBIE SHADES

During a game, press R1 + R2 + L1 + L2 and enter future.

ZOMBIES HAVE A MUSTACHE

During a game, press R1 + R2 + L1 + L2 and enter mustache.

ZOMBIES DANCE

During a game, press R1 + R2 + L1 + L2 and enter dance.

DEAD ZOMBIES LEAVE DAISIES BEHIND

During a game, press R1 + R2 + L1 + L2 and enter daisies.

CANDY SHOWER WHEN ZOMBIE DIES

During a game, press R1 + R2 + L1 + L2 and enter piñata.

CHANGES ZOMBIES SOUND

During a game, press R1 + R2 + L1 + L2 and enter sukhbir.

RAYMAN ORIGINS

LAND OF THE LIVING DEAD LEVEL

Collect all ten Skull Teeth and turn them in.

REALITY FIGHTERS

STORY MODE: FULL STEAM

Complete the regular Story Mode.

MR. MIYAGI

Defeat Mr. Miyagi in Story mode and Story Mode: Full Steam.

SURVIVAL EXTREME

In Survival Classic mode, win 15 fights.

UNCHARTED: GOLDEN ABYSS

CRUSHING DIFFICULTY

Complete the game on Hard.

WIPEOUT 2048

BOOST AT START

Use turbo just as the timer reaches Go.

PLAYSTATION® PORTABLE

ASTRO BOY: THE VIDEO GAME

INVULNERABLE

Pause the game and press Up, Down, Down, Up, L, R.

MAX STATS

Pause the game and press Left, Left, R, Down, Down, L.

INFINITE SUPERS

Pause the game and press Left, L, Right, L, Up, Down.

INFINITE DASHES

Pause the game and press R, R, L, R, Left, Up.

DISABLE SUPERS

Pause the game and press L, L, R, R, L, Left.

COSTUME SWAP (ARENA AND CLASSIC COSTUMES)

Pause the game and press R, Up, L, Up, Down, R.

UNLOCK LEVELS

Pause the game and press Up, L, Right, L, Down, L. This allows you to travel to any level from the Story menu.

BEN 10: ALIEN FORCE THE GAME

LEVEL LORD

Enter Gwen, Kevin, Big Chill, Gwen as a code.

INVINCIBILITY

Enter Kevin, Big Chill, Swampfire, Kevin as a code.

ALL COMBOS

Enter Swampfire, Gwen, Kevin, Ben as a code.

INFINITE ALIENS

Enter Ben, Swampfire, Gwen, Big Chill as a code.

BEN 10: ALIEN FORCE VILGAX ATTACKS

LEVEL SKIP

Pause the game and enter Portal in the Cheats menu.

UNLOCK ALL SPECIAL ATTACKS FOR ALL FORMS

Pause the game and enter Everythingproof in the Cheats menu.

UNLOCK ALL ALIEN FORMS

Pause the game and enter Primus in the Cheats menu.

TOGGLE INVULNERABILITY ON AND OFF

Pause the game and enter Xlmrsmoothy in the Cheats menu.

GIVES PLAYER FULL HEALTH

Pause the game and enter Herotime in the Cheats menu.

QUICK ENERGY REGENERATION

Pause the game and enter Generator in the Cheats menu.

BEN 10: PROTECTOR OF EARTH

INVINCIBILITY

Select a game from the Continue option. Go to the Map Selection screen, press Start and choose Extras. Select Enter Secret Code and enter XLR8, Heatblast, Wildvine, Fourarms.

ALL COMBOS

Select a game from the Continue option. Go to the Map Selection screen, press Start and choose Extras. Select Enter Secret Code and enter Cannonblot, Heatblast, Fourarms, Heatblast.

ALL LOCATIONS

Select a game from the Continue option. Go to the Map Selection screen, press Start and choose Extras. Select Enter Secret Code and enter Heatblast, XLR8, XLR8, Cannonblot.

DNA FORCE SKINS

Select a game from the Continue option. Go to the Map Selection screen, press Start and choose Extras. Select Enter Secret Code and enter Wildvine, Fourarms, Heatblast, Cannonbolt.

BEN 10 ULTIMATE ALIEN: COSMIC DESTRUCTION

To remove the cheats, you will need to start a new game.

1,000,000 DNA

Pause the game, select Cheats, and enter Cash.

REGENERATE HEALTH

Pause the game, select Cheats, and enter Health.

REGENERATE ENERGY

Pause the game, select Cheats, and enter Energy.

UPGRADE EVERYTHING

Pause the game, select Cheats, and enter Upgrade.

ALL LEVELS

Pause the game, select Cheats, and enter Levels.

ENEMIES DO DOUBLE DAMAGE/ PLAYER DOES 1/2 DAMAGE

Pause the game, select Cheats, and enter Hard.

CAPCOM CLASSICS COLLECTION REMIXED

UNLOCK EVERYTHING

At the title screen, press Left on D-pad, Right on D-pad, Left on Analog stick, Right on Analog stick, ⬤, ⬤, Up on D-pad, Down on D-pad.

CAPCOM PUZZLE WORLD

SUPER BUSTER BROS.

LEVEL SELECT IN TOUR MODE

At the Main menu, highlight Tour Mode, hold Down and press ❌.

SUPER PUZZLE FIGHTER

PLAY AS AKUMA

At the character select, highlight Hsien-Ko and press Down.

PLAY AS ANITA

At the character select, hold L + R and choose Donovan.

PLAY AS DAN

At the character select, highlight Donovan and press Down.

PLAY AS HSIEN-KO'S TALISMAN

At the character select, hold L + R and choose Hsien-Ko.

PLAY AS DEVILOT

At the character select, highlight Morrigan and press Down.

PLAY AS MORRIGAN AS A BAT

At the character select, hold L + R and choose Morrigan.

CRASH: MIND OVER MUTANT

A cheat can be deactivated by re-entering the code.

FREEZE ENEMIES WITH TOUCH

Pause the game, hold R and press Down, Down, Down, Up.

ENIMIES DROP WUMPA FRUIT

Pause the game, hold R and press Right, Right, Right, Up.

ENEMIES DROP X4 DAMAGE

Pause the game, hold R and press Up, Up, Up, Left.

SHADOW CRASH

Pause the game, hold R and press Left, Right, Left, Right.

ENEMIES DROP PURPLE FRUIT

Pause the game, hold R and press Up, Down, Down, Up.

DEFORMED CRASH

Pause the game, hold R and press Left, Left, Left, Down.

ENEMIES DROP SUPER KICK

Pause the game, hold R and press Up, Right, Down, Left.

CRISIS CORE— FINAL FANTASY VII

NEW GAME+

After completing the game, you'll be prompted to make a new save. Loading a game from this new save will begin a New Game+, starting the game over while allowing Zack to retain almost everything he's earned.

The following items transfer to a New Game+:

Level, Experience, SP, Gil, Playtime, Non-Key Items, Materia, and DMW Completion Rate

The following items do not transfer:

Key Items, Materia/Accessory Slot Expansion, Ability to SP Convert, DMW Images, Mission Progress, Mail, and Unlocked Shops

DESPICABLE ME: THE GAME

MINIONETTES COSTUME SET

In Gru's Lab, select cheats from the bonus menu and enter ◉, ◉, ▣, ▲, ✕.

VILLAGE FOLK COSTUME SET

In Gru's Lab, select cheats from the bonus menu and enter ▲, ✕, ✕, ◉, ✕.

TAFFY WEB GUN

In Gru's Lab, select cheats from the bonus menu and enter ✕, ◉, ▣, ✕, ▲.

DISGAEA 2: DARK HERO DAYS

AXEL MODE

Highlight New Game and press ▲, ▣, ◉, ▲, ▣, ◉, ✕.

FLATOUT: HEAD ON

1 MILLION CREDITS

Select Enter Code from the Extras menu and enter GIVECASH.

ALL CARS AND 1 MILLION CREDITS

Select Enter Code from the Extras menu and enter GIEVEPIX.

BIG RIG

Select Enter Code from the Extras menu and enter ELPUEBLO.

BIG RIG TRUCK

Select Enter Code from the Extras menu and enter RAIDERS.

FLATMOBILE CAR

Select Enter Code from the Extras menu and enter WOTKINS.

MOB CAR

Select Enter Code from the Extras menu and enter BIGTRUCK.

PIMPSTER CAR

Select Enter Code from the Extras menu and enter RUTTO.

ROCKET CAR

Select Enter Code from the Extras menu and enter KALJAKOPPA.

SCHOOL BUS

Select Enter Code from the Extras menu and enter GIEVCARPLZ.

G.I. JOE: THE RISE OF COBRA

CLASSIC DUKE

At the main menu, press Left, Up, Square, Up, Right, ▲.

CLASSIC SCARLET

At the main menu, press Right, Up, Down, Down, ▲.

GODS EATER BURST

CONTINUE + MODE

After defeating Arda Nova and completing the game, save the game. Load this saved game to continue with new missions.

CONTINUE ++ MODE

After defeating Corrosive Hannibal and completing Continue + Mode, save the game. Load this saved game to continue with new missions.

GUILTY GEAR JUDGMENT

EXTRA SOUL IN MAIN STORY

Pause the game, press Select, and press Up, Up, Down, Left, Start.

LIFE + TENSION MAX IN MAIN STORY AND SURVIVAL

Pause the game, press Select, and press Down, Right, Right, Up, Start.

HIDDEN GALLERY TEST

First you must complete the game with each character. Then, highlight Quit on the Main Menu and press L + R + ◉.

SOFT RESET

Press Start + Select + L + R.

GOLD CHARACTERS

While selecting your character, press L + R.

HOT BRAIN

119.99 TEMPERATURE IN ALL 5 CATEGORIES

Select New Game and enter Cheat.

INVIZIMALS

SPECIAL INVIZIMAL

At the World Map, hold Select and press Up, Right, Down, Left. At the Big Secret select Capture Invizimals.

IRON MAN

Iron Man's different armor suits are unlocked by completing certain missions.

COMPLETE MISSION	SUIT UNLOCKED
1, Escape	Mark I
2, First Flight	Mark II
3, Fight Back	Mark III
5, Maggia Compound	Gold Tin Can
8, Frozen Ship	Classic
11, Island Meltdown	Stealth
13, Showdown	Titanium Man

PSP MINIGAMES

Minigames can be unlocked by completing the following missions. Access the minigames through the Bonus menu.

COMPLETE MISSION	PSP MINIGAME UNLOCKED
1, Escape	Tin Can Challenge 1 + 2
2, First Flight	DEATH RACE: STARK INDUSTRY
3, Fight Back	BOSS FIGHT: DREADNOUGHT
4, Weapons Transport	DEATH RACE: AFGHAN DESERT BOSS FIGHT: WHIPLASH
5, Maggia Compound	DEATH RACE: MAGGIA MANSION
6, Flying Fortress	SPEED KILL: FLYING FORTRESS SURVIVAL: FLYING FORTRESS
7, Nuclear Winter	DEATH RACE: ARTIC CIRCLE
8, Frozen Ship	SPEED KILL: FROZEN SHIP SURVIVAL: FROZEN SHIP
9, Home Front	BOSS FIGHT: TITANIUM MAN
10, Save Pepper	DEATH RACE: DAM BASSIN
11, Island Meltdown	SPEED KILL: GREEK ISLANDS SURVIVAL: GREEK ISLANDS
12, Battlesuit Factory	SPEED KILL: TINMEN FACTORY SURVIVAL: TINMEN FACTORY
13, Showdown	BOSS FIGHT: IRON MONGER

CONCEPT ART

As you progress through the game and destroy the Weapon Crates, bonuses are unlocked. You can find all of these in the Bonus menu once unlocked.

CONCEPT ART UNLOCKED	NUMBER OF WEAPON CRATES FOUND
Environments Set 1	6
Environments Set 2	12
Iron Man	18
Environments Set 3	24
Enemies	30
Environments Set 4	36
Villains	42
Vehicles	48
Covers	50

JUICED 2: HOT IMPORT NIGHTS

LAST MAN STANDING CHALLENGE AND AN ASCARI KZ1

Select Cheats and Challenges from the DNA Lab menu and enter KNOX. Defeat the challenge to earn the Ascari KZ1.

SPECIAL CHALLENGE AND AN AUDI TT 1.8 QUATTRO

Select Cheats and Challenges from the DNA Lab menu and enter YTHZ. Defeat the challenge to earn the Audi TT 1.8 Quattro.

SPECIAL CHALLENGE AND A BMW Z4

Select Cheats and Challenges from the DNA Lab menu and enter GVDL. Defeat the challenge to earn the BMW Z4.

SPECIAL CHALLENGE AND A HOLDEN MONARO

Select Cheats and Challenges from the DNA Lab menu and enter RBSG. Defeat the challenge to earn the Holden Monaro.

SPECIAL CHALLENGE AND A HYUNDAI COUPE 2.7 V6

Select Cheats and Challenges from the DNA Lab menu and enter BSLU. Defeat the challenge to earn the Hyundai Coupe 2.7 V6.

SPECIAL CHALLENGE AND AN INFINITY G35

Select Cheats and Challenges from the DNA Lab menu and enter MRHC. Defeat the challenge to earn the Infinity G35.

SPECIAL CHALLENGE AND AN INFINITY RED G35

Select Cheats and Challenges from the DNA Lab menu and enter MNCH. Defeat the challenge to earn the Infinity G35.

SPECIAL CHALLENGE AND A KOENIGSEGG CCX

Select Cheats and Challenges from the DNA Lab menu and enter KDTR. Defeat the challenge to earn the Koenigsegg CCX.

SPECIAL CHALLENGE AND A MITSUBISHI PROTOTYPE X

Select Cheats and Challenges from the DNA Lab menu and enter DOPX. Defeat the challenge to earn the Mitsubishi Prototype X.

SPECIAL CHALLENGE AND A NISSAN 350Z

Select Cheats and Challenges from the DNA Lab menu and enter PRGN. Defeat the challenge to earn the Nissan 350Z.

SPECIAL CHALLENGE AND A NISSAN SKYLINE R34 GT-R

Select Cheats and Challenges from the DNA Lab menu and enter JWRS. Defeat the challenge to earn the Nissan Skyline R34 GT-R.

SPECIAL CHALLENGE AND A SALEEN S7

Select Cheats and Challenges from the DNA Lab menu and enter WIKF. Defeat the challenge to earn the Saleen S7.

SPECIAL CHALLENGE AND A SEAT LEON CUPRA R

Select Cheats and Challenges from the DNA Lab menu and enter FAMQ. Defeat the challenge to earn the Seat Leon Cupra R.

KINGDOM HEARTS: BIRTH BY SLEEP

FINAL EPISODE

Find all of the Xehanort Reports and complete all three stories.

TRINITY ARCHIVES

Complete the story with any character.

TRINITY ARCHIVES TROPHY LIST

TROPHY	UNLOCKED BY[EL]
Power Walker	Take 99,999 steps.
Keyslinger	Defeat 9,999 Unversed.
Clockworks	Accumulate 80 hours or more of gameplay.
Arena Sweeper	Complete all arena matches.
Dairy Devotee	Activate Frozen Fortune 30 times.
In the Munny	Earn 33,333 munny.
One Down	Complete the story with any character.
Trinity	Complete all stories in at least Proud Mode.

LEGO BATMAN

BATCAVE CODES

Using the computer in the Batcave, select Enter Code and enter the following codes:

CHARACTERS

CHARACTER	CODE	CHARACTER	CODE
Alfred	ZAQ637	Penguin Goon	NKA238
Batgirl	JKR331	Penguin Henchman	BJH782
Bruce Wayne	BDJ327	Penguin Minion	KJP748
Catwoman (Classic)	M1AAWW	Poison Ivy Goon	GTB899
Clown Goon	HJK327	Police Marksman	HKG984
Commissioner Gordon	DDP967	Police Officer	JRY983
Fishmonger	HGY748	Riddler Goon	CRY928
Freeze Girl	XVK541	Riddler Henchman	XEU824
Joker Goon	UTF782	S.W.A.T.	HTF114
Joker Henchman	YUN924	Sailor	NAV592
Mad Hatter	JCA283	Scientist	JFL786
Man-Bat	NYU942	Security Guard	PLB946
Military Policeman	MKL382	The Joker (Tropical)	CCB199
Nightwing	MVY759	Yeti	NJL412
		Zoo Sweeper	DWR243

VEHICLES

VEHICLE	CODE
Bat-Tank	KNTT4B
Bruce Wayne's Private Jet	LEA664
Catwoman's Motorcycle	HPL826
Garbage Truck	DUS483
Goon Helicopter	GCH328
Harbor Helicopter	CHP735
Harley Quinn's Hammer Truck	RDT637
Mad Hatter's Glider	HS000W
Mad Hatter's Steamboat	M4DM4N
Mr. Freeze's Iceberg	ICYICE
The Joker's Van	JUK657

VEHICLE	CODE
Mr. Freeze's Kart	BCT229
Penguin Goon Submarine	BTN248
Police Bike	LJP234
Police Boat	PLC999
Police Car	KJL832
Police Helicopter	CWR732
Police Van	MAC788
Police Watercraft	VJD328
Riddler's Jet	HAHAHA
Robin's Submarine	TTF453
Two-Face's Armored Truck	EFE933

CHEATS

CHEAT	CODE
Always Score Multiply	9LRGNB
Fast Batarangs	JRBDCB
Fast Walk	ZOLM6N
Flame Batarang	D8NYWH
Freeze Batarang	XPN4NG
Extra Hearts	ML3KHP
Fast Build	EVG26J
Immune to Freeze	JXUDY6
Invincibility	WYD5CP
Minikit Detector	ZXGH9J

CHEAT	CODE
More Batarang Targets	XWP645
Piece Detector	KHJ554
Power Brick Detector	MMN786
Regenerate Hearts	HJH7HJ
Score x2	N4NR3E
Score x4	CX9MAT
Score x6	MLVNF2
Score x8	WCCDB9
Score x10	18HW07

LEGO INDIANA JONES: THE ORIGINAL ADVENTURES

CHARACTERS

Approach the blackboard in the Classsroom and enter the following codes.

CHARACTER	CODE	CHARACTER	CODE
Bandit	12N68W	Enemy Soldier (Desert)	4NSU7Q
Bandit Swordsman	1MK4RT	Fedora	V75YSP
Barranca	04EM94	First Mate	0GIN24
Bazooka Trooper (Crusade)	MK83R7	Grail Knight	NE6THI
Bazooka Trooper (Raiders)	S93Y5R	Hovitos Tribesman	HOV1SS
Belloq	CHN3YU	Indiana Jones (Desert Disguise)	4J8S4M
Belloq (Jungle)	TDR197	Indiana Jones (Officer)	VJ850S
Belloq (Robes)	VEO29L	Jungle Guide	24PF34
British Commander	B73EUA	Kao Kan	WMO46L
British Officer	VJ5TI9	Kazim	NRH23J
British Soldier	DJ5I2W	Kazim (Desert)	3M29TJ
Captain Katanga	VJ3TT3	Lao Che	2NK479
Chatter Lal	ENW936	Maharajah	NFK5N2
Chatter Lal (Thuggee)	CNH4RY	Major Toht	13NS01
Chen	3NK48T	Masked Bandit	N48SFO
Colonel Dietrich	2K9RKS	Mola Ram	FJUR31
Colonel Vogel	8EAL4H	Monkey Man	3RF6YJ
Dancing Girl	C7EJ21	Pankot Assassin	2NKT72
Donovan	3NFTU8	Pankot Guard	VN28RH
Elsa (Desert)	JSNRT9	Sherpa Brawler	VJ37WJ
Elsa (Officer)	VMJ5US	Sherpa Gunner	ND762W
Enemy Boxer	8246RB	Slave Child	OE3ENW
Enemy Butler	VJ48W3	Thuggee	VM683E
Enemy Guard	VJ7R51	Thuggee Acolyte	T2R3F9
Enemy Guard (Mountains)	YR47WM	Thuggee Slave Driver	VBS7GW
Enemy Officer	572E61	Village Dignitary	KD48TN
Enemy Officer (Desert)	2MK450	Village Elder	4682E1
Enemy Pilot	B84ELP	Willie (Dinner Suit)	VK93R7
Enemy Radio Operator	1MF94R	Willie (Pajamas)	MEN4IP
		Wu Han	3NSLT8

EXTRAS

Approach the blackboard in the Classsroom and enter the following codes. Some cheats need to be enabled by selecting Extras from the pause menu.

CHEAT	CODE
Artifact Detector	VIKED7
Beep Beep	VNF59Q
Character Treasure	VIES2R
Disarm Enemies	VKRNS9
Disguises	4ID1N6
Fast Build	V83SLO
Fast Dig	378RS6
Fast Fix	FJ59WS
Fertilizer	B1GW1F
Ice Rink	33GM7J
Parcel Detector	VUT673
Pao Treasure	WWQ1SA

CHEAT	CODE
Regenerate Hearts	MDLP69
Secret Characters	3X44AA
Silhouettes	3HE85H
Super Scream	VN3R7S
Super Slap	OP1TA5
Treasure Magnet	H86LA2
Treasure x10	VI3PS8
Treasure x2	VM4TS9
Treasure x4	VLWEN3
Treasure x6	V84RYS
Treasure x8	A72E1M

LEGO STAR WARS II: THE ORIGINAL TRILOGY

BEACH TROOPER

At Mos Eisley Canteena, select Enter Code and enter UCK868. You still need to select Characters and purchase this character for 20,000 studs.

BEN KENOBI (GHOST)

At Mos Eisley Canteena, select Enter Code and enter BEN917. You still need to select Characters and purchase this character for 1,100,000 studs.

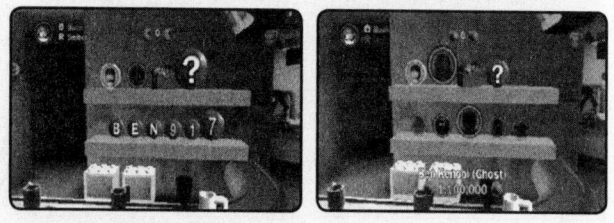

BESPIN GUARD

At Mos Eisley Canteena, select Enter Code and enter VHY832. You still need to select Characters and purchase this character for 15,000 studs.

BIB FORTUNA

At Mos Eisley Canteena, select Enter Code and enter WTY721. You still need to select Characters and purchase this character for 16,000 studs.

BOBA FETT

At Mos Eisley Canteena, select Enter Code and enter HLP221. You still need to select Characters and purchase this character for 175,000 studs.

DEATH STAR TROOPER

At Mos Eisley Canteena, select Enter Code and enter BNC332. You still need to select Characters and purchase this character for 19,000 studs.

EWOK

At Mos Eisley Canteena, select Enter Code and enter TTT289. You still need to select Characters and purchase this character for 34,000 studs.

GAMORREAN GUARD

At Mos Eisley Canteena, select Enter Code and enter YZF999. You still need to select Characters and purchase this character for 40,000 studs.

GONK DROID

At Mos Eisley Canteena, select Enter Code and enter NFX582. You still need to select Characters and purchase this character for 1,550 studs.

GRAND MOFF TARKIN

At Mos Eisley Canteena, select Enter Code and enter SMG219. You still need to select Characters and purchase this character for 38,000 studs.

GREEDO

At Mos Eisley Canteena, select Enter Code and enter NAH118. You still need to select Characters and purchase this character for 60,000 studs.

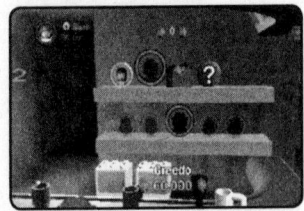

HAN SOLO (HOOD)

At Mos Eisley Canteena, select Enter Code and enter YWM840. You still need to select Characters and purchase this character for 20,000 studs.

IG-88

At Mos Eisley Canteena, select Enter Code and enter NXL973. You still need to select Characters and purchase this character for 30,000 studs.

IMPERIAL GUARD

At Mos Eisley Canteena, select Enter Code and enter MMM111. You still need to select Characters and purchase this character for 45,000 studs.

IMPERIAL OFFICER

At Mos Eisley Canteena, select Enter Code and enter BBV889. You still need to select Characters and purchase this character for 28,000 studs.

IMPERIAL SHUTTLE PILOT

At Mos Eisley Canteena, select Enter Code and enter VAP664. You still need to select Characters and purchase this character for 29,000 studs.

HAN SOLO (HOOD)

At Mos Eisley Canteena, select Enter Code and enter YWM840. You still need to select Characters and purchase this character for 20,000 studs.

IG-88

At Mos Eisley Canteena, select Enter Code and enter NXL973. You still need to select Characters and purchase this character for 30,000 studs.

IMPERIAL GUARD

At Mos Eisley Canteena, select Enter Code and enter MMM111. You still need to select Characters and purchase this character for 45,000 studs.

IMPERIAL OFFICER

At Mos Eisley Canteena, select Enter Code and enter BBV889. You still need to select Characters and purchase this character for 28,000 studs.

IMPERIAL SHUTTLE PILOT

At Mos Eisley Canteena, select Enter Code and enter VAP664. You still need to select Characters and purchase this character for 29,000 studs.

IMPERIAL SPY

At Mos Eisley Canteena, select Enter Code and enter CVT125. You still need to select Characters and purchase this character for 13,500 studs.

JAWA

At Mos Eisley Canteena, select Enter Code and enter JAW499. You still need to select Characters and purchase this character for 24,000 studs.

LOBOT

At Mos Eisley Canteena, select Enter Code and enter UUB319. You still need to select Characters and purchase this character for 11,000 studs.

PALACE GUARD

At Mos Eisley Canteena, select Enter Code and enter SGE549. You still need to select Characters and purchase this character for 14,000 studs.

REBEL PILOT

At Mos Eisley Canteena, select Enter Code and enter CYG336. You still need to select Characters and purchase this character for 15,000 studs.

REBEL TROOPER (HOTH)

At Mos Eisley Canteena, select Enter Code and enter EKU849. You still need to select Characters and purchase this character for 16,000 studs.

SANDTROOPER

At Mos Eisley Canteena, select Enter Code and enter YDV451. You still need to select Characters and purchase this character for 14,000 studs.

SKIFF GUARD

At Mos Eisley Canteena, select Enter Code and enter GBU888. You still need to select Characters and purchase this character for 12,000 studs.

SNOWTROOPER

At Mos Eisley Canteena, select Enter Code and enter NYU989. You still need to select Characters and purchase this character for 16,000 studs.

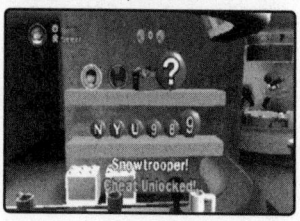

STORMTROOPER

At Mos Eisley Canteena, select Enter Code and enter PTR345. You still need to select Characters and purchase this character for 10,000 studs.

THE EMPEROR

At Mos Eisley Canteena, select Enter Code and enter HHY382. You still need to select Characters and purchase this character for 275,000 studs.

TIE FIGHTER

At Mos Eisley Canteena, select Enter Code and enter HDY739. You still need to select Characters and purchase this character for 60,000 studs.

TIE FIGHTER PILOT

At Mos Eisley Canteena, select Enter Code and enter NNZ316. You still need to select Characters and purchase this character for 21,000 studs.

TIE INTERCEPTOR

At Mos Eisley Canteena, select Enter Code and enter QYA828. You still need to select Characters and purchase this character for 40,000 studs.

TUSKEN RAIDER

At Mos Eisley Canteena, select Enter Code and enter PEJ821. You still need to select Characters and purchase this character for 23,000 studs.

UGNAUGHT

At Mos Eisley Canteena, select Enter Code and enter UGN694. You still need to select Characters and purchase this character for 36,000 studs.

MARVEL SUPER HERO SQUAD

IRON MAN, BONUS COSTUME "WAR MACHINE"

Select Enter Code from the Options and enter 111111.

HULK, BONUS COSTUMES "GREY HULK" & "RED HULK"

Select Enter Code from the Options and enter 222222.

WOLVERINE, BONUS COSTUMES "WOLVERINE (BROWN COSTUME)" & "FERAL WOLVERINE"

Select Enter Code from the Options and enter 333333.

THOR, BONUS COSTUMES "THOR (CHAIN ARMOR)" & "LOKI-THOR"

Select Enter Code from the Options and enter 444444.

SILVER SURFER, BONUS COSTUMES "ANTI-SURFER" & "GOLD SURFER"

Select Enter Code from the Options and enter 555555.

FALCON, BONUS COSTUME "ULTIMATE FALCON"

Select Enter Code from the Options and enter 666666.

DOCTOR DOOM, BONUS COSTUMES "ULTIMATE DOCTOR DOOM" & "PROFESSOR DOOM"

Select Enter Code from the Options and enter 999999.

CAPTAIN AMERICA, BONUS COSTUME "ULTIMATE CAPTAIN AMERICA COSTUME"

Select Enter Code from the Options and enter 177674

A.I.M. AGENT, BONUS COSTUME "BLUE SUIT A.I.M."

Select Enter Code from the Options and enter 246246

CHEAT "SUPER KNOCKBACK"

Select Enter Code from the Options and enter 777777.

CHEAT "NO BLOCK MODE"

Select Enter Code from the Options and enter 888888.

CHEAT "GROUNDED"

Select Enter Code from the Options and enter 476863

CHEAT "ONE-HIT TAKEDOWN"

Select Enter Code from the Options and enter 663448

CHEAT "INFINITE SHARD DURATION"

Select Enter Code from the Options and enter 742737

CHEAT "THROWN OBJECT TAKEDOWN"

Select Enter Code from the Options and enter 847936

MARVEL ULTIMATE ALLIANCE

UNLOCK ALL SKINS

At the Team menu, press Up, Down, Left, Right, Left, Right, Start.

UNLOCKS ALL HERO POWERS

At the Team menu, press Left, Right, Up, Down, Up, Down, Start.

ALL HEROES TO LEVEL 99

At the Team menu, press Up, Left, Up, Left, Down, Right, Down, Right, Start.

UNLOCK ALL HEROES

At the Team menu, press Up, Up, Down, Down, Left, Left, Left, Start.

UNLOCK DAREDEVIL

At the Team menu, press Left, Left, Right, Right, Up, Down, Up, Down, Start.

UNLOCK SILVER SURFER

At the Team menu, press Down, Left, Left, Up, Right, Up, Down, Left, Start.

GOD MODE

During gameplay, press Up, Down, Up, Down, Up, Left, Down, Right, Start.

TOUCH OF DEATH

During gameplay, press Left, Right, Down, Down, Right, Left, Start.

SUPER SPEED

During gameplay, press Up, Left, Up, Right, Down, Right, Start.

FILL MOMENTUM

During gameplay, press Left, Right, Right, Left, Up, Down, Down, Up, Start.

UNLOCK ALL COMICS

At the Review menu, press Left, Right, Right, Left, Up, Up, Right, Start.

UNLOCK ALL CONCEPT ART

At the Review menu, press Down, Down, Down, Right, Right, Left, Down, Start.

UNLOCK ALL CINEMATICS

At the Review menu, press Up, Left, Left, Up, Right, Right, Up, Start.

UNLOCK ALL LOAD SCREENS

At the Review menu, press Up, Down, Right, Left, Up, Up Down, Start.

UNLOCK ALL COURSES

At the Comic Missions menu, press Up, Right, Left, Down, Up, Right, Left, Down, Start.

MARVEL ULTIMATE ALLIANCE 2

GOD MODE

At any point during a game, press Up, Up, Down, Down, Left, Right, Down.

GIVE MONEY

At the Team Select or Hero Details screen press Up, Up, Down, Down, Up, Up, Up, Down.

UNLOCK ALL POWERS

At the Team Select or Hero Details screen press Up, Up, Down, Down, Left, Right, Right, Left.

ADVANCE ALL CHARACTERS TO L99

At the Hero Details screen press Down, Up, Left, Up, Right, Up, Left, Down.

UNLOCK ALL BONUS MISSIONS

While using the Bonus Mission Simulator, press Up, Right, Down, Left, Left, Right, Up, Up.

ADD 1 CHARACTER LEVEL

During a game, press Down, Up, Right, Up, Right, Up, Right, Down.

ADD 10 CHARACTER LEVELS

During a game, press Down, Up, Left, Up, Left, Up, Left, Down.

MLB 08: THE SHOW

CLASSIC FREE AGENTS AT THE PLAYER MOVEMENT MENU

At the main menu, press Left, Right, Up, Left, Right, Up, Right, Down.

SILVER ERA AND GOLDEN ERA TEAMS

At the main menu, press Right, Up, Right, Down, Down, Left, Up, Down.

BIG BALL

Pause the game and press Right, Down, Up, Left, Right, Left, Down, Up.

BIG HEAD MODE

Pause the game and press Right, Left, Down, Up, Left, Up, Down, Left.

SMALL HEAD MODE

Pause the game and press Left, Right, Down, Up, Right, Left, Down, Left.

N+

25 EXTRA LEVELS

At the main menu, hold L + R and press ✖, ⬤, ✖, ⬤, ✖, ✖, ⬤.

NARUTO SHIPPUDEN: ULTIMATE NINJA HEROES 3

FIGURES

At the Tree of Mettle, select Enter Password and enter the following passwords:

FIGURE	PASSWORD
Gods and Angels	Fire, Sheep, Ox, Tiger
Inheritor of the Will	Water, Dog, Snake, Ox
One Who Lurks in Darkness	Thunder, Dog, Tiger, Boar
Rivals	Earth, Sheep, Boar, Dog
Team Asuma	Fire, Dog, Rabbit, Tiger
Team Guy	Water, Dog, Rat, Rooster
Team Kurenai	Thunder, Snake, Dragon, Monkey
The Hokage's Office	Wind, Rabbit, Dragon, Ox
The Innocent Maiden	Water, Snake, Dragon, Ox
The Three Sand Siblings	Earth, Rooster, Ox, Snake

JUTSU

At the Tree of Mettle, select Enter Password and enter the following passwords:

NINJUTSU	PASSWORD
100m Punch	Thunder, Rat, Snake, Horse
Assault Blade	Wind, Rat, Rabbit, Ox
Bring Down the House Jutsu	Thunder, Sheep, Ox, Rooster
Cherry Blossom Clash	Fire, Monkey, Boar, Rabbit
Dead Soul Jutsu	Thunder, Monkey, Dog, Ox
Detonation Dispersion	Wind, Dragon, Horse, Rat
Dynamic Entry	Fire, Rooster, Rabbit, Boar
Feather Illusion Jutsu	Water, Dragon, Boar, Dog
Fire Style: Burning Ash	Fire, Rat, Rabbit, Monkey
Fire Style: Dragon Flame Bomb	Fire, Snake, Dragon, Rabbit
Fire Style: Fire Ball Jutsu	Fire, Dragon, Rat, Monkey
Fire Style: Yoruho'o	Fire, Horse, Rabbit, Sheep
Genjutsu: Haze	Wind, Dragon, Sheep, Rooster
Genjutsu: Madder Mist	Thunder, Rooster, Boar, Dog
Heaven Defending Kick	Earth, Rat, Boar, Monkey
Intensive Healing	Water, Rat, Tiger, Rat
Leaf Repeating Wind	Wind, Rooster, Ox, Tiger
Lightning Blade	Thunder, Monkey, Rooster, Snake
Lightning Style: Thunderbolt Flash	Thunder, Sheep, Ox, Dog
Slithering Snakes	Thunder, Tiger, Rooster, Dog
Summoning: Rashomon	Earth, Monkey, Boar, Rooster
Tunneling Fang	Wind, Dog, Boar, Horse
Water Style: Ripping Torrent	Water, Ox, Dog, Sheep
Water Style: Water Fang Bomb	Water, Horse, Rat, Ox
Weapon: Flash Kunai Ball	Fire, Sheep, Boar, Ox
Wind Style: Air Bullets	Wind, Ox, Boar, Rabbit

HOKAGE NARUTO WALLPAPER

At the Tree of Mettle, select Enter Password and enter Fire, Ox, Rabbit, Horse.

NBA 2K10

ABA BALL

Select Codes from the Options menu. Then select Enter Code and enter payrespect.

NBA 2K TEAM

Select Codes from the Options menu. Then select Enter Code and enter nba2k.

2K CHINA TEAM

Select Codes from the Options menu. Then select Enter Code and enter 2kchina.

2K SPORTS TEAM

Select Codes from the Options menu. Then select Enter Code and enter 2ksports.

VISUAL CONCEPTS TEAM

Select Codes from the Options menu. Then select Enter Code and enter vcteam.

2010 ALL-STAR UNIFORMS

Select Codes from the Options menu. Then select Enter Code and enter otnresla.

HARDWOOD CLASSIC UNIFORMS

Select Codes from the Options menu. Then select Enter Code and enter wasshcicsl. This code gives Hardwood Classic Uniforms for the Cavaliers, Jazz, Magic, Raptors, timberwolves, Trail Blazers, and Warriors.

LATIN NIGHTS UNIFORMS

Select Codes from the Options menu. Then select Enter Code and enter aihinntslgt. This code gives Latin Nights jerseys for Bulls, Heat, Knicks, Lakers, Mavericks, Rockets, Spurs, and Suns.

NBA GREEN UNIFORMS

Select Codes from the Options menu. Then select Enter Code and enter nreogge. This code gives green uniforms for the Bobcats, Bulls, and Nuggets.

SECONDARY ROAD UNIFORMS

Select Codes from the Options menu. Then select Enter Code and enter eydonscar. This code gives Second Road Uniforms for the Grizzlies, Hawks, Mavericks, and Rockets.

ST. PATRICK'S DAY UNIFORMS

Select Codes from the Options menu. Then select Enter Code and enter riiasgerh. This code gives St. Patrick's Day jerseys for the Bulls, Celtics, Knicks, and Raptors.

BOBCATS RACING UNIFORM

Select Codes from the Options menu. Then select Enter Code and enter agsntrccai.

CAVALIERS CAVFANATICS UNIFORM

Select Codes from the Options menu. Then select Enter Code and enter aifnaatccv.

HORNETS MARDI GRAS UNIFORM

Select Codes from the Options menu. Then select Enter Code and enter asrdirmga.

TRAIL BLAZERS RIP CITY UNIFORM

Select Codes from the Options menu. Then select Enter Code and enter ycprtii.

NBA 2K11

2K CHINA TEAM

In Features, select Codes from the Extras menu. Choose Enter Code and enter 2kchina.

2K SPORTS TEAM

In Features, select Codes from the Extras menu. Choose Enter Code and enter 2Ksports.

NBA 2K TEAM

In Features, select Codes from the Extras menu. Choose Enter Code and enter nba2k.

VC TEAM

In Features, select Codes from the Extras menu. Choose Enter Code and enter vcteam.

ABA BALL

In Features, select Codes from the Extras menu. Choose Enter Code and enter payrespect.

NBA 2K12

ABA BALL

Select Cheats from the Features menu and enter payrespect.

BOBCATS NASCAR RACING UNIFORM

Select Cheats from the Features menu and enter agsntrccai.

CAVS CAVFANATIC UNIFORM

Select Cheats from the Features menu and enter aifnaatccv.

HARDWOOD CLASSICS UNIFORMS

Select Cheats from the Features menu and enter Wasshcicsl. This unlocks uniforms for the Cavaliers, Jazz, Magic, Raptors, Timberwolves, Trail Blazers, and Warriors.

MARDI GRAS UNIFORMS

Select Cheats from the Features menu and enter asrdirmga. This unlocks uniforms for the Bulls, Celtics, Knicks, and Raptors.

SECONDARY ROAD UNIFORMS

Select Cheats from the Features menu and enter eydonscar. This unlocks uniforms for the Grizzlies, Hawks, Mavs, and Rockets.

ST PATRICK'S DAY UNIFORMS

Select Cheats from the Features menu and enter riiasgerh. This unlocks uniforms for the Bulls, Celtics, Knicks, and Raptors.

TRAIL BLAZERS RIP CITY UNIFORM

Select Cheats from the Features menu and enter ycprtii.

NBA LIVE 10

CHARLOTTE BOBCATS' 2009/2010 RACE DAY ALTERNATE JERSEYS

Select Options from My NBA Live and go to Select Codes. Enter ceobdabacarstcy.

NEW ORLEANS HORNETS' 2009/2010 MARDI GRAS ALTERNATE JERSEYS

Select Options from My NBA Live and go to Select Codes. Enter nishrag1rosmad0.

ALTERNATE JERSEYS

Select Options from My NBA Live and go to Select Codes. Enter ndnba1rooaesdc0. This unlocks alternate jerseys for Atlanta Hawks, Dallas Mavericks, Houston Rockets, and Memphis Grizzlies.

MORE HARDWOOD CLASSICS NIGHTS JERSEYS

Select Options from My NBA Live and go to Select Codes. Enter hdogdrawhoticns. This unlocks Hardwood Classics Nights jerseys for Cleveland Cavaliers, Golden State Warriors, Minnesota Timberwolves, Orlando Magic, Philadelphia 76ers.

ADIDAS EQUATIONS

Select Options from My NBA Live and go to Select Codes. Enter adaodqauieints1.

ADIDAS TS CREATORS WITH ANKLE BRACES

Select Options from My NBA Live and go to Select Codes. Enter atciadsstsdhecf.

ADIDAS TS SUPERNATURAL COMMANDERS

Select Options from My NBA Live and go to Select Codes. Enter andsicdsmatdnsr.

ADIDAS TS SUPERNATURAL CREATORS

Select Options from My NBA Live and go to Select Codes. Enter ard8siscdnatstr.

AIR MAX LEBRON VII

Select Options from My NBA Live and go to Select Codes. Enter ere1nbvlaoeknii, 2ovnaebnkrielei, 3rioabeneikenvl, ri4boenanekilve, ivl5brieekaeonn, or n6ieirvalkeeobn.

KOBE V

Select Options from My NBA Live and go to Select Codes. Enter ovze1bimenkoko0, m0kveokoiebozn2, eev0nbimokk3ozo, or bmo4inozeeo0kvk.

JORDAN CP3 IIIS

Select Options from My NBA Live and go to Select Codes. Enter iaporcdian3ejis.

JORDAN MELO M6S

Select Options from My NBA Live and go to Select Codes. Enter emlarmeoo6ajdsn.

JORDAN SIXTY PLUSES

Select Options from My NBA Live and go to Select Codes. Enter aondsuilyjrspxt.

NIKE HUARACHE LEGIONS

Select Options from My NBA Live and go to Select Codes. Enter aoieuchrahelgn.

NIKE KD 2S

Select Options from My NBA Live and go to Select Codes. Enter kk2tesaosepinrd.

NIKE ZOOM FLIP'NS

Select Options from My NBA Live and go to Select Codes. Enter epfnozaeminolki.

NEED FOR SPEED CARBON: OWN THE CITY

UNLOCK EVERYTHING

At the start menu, press ✖, ✖, Right, Left, ⬤, Up, Down.

JET CAR

At the start menu, press Up, Down, Left, **R1**, **L1**, ⬤, ▲.

LAMBORGINI MERCIALAGO

At the start menu, press ✖, ✖, Up, Down, Left, Right, ⬤, ⬤.

TRANSFORMERS CAR

At the start menu, press ✖, ✖, ✖, ⬤, ▲, ▲, Up, Down.

NEOPETS PETPET ADVENTURE: THE WAND OF WISHING

START GAME WITH 5 CHOCOLATE TREATS

Enter treat4u as your Petpet's name. You can then rename name your character. The chocolate treats are shaped according to the character you chose.

VISION PHONE

Use your Vision Phone to enter the following:

EFFECT	PASSWORD	EFFECT	PASSWORD
Akahara Reisou	24932278	Miku's T. Leek Sabers	39395344
Akahara Reisou	24932279	Mr. Ekoeko Stick	55687362
Akahara Reisou	24932280	Ogi's Head	74612418
Alis Landale Poster	41325468	Pizza Shack D Box	89747981
Angry Marshmellow	32549410	Platinum Tiger	32549412
Art Javelin	72401990	Platinum Tiger	32549414
Blank Epoch	48168861	Platinum Tiger	32549411
Blank Epoch	48168862	Platinum Tiger	32549413
Bullet Lancer	32091120	Plug Suit Asuka	34336181
Clarita Visas	29888026	Plug Suit Asuka	34336182
Crutches	98443460	Plug Suit Rei	46211351
Edelweiss Figurine	54333358	Plug Suit Rei	46211352
Hanhei Tsunagin	41761771	Plug Suit Shinji	15644322
Hanhei Tsunagin	41761772	Puyo Pop Fever Gun	54186516
Hatsune Miku's Leek Wand	12344321	Puyo Pop Fists	11293398
Kansho Bayuka	46815464	Scouring Bubble	33286491
Longinus Lance	32143166	Sonic Knuckles	34819852
Lovely Feathers	72401991	Special Pizza Cutter	34162313
Lovely Feathers	72401992	Telltale Hearts	48168860
Magical Princess	55687361	The Rappy of Hope	54684698
Magical Princess	55687362	Toop Nasur	30495153
Maverick Rifle	53962481	Trauma Bandages	98443462
Miku Hatsune Dress	39395341	Trauma Bandages	98443464
Miku Hatsune Dress	39395342	Trauma Bandages	98443461
Miku's Leek Rifle	39395345	Trauma Bandages	98443463
Miku's Leek Saber	39395343	True Hash	41761770

POCKET POOL

ALL PICTURES AND VIDEOS

At the title screen, press L, R, L, L, R, R, L (x3), R (x3), L (x4), R (x4).

PRINNY: CAN I REALLY BE THE HERO?

START A NEW GAME WITH THE ALTERNATE STORYLINE

At the main menu, highlight New Game and press ▲, ■, ●, ▲, ■, ●, ✕.

ROCKET RACING

TRIGGER MODE

At the main menu or during a game, hold L and press Up, Down, Left, Right, ▲, release L.

TRIGGER MODE (REVERSED)

At the main menu or during a game, hold L and press Up, Down, Left, Right, ■, release L.

STICK MODE (DEFAULT)

At the main menu or during a game, hold L and press Up, Down, Left, Right, R, release L.

SECRET AGENT CLANK

ACTIVATE CHALICE OF POWER

Press Up, Up, Down, Down, Left, Right, Left, Right to regain health once per level.

THE SECRET SATURDAYS: BEASTS OF THE 5TH SUN

ALL LEVELS

Select Enter Secret Code from the Secrets menu and enter Zon, Zon, Zon, Zon.

UNLOCK AMAROK TO BE SCANNED IN LEVEL 2

Select Enter Secret Code from the Secrets menu and enter Fiskerton, Zak, Zon, Komodo.

UNLOCK BISHOPVILLE LIZARDMAN TO BE SCANNED IN LEVEL 3

Select Enter Secret Code from the Secrets menu and enter Komodo, Zon, Zak, Komodo.

UNLOCK NAGA TO BE SCANNED IN LEVEL 7

Select Enter Secret Code from the Secrets menu and enter Zak, Zak, Zon, Fiskerton.

UNLOCK RAKSHASA TO BE SCANNED IN LEVEL 8

Select Enter Secret Code from the Secrets menu and enter Zak, Komodo, Fiskerton, Fiskerton.

UNLOCK BILOKO TO BE SCANNED IN LEVEL 9

Select Enter Secret Code from the Secrets menu and enter Zon, Zak, Zon, Fiskerton.

SEGA GENESIS COLLECTION

Before using the following cheats, select the ABC Control option. This sets the controller to the following: ● is A, ✖ is B, ◉ is C.

ALTERED BEAST

OPTIONS MENU

At the title screen, hold ✖ and press Start.

LEVEL SELECT

After enabling the Options menu, select a level from the menu. At the title screen, hold ● and press Start.

BEAST SELECT

At the title screen, hold ● + ✖ + ◉ + Down/Left and then press Start

SOUND TEST

At the title screen, hold ● + ◉ + Up/Right and press Start.

COMIX ZONE

INVINCIBILITY

At the jukebox screen, press C on the following sounds:

3, 12, 17, 2, 2, 10, 2, 7, 7, 11

LEVEL SELECT

At the jukebox screen, press C on the following sounds:

14, 15, 18, 5, 13, 1, 3, 18, 15, 6

Press C on the desired level.

ECCO THE DOLPHIN

INVINCIBILITY

When the level name appears, hold ⏺ + Start until the level begins.

DEBUG MENU

Pause the game with Ecco facing the screen and press Right, ⊗,◉, ⊗,◉, Down,◉, Up.

INFINITE AIR

Enter LIFEFISH as a password

PASSWORDS

LEVEL	PASSWORD	LEVEL	PASSWORD
The Undercaves	WEFIDNMP	Deep City	DDXPQQLJ
The Vents	BQDPXJDS	City of Forever	MSDBRQLA
The Lagoon	JNSBRIKY	Jurassic Beach	IYCBUNLB
Ridge Water	NTSBZTKB	Pteranodon Pond	DMXEUNLI
Open Ocean	YWGTTJNI	Origin Beach	EGRIUNLB
Ice Zone	HZIFZBMF	Trilobite Circle	IELMUNLB
Hard Water	LRFJRQLI	Dark Water	RKEQUNLN
Cold Water	UYNFRQLC	City of Forever 2	HPQIGPLA
Island Zone	LYTIOQLZ	The Tube	JUMFKMLB
Deep Water	MNOPOQLR	The Machine	GXUBKMLF
The Marble	RJNTQQLZ	The Last Fight	TSONLMLU
The Library	RTGXQQLE		

FLICKY

ROUND SELECT

Begin a new game. Before the first round appears, hold ⏺ + ◉ + Up + Start. Press Up or Down to select a Round.

GAIN GROUND

LEVEL SELECT

At the Options screen, press ◉, ◉, ✖, ◉.

GOLDEN AXE

LEVEL SELECT

Select Arcade Mode. At the character select, hold Down/Left +✖ and press Start. Press Up or Down to select a level.

RISTAR

Select Passwords from the Options menu and enter the following:

LEVEL SELECT

ILOVEU

BOSS RUSH MODE

MUSEUM

TIME ATTACK MODE

DOFEEL

TOUGHER DIFFICULTY

SUPER

ONCHI MUSIC

MAGURO. Activate this from the Sound Test.

CLEARS PASSWORD

XXXXXX

GAME COPYRIGHT INFO

AGES

SONIC THE HEDGEHOG

LEVEL SELECT

At the title screen, press Up, Down, Left, Right. Hold ◉ and press Start.

SONIC THE HEDGEHOG 2

LEVEL SELECT

Select Sound Test from the options. Press C on the following sounds in order: 19, 65, 09, 17. At the title screen, hold ◉ and press Start.

VECTORMAN

DEBUG MODE

At the options screen, press ◉, ✖, ✖, ◉, Down, ◉, ✖, ✖, ◉.

REFILL LIFE

Pause the game and press ◉, ✖, Right, ◉, ◉, ◉, Down, ◉, ✖, Right, ◉.

VECTORMAN 2

LEVEL SELECT

Pause the game and press Up, Right, ●, ✕, ●, Down, Left, ●, Down.

EXTRA LIFE

Pause the game and press Right, Up, ✕, ●, Down, Up, ✕, Down, Up, ✕. Repeat for more lives.

FULL ENERGY

Pause the game and press ✕, ●, ✕, ●, Left, Up, Up.

NEW WEAPON

Pause the game and press ●, ●, Left, Left, Down, ●, Down. Repeat for more weapons.

THE SIMPSONS GAME

UNLIMITED POWER FOR ALL CHARACTERS

At the Extras menu, press ▲, Left, Right, ▲, ●, L.

ALL MOVIES

At the Extras menu, press ●, Left, ●, Right, ▲, R.

ALL CLICHÉS

At the Extras menu, press Left, ●, Right, ▲, Right, L.

A SPACE SHOOTER FOR TWO BUCKS!

INVINCIBILITY

At the credits screen, press Up, Up, Down, Down, Left, Right, Left, Right, ●, Start.

MAXIMUM CASH

At the credits screen, press Left, Right, Left, Right, +, Right, ▲, ▲, ●, Start.

DISABLE SHIP INERTIA

At the credits screen, press ▲, ▲, ▲, ▲, +, +, +, +, ●, Start.

FULL OVERDRIVE

At the credits screen, press Down, Left, Up, Right, ▲, ▲, +, +, ●, Start.

HIGH SPEED

At the credits screen, press ▲, +, ●, Left, Right, Left, Left, Up, ●, Start.

SLOW MOTION

At the credits screen, press +, ▲, ●, Right, Left, Right, Right, ●, ●, Start.

119

SPIDER-MAN: FRIEND OR FOE

NEW GOBLIN

At the stage complete screen, hold L + R and press ●, Down, ✖, Right, ◉, Up, ▲, Left.

STAR WARS: THE FORCE UNLEASHED

CHEATS

Once you have accessed the Rogue Shadow, select Enter Code from the Extras menu. Now you can enter the following codes:

CHEAT	CODE	CHEAT	CODE
Invincibility	CORTOSIS	Max Force Power Level	KATARN
Unlimited Force	VERGENCE	Max Combo Level	COUNTDOOKU
1,000,000 Force Points	SPEEDER	Amplified Lightsaber Damage	LIGHTSABER
All Force Powers	TYRANUS		

COSTUMES

Once you have accessed the Rogue Shadow, select Enter Code from the Extras menu. Now you can enter the following codes:

COSTUME	CODE	COSTUME	CODE
All Costumes	GRANDMOFF	Juno Eclipse	ECLIPSE
501st Legion	LEGION	Kento's Robe	WOOKIEE
Aayla Secura	AAYLA	Kleef	KLEEF
Admiral Ackbar	ITSATWAP	Lando Calrissian	SCOUNDREL
Anakin Skywalker	CHOSENONE	Luke Skywalker	T16WOMPRAT
Asajj Ventress	ACOLYTE	Luke Skywalker (Yavin)	YELLOWJCKT
Ceremonial Jedi Robes	DANTOOINE	Mace Windu	JEDIMASTER
Chop'aa Notimo	NOTIMO	Mara Jade	MARAJADE
Classic stormtrooper	TK421	Maris Brook	MARISBROOD
Count Dooku	SERENNO	Navy commando	STORMTROOP
Darth Desolous	PAUAN	Obi Wan Kenobi	BENKENOBI
Darth Maul	ZABRAK	Proxy	HOLOGRAM
Darth Phobos	HIDDENFEAR	Qui Gon Jinn	MAVERICK
Darth Vader	SITHLORD	Shaak Ti	TOGRUTA
Drexl Roosh	DREXLROOSH	Shadow trooper	INTHEDARK
Emperor Palpatine	PALPATINE	Sith Robes	HOLOCRON
General Rahm Kota	MANDALORE	Sith Stalker Armor	KORRIBAN
Han Solo	NERFHERDER	Twi'lek	SECURA
Heavy trooper	SHOCKTROOP		

STAR WARS: LETHAL ALLIANCE

ALL LEVELS

Select Create Profile from the Profiles menu and enter HANSOLO.

ALL LEVELS AND REFILL HEALTH WHEN DEPLETED

Select Create Profile from the Profiles menu and enter JD1MSTR.

REFILL HEALTH WHEN DEPLETED

Select Create Profile from the Profiles menu and enter BOBAF3T.

STRIKERS 1945 PLUS PORTABLE

XP-55 ASCENDER

At the random select, press Down, Up, Down, Up, Down, Down, Down, Down, Up.

SUPER MONKEY BALL ADVENTURE

ALL CARDS

At the mode select, press ■, ▲, ◉, ■, ▲, ◉, ■, ▲, ◉, ■, ▲, ◉.

THRILLVILLE: OFF THE RAILS

$50,000

During a game, press ■, ◉, ▲, ■, ◉, ▲, ✕. Repeat this code as much as desired.

ALL PARKS

During a game, press ■, ◉, ▲, ■, ◉, ▲, ■.

ALL RIDES

During a game, press ■, ◉, ▲, ■ ◉, ▲, ▲. Some rides still need to be researched.

COMPLETE MISSIONS

During a game, press ■, ◉, ▲, ■, ◉, ▲, ◉. Then, at the Missions menu, highlight a mission and press ◉ to complete that mission. Some missions have Bronze, Silver, and Gold objectives. For these missions the first press of ◉ earns the Bronze, the second earns the Silver, and the third earns the Gold.

TIGER WOODS PGA TOUR 09

UNLOCK PGA TOUR EVENTS

Enter BEATIT as a password.

$1,000,000

Enter JACKPOT as a password.

UNLOCK ALL CLOTHING AND EQUIPMENT

Enter SHOP2DROP as a password.

MAX SKILL POINTS AND ALL CLOTHING AND EQUIPMENT

Enter IAMRUBBISH as a password.

UNLOCK ALL COVER STORIES

Enter HEADLINER as a password.

TOY STORY 2: BUZZ LIGHTYEAR TO THE RESCUE!

LEVEL SELECT

At the Options menu, press Right, Left, ●, ▲, ▲.

ALL LEVELS

At the title screen, press Up (x4), Down, Down, Up, Up, Down (x3).

DEBUG MODE

At the title screen, press ✖, ●, ■.

TOY STORY 3

BUZZ USES LASER IN ALL STORY LEVELS

Select Cheat Codes from the Bonus menu and enter BLASER. Activate the cheat from the pause menu.

WOODY'S BANDIT OUTFIT

Select Cheat Codes from the Bonus menu and enter BANDIT. Activate the cheat from the pause menu.

TOY ALIENS WEAR 3D GLASSES

Select Cheat Codes from the Bonus menu and enter 3DGLAS. Activate the cheat from the pause menu.

OLD MOVIE EFFECT

Select Cheat Codes from the Bonus menu and enter OLDMOV. Activate the cheat from the pause menu.

VALKYRIA CHRONICLES II

TANK STICKERS

Enter the following codes in Extra Mode for the desired effect.

STICKER	CODE	STICKER	CODE
Alicia Gunther	K1C7XKLJMXUHRD8S	Isara Gunther and Isara's Dream	37LRK5D214VQVFYH
Blitz Logo	VWUYNJQ8HGSVXR7J	Prince Maximilian and Imperial Flag	H73G4L9GLJR1CHJP
Edy Nelson	R5PT1MXEY3BW8VBE	Selvaria	53K8FKGP1GHQ4SBN
Edy's Squad	CR6BG1A9LYQKB6WJ	Sonic the Hedgehog	CUP34ASEZ9WDKBYV
SEGA Logo	6RK45S59F7U2JLTD	Super Monkey Ball	7JMNHZ83TGH7XFKT
Skies of Arcadia	WVZLPTYXURS1Q8TV	Yakuza	QAKVXZTALF4TU7SK
Crazy Taxi	38WV17PK45TYAF8V	Vanquish Tank	BUNLT4EXDS74QRCR
Faldio	GWNU95RSETW1VGNQ		
Gallian Military	TXU14EUV74PCR3TE		

CHARACTERS

Enter the following codes in Extra Mode for the desired effect.

CHARACTER	CODE	CHARACTER	CODE
Alicia Gunther	KBAFLFHICAJTKMIY	Mintz	CKRJWNSXTYMNGZRT
Edy's Detachment	TKBHCNBERHRKJNFG	Selvaria	KSNEGA56LPY7CTQ9
Julius Kroze	AMNKZKYTKNBNKYMT	Support-class Aliasse, Lancer-class Cosette and Armor-type Zeri	PZRJQM7SK4HPXTYM
Lamar/Ramal	LITSGAAMEORFRCRQ		
Landzaat Farudio	KNWRJRGSMLASTNSQ		
Maximillian	KBFHZRJTKMKSKNKP		

VIRTUA TENNIS 3

ALL COURTS

At the Game Mode screen, press Up, Up, Down, Down, Left, Right, Left, Right.

ALL GEAR

At the Game Mode screen, press Left, Right, ⊙, Left, Right, ⊙, Up, Down.

KING & DUKE

At the Game Mode screen, press Up, Up, Down, Down, Left, Right, L, R.

WALL-E

KILL ALL

Select Cheats and then Secret Codes. Enter BOTOFWAR.

UNDETECTED BY ENEMIES

Select Cheats and then Secret Codes. Enter STEALTHARMOR.

LASERS CHANGE COLORS

Select Cheats and then Secret Codes. Enter RAINBOWLAZER.

CUBES ARE EXPLOSIVE

Select Cheats and then Secret Codes. Enter EXPLOSIVEWORLD.

LIGHTEN DARK AREAS

Select Cheats and then Secret Codes. Enter GLOWINTHEDARK.

GOGGLES

Select Cheats and then Secret Codes. Enter BOTOFMYSTERY.

GOLD TRACKS

Select Cheats and then Secret Codes. Enter GOLDENTRACKS.

WHAT DID I DO TO DESERVE THIS, MY LORD!? 2

WHAT DID I DO TO DESERVE THIS, MY LORD!?

At the title screen, press L, R, L, R, L, R, L, R, L, R to play the first What Did I Do to Deserve This, My Lord!?

WHAT DID I NOT DO TO DESERVE THIS, MY LORD!?

After entering the above code and the game loads, enter the same code again at the title screen. This is the Hard Mode of What Did I Do to Deserve This, My Lord!?.

WORLD CHAMPIONSHIP POKER 2:FEATURING HOWARD LEDERER

SKIP WEEK AND MONEY CHEATS

At the career world map, hold R. Hold L and release R. Hold Up and release L. Hold L and release Up. Hold R and release L. While still holding R, press Up/Down to skip weeks and Right/Left for money.

WTF: WORK TIME FUN

$20 ON CHRISTMAS

Play on December 25th to receive $20 by e-mail.

$30 ON NEW YEAR'S DAY

Play on January 1st to receive $30 by e-mail.

$50 FOR BIRTHDAY

Play on your birthday to receive $50 by e-mail.

WWE ALL STARS

UNLOCK EVERYTHING

At the main menu, press Left, Right, Left, Down, Up, Left, Right, Up.

STEVE AUSTIN AND CM PUNK ATTIRES

At the main menu, press Left, Left, Right, Right, Up, Down, Up, Down.

RANDY ORTON AND JAKE ROBERTS ATTIRES

At the main menu, press Up, Down, Left, Right, Up, Up, Down, Down.

JOHN MORRISON AND RANDY SAVAGE ATTIRES

At the main menu, press Down, Left, Up, Right, Right, Up, Left, Down.

WWE SMACKDOWN VS. RAW 2010

THE ROCK

Select Cheat Codes from the Options and enter The Great One.

VINCE'S OFFICE AND DIRT SHEET FOR BACKSTAGE BRAWL

Select Cheat Codes from the Options menu and enter BonusBrawl.

HBK/SHAWN MICHAEL'S ALTERNATE COSTUME

Select Cheat Codes from the Options menu and enter Bow Down.

JOHN CENA'S ALTERNATE COSTUME

Select Cheat Codes from the Options menu and enter CENATION.

RANDY ORTON'S ALTERNATE COSTUME

Select Cheat Codes from the Options menu and enter ViperRKO.

SANTINO MARELLA'S ALTERNATE COSTUME

Select Cheat Codes from the Options menu and enter Milan Miracle.

TRIPLE H'S ALTERNATE COSTUME

Select Cheat Codes from the Options menu and enter Suck IT!.

WWE SMACKDOWN VS. RAW 2011

JOHN CENA (ENTRANCE/CIVILIAN)

In My WWE, select Cheat Codes from the Options and enter SLURPEE.

ALL OF RANDY ORTON'S COSTUMES

In My WWE, select Cheat Codes from the Options and enter apexpredator.

TRIBUTE TO THE TROOPS ARENA

In My WWE, select Cheat Codes from the Options and enter 8thannualtribute.

CRUISERWEIGHT TITLE, HARDCORE TITLE, AND MILLION DOLLAR TITLE

In My WWE, select Cheat Codes from the Options and enter Historicalbelts.

ALL CHARACTERS

At the Team Management screen, press Right, Left, Left, Right, Up, Up, Up, Start.

LEVEL 99 CHARACTERS

At the Team Management screen, press Up, Down, Up, Down, Left, Up, Left, Right, Start.

ALL SKILLS

At the Team Management screen, press Left, Right, Left, Right, Down, Up, Start.

SUPER SPEED

Pause the game and press Up, Up, Up, Down, Up, Down, Start.

UNLIMITED XTREME POWER

Pause the game and press Left, Down, Right, Down, Up, Up, Down, Up Start.

100,000 TECHBITS

At Forge or Beast's equipment screen, press Up, Up, Up, Down, Right, Right, Start.

ALL CINEMATICS

A the Review menu, press Left, Right, Right, Left, Down, Down, Left, Start.

ALL COMIC BOOKS

At the Review menu, press Right, Left, Left, Right, Up, Up, Right, Start.

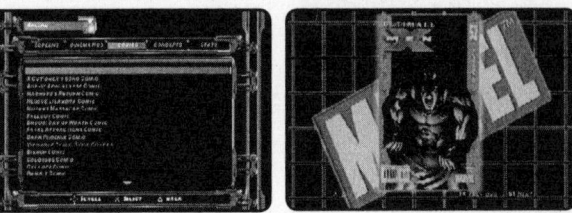

YS: THE OATH IN FELGHANA

GAME COMPLETION BONUSES

Complete the game and save after the credits to unlock New Game +, Time Attack, and the Inferno Difficulty.

BLACK PICCARD

Complete the Game on Inferno difficulty.

BERNHARDT

Complete Time Attack on any difficulty.

EXTRA BATTLE WITH BERNHARDT

Complete Boss Rush Mode on very easy.

YU-GI-OH! 5D'S TAG FORCE 4

HIGH NOON CONSTELLATION PACK

At the card shop, press Right (x5), ● (x7), Select (x3).

YU-GI-OH! 5D'S TAG FORCE 5

HIGH NOON CONSTELLATION PACK

At the card shop, press Up, Up, Down, Down, L, R, L, R, ●, ▲.

YU-GI-OH! DUEL MONSTERS GX: TAG FORCE 3

MIDDAY CONSTELLATION BOOSTER PACK

At the store, get to the booster pack menu and press Up, Up, Down, Down, Left, Right, Left, Right, ✖, ●. The pack will now be available at the store.